A CONSTITUTION FOR THE SOCIALIST COMMONWEALTH OF GREAT BRITAIN

A Constitution for the Socialist Commonwealth of Great Britain

by Sidney and Beatrice Webb

———

with an introduction by
Samuel H. Beer

Eaton Professor of the Science of Government
Harvard University

London School of Economics and Political Science
Cambridge University Press

Published by the Syndics of the Cambridge University Press
The Pitt Building, Trumpington Street, Cambridge CB2 1RP
Bentley House, 200 Euston Road, London NW1 2DB
32 East 57th Street, New York, NY 10022, USA
296 Beaconsfield Parade, Middle Park, Melbourne 3206, Australia

ISBN: 0 521 20851 3

First published 1920
This edition 1975

Printed in Great Britain
at the University Printing House, Cambridge
(Euan Phillips, University Printer)

CONTENTS

Cabinet – Cabinet Dictatorship – Hypertrophy – A Vicious
Mixture of Functions – The Task of the M.P. – The Failure of
the Elector – The Warping of Political Democracy by a
Capitalist Environment – Political Parties – The Labour Party –
The Success of Political Democracy in general, and of British
Democracy in particular – The Need for Constitutional Reform.

PART II

THE CO-OPERATIVE
COMMONWEALTH OF TOMORROW

CHAPTER I

The King – The House of Lords – The National Parliament –
The Political Parliament and its Executive – The Social Parliament and its Executive – The Relation between the Political
and the Social Parliaments – Devolution as an Alternative
Scheme of Reform – The Argument summarised – The Political
Complex – The Social Complex – The Protection of the Individual against the Government.

CHAPTER II

Three Separate Aspects of Economic Man – The Relative
Functions of Democracies of Consumers and Democracies of
Producers – Democracies of Citizen-Consumers – Democracies
of Producers – Ownership and Direction – The Participation in
Management by the Producers.

CHAPTER III

The Abandonment of Ministerial Responsibility – The Differentiation of Control from Administration – The Administrative Machine – District Councils – Works Committees – The
Recruitment of the Staff – Discipline Boards – Collective Bargaining – Advisory Committees – The Sphere of the Social
Parliament – How the Administration will work – Initiative and

Publicity – The Transformation of Authority – Co-ordinated instead of Chaotic Complexity – The Price of Liberty.

INTRODUCTION TO THIS EDITION

SAMUEL H. BEER

SERIOUS STUDIES of the history or theory of socialism devote little or no attention, favourable or unfavourable, to the Webbs' *Constitution for the Socialist Commonwealth of Great Britain*; yet I would contend that there is a good case to be made for reading the book, indeed for studying it, and so for this reprinting. In the first place it is exceptionally valuable for anyone concerned with understanding the 'mind of the Webbs'. They were not given to theorizing or system-building and of their books this is the most general in scope – Beatrice calls it a 'summing up'. It reveals a great deal about the ideology of the great partnership, not least because, as its critics note, the book is deductive in approach and was hastily composed. And since the mind of the Webbs was also in no small degree the mind (though not the heart) of British socialism, an appreciation of this ideology, considered with regard not only to its confusions and blind spots, but also its insights and intellectual sensitivities, helps one understand the Labour party and what is still sometimes called 'the Movement'.

The book can also be made to tell one a great deal about the times in which it was written. In 1920, its year of publication, nineteenth-century democratic hopes were being assailed by storms of criticism that came from both left and right and had risen suddenly and with great force. These attacks revealed new problems of economic and political power for which the older democrats, whether liberals or socialists, had no ready solutions. The Webbs were highly sensitive to these criticisms and did grapple with the problems they brought forward. In important ways I find their perceptions prescient and their proposals sensible. That they were also very wrong on many points is no cause for ridicule, since these same political and economic problems are to this day only imperfectly understood by students of society and have by no means been mastered by the institutions of the welfare state and managed economy. To review these pages is an instructive experience for anyone who thinks that for his own day he can read the trends of the times.

How the Book was Written and Received

In her diary for 11 May 1920, Beatrice Webb wrote:

> The last six weeks has been strenuous work, day after day finishing our book on *A Constitution for the Socialist Commonwealth of Great Britain*. It has been a great lark writing it – I have never enjoyed writing a book so much – it has been real sport thinking out each separate part and making each part fit the others. . . I have still the last chapter to devise and Sidney has the summary to prepare and all the proof corrections. Neither of us could have written the book alone – it is the jointest of our joint efforts. No one will like our constitution; we shall offend all sides and sections with some of our proposals. But someone must begin to think things out, and our task in life is to be pioneers in social engineering.

The Webbs (certainly Beatrice) not only enjoyed writing the book, but also took this piece of 'social engineering' very seriously then and afterwards. Its publication, wrote Beatrice, was 'an event in our lives – the summing up of our observation and reasoning about political and industrial organisation'. Many years later when the Webbs were embarking on their study of Soviet Communism, Beatrice in seeking to express their high regard for the Russian system professed to find in it the embodiment of their *Constitution for a Socialist Commonwealth*, 'the same tripod of political democracy, vocational organisation, and consumers' cooperative movement', together with '. . . no damned nonsense about Guild Socialism!' Yet the Constitution was written quickly, even hastily, and originated from an outside request, not their own inspiration, which at that time engaged them in revisions of their great works on trade unionism and in preparation of the manuscript that became the *Decay of Capitalist Civilisation*.

The request came from the Second International. Transmitted by Camille Huysmans, secretary of the bureau of the International and a friend of the Webbs, it sought to prompt the constituent bodies to prepare reports on two questions of urgent importance to the socialist movement in those years – the socialization of industry and the constitution of a socialist state – for submission to the forthcoming Congress. In the latter part of November 1919, delegates from the four member organizations of the British section, the Labour Party, the TUC, the ILP and the Fabians, appointed a committee to comply with the request, Sidney representing the Labour Party and Beatrice the Fabians. Elaborated to book length, as its Preface explains a little defensively, this report became the *Constitution*, completed in May and published in July 1920.

Initially a submission to the Fabian society, the book was presumably put before the Congress of the Second International, held in Geneva in August. There Sidney was chairman of the Commission for the Political Systems of Socialism and Socialization, Beatrice served on the subcommittee on Socialization and the Webb resolution on the two topics was adopted unanimously, except for a few rebel voices among the British delegates. 'Fabianism', recorded Beatrice, '[was] in fact dominating the Second International through the medium of British trade unionism'. Later in the year the Fabian Society sponsored a series of lectures at King's Hall in which the Webbs explained the proposals of their new book to an audience largely non-socialist – it included 'two Rothschilds, peers and princes and a minor Royalty' – and which George Bernard Shaw concluded with a criticism of 'the Webb Constitution'. In spite of Beatrice's initial misgivings, the lectures 'went off well' and earned a modest profit for the Fabians. In the January after publication Beatrice wrote that 'on the whole, the book has been well, though hardly enthusiastically received'. What some of the reviewers said will indicate the climate of opinion in which the Webbs wrote.

A sputtering, right-wing review in *Blackwood's* compared the Webbs to Lenin, 'their great exemplar', and accused them of being 'prepared to plunge the country into a sea of blood' to bring about their 'revolution'. Its author defended the House of Lords, denounced democracy, and assailed at length the Webbs' proposal to use country houses as convalescent homes. While writing with as little knowledge of politics and economics as of the book itself, he showed a hack journalist's sense of what his readers wanted to hear. For this was a time when the threats of Bolshevik and syndicalist revolution had spread through Europe a panic fear which lapped over into the mounting apprehension aroused by the rapid growth of social democracy and trade unionism. In some quarters, therefore, 'Fabian socialism', far from being that friendly toothless creature later times were taught to picture, enjoyed a fearsome reputation that survives today only in the mythology of the John Birch Society.

While less ill-tempered, most British reviews were severely critical, their attention being mainly drawn to the proposal of two parliaments, one to control external relations, defence and justice, the other to control social and economic affairs. This was called 'a staggering proposition' (*Contemporary Review*), 'mutually destructive' (*Economist*), 'prolific of awkward deadlocks' (*London Mercury*). Even Clifford Sharp, writing in the *New Statesman*, of which the Webbs had made him editor eight years earlier when founding the journal,

wrote with evident embarrassment and not much understanding. While admiring in general, he could find
specific cause for praise only in the Webbs' negative conclusions regarding 'the proved inadequacy of the present
machinery of democracy' and the 'decay of Parliament'.

Perhaps the most thoughtful British comment came
from the *Spectator*, where J. B. Atkins, a general
feature writer and long associate of the magazine,
launched an earnest, although inexpert counter-attack.
Taking up a familiar but fundamental question, he
asked what motives would power the 'Co-operative
Commonwealth of Tomorrow'. His own answer was
to doubt that the 'ideal motives' supposed by the
Webbs could take the place of the 'incentive' provided
by 'competitive industry'. In foreseeing 'rivalry' between the two parliaments, he wondered what would
happen if the Social Parliament, 'backed by a carefully
contrived strike', were to resist 'a policy of war' adopted
by the Political Parliament and he gave contemporary
relevance to the criticism by pointing out that the
materials for such a clash were present 'at this very
moment'. His readers would have understood his
reference. On 13 August, only seven days before the
review appeared, a conference of trade unions and the
Labour party had approved a threat to use 'the whole
industrial power of the workers' to prevent British
intervention in the war between Poland and Soviet
Russia. This threat achieved one of the greatest victories
of the post-war period for the syndicalist doctrine of
'direct action' when it forced Lloyd George to reverse
his Polish plans.

As compared with British reviewers Americans took
the book more seriously and gave it more scholarly
consideration. This was not only because of the rather
colonial relation of American left-wing thought to
British socialism, but also because the reviews were by
professors rather than journalists: Robert Hale of

Columbia in *The Survey*; Harold Laski, fresh from Harvard, in *The New Republic*; Charles Beard, ex-Columbia in *The Nation*, and John R. Commons of Wisconsin in *The American Economic Review*. The counterpoint between Beard and Commons is worth remarking as it goes to the heart of the analysis of the forces the Webbs were trying to master in thought and practice. Beard, the political scientist, saw economic power as fundamental in the state. 'Which assembly would dominate', he asked rhetorically, 'the one dwelling in the windy realm of purified politics, or the one possessing the real goods?' For Commons, the economist, on the other hand, it was political power that would constitute the stakes of future conflict. Commons did not question the basic economics of the Webbs' proposals for total socialization, the concept of the 'super-trust'. He did warn that political conflict could produce distortions of the socialized economy greater even than those arising from profit-seeking under capitalism. In a prescient conclusion, which allowed for the trends toward collectivism identified by the Webbs, but which showed a more sophisticated appreciation of political possibilities and limitations, he put forward a plea for a controlled, reformed and counterbalanced capitalism which looks remarkably like the welfare state that ultimately did emerge in Britain and generally in the Western world.

While differing among themselves, Beard, Commons and the Webbs were united in perceiving that power in the Western polity was being transformed with regard to sources and form. The *Constitution* can be regarded as the Webbs' effort to adjust British institutions to these emerging forms of power. To see where they read the trends of the times correctly and where incorrectly will tell us something about the problems they confronted and about the outlook they brought to the task of understanding and solving them.

CHANGING SOURCES OF POWER IN THE MODERN STATE

As Charles Beard observed in his review, the central problems with which the Webbs were grappling arose from 'the great society'. Beard took this term from the title of a remarkable book published six years earlier by another Fabian, Graham Wallas, who in turn had adapted it from Emile Durkheim. According to this way of looking at modern history, increasing specialization, sustained by an expanding science and technology, was continually extending the scale of society in all spheres, creating ever wider networks of human interdependence. By the latter part of the nineteenth century, this development confronted the modern state with a new problem of power. Interdependence on such a scale meant that a group controlling a specialized function within a system could paralyse the whole system by a withdrawal of its activity.

Power of this sort had grown up in many spheres – governmental, political, social – wherever interdependence had reached the new order of magnitude. Its presence and threat, however, were most evident in the form of 'economic power', i.e. the control by a group over a specialized function within the mode of production, as in a trade union's power to strike a vital industry. On this power of industrial labour, some socialist leaders hoped to build a comprehensive working class movement. There was, however, a fundamental difficulty with this plan which the Webbs themselves had brought out in 1894 when they wrote in their study of trade unionism:

the basis of association of these million and a half workers is sectional in nature. They come together, and contribute their pence, for the defence of their interest as Boilermakers, Miners, Cotton-spinners, and not directly for the advancement of the whole working class.

Since those days, organizations of workers (as of managers and professional people) have on occasions created alliances with a complex vocational base. The narrow foundation of the economic power of the constituent bodies, however, has continued powerfully to condition the behaviour of these wider associations.

The rise of economic power was closely related to two other broad trends: the spread of democracy and of organization. Changes in British government display both. Between the election of 1880 and 1918, the percentage of the British population numbered in the electorate rose from 8.8 to 45.6. In the same period, the activity of government grew immensely. After falling as a percentage of national income during the middle years of the nineteenth century, government expenditure (central and local) reversed this trend and began to rise between 1890 and 1900. Government employment told the same story. After unsteady movements up and down in the mid-century years, the total of non-industrial staff of the central government moved sharply upward after 1880. Both trends have continued unabated to this day, constituting major signs of the rise and dominance of the welfare state.

As big government appeared so also did big business and big unionism. By the nineties British managers were using the new corporate forms of the joint stock company to make their first large-scale experiments with industrial combinations. After 1880 trade associations had begun to appear in substantial numbers, but effective peak associations were not set up until World War I. In creating inter-industry association and in organizing generally, the trade unions outpaced business. Dating from 1868 the TUC increased its membership from 1.5 million in 1880 to 6.5 million in 1920. In both sorts of organization, it must be stressed, the great surge forward took place during World War I when government policy deliberately and energetically encouraged and sometimes even forced economic concentration for the sake of the war effort.

In sum, as the great society extended its circles of interdependence, the democratic impulse mobilized new strata for political and economic activity, while the effort to control these vast complexes of activity fostered large-scale organization on the part of both the state and private groups.

An examination of these two tendencies – toward extending human control over society and toward democratizing this control – was a major theme of the Webbs' life work. For the *Constitution of the Socialist Commonwealth*, this theme constitutes the organizing principle. As socialists, the Webbs' purpose was to substitute for the incoherence of capitalism a system of conscious human direction, which, moreover, would involve 'a progressive democratisation of industry' (p. 97). Their approach to this task of reform may be called functionalist. That is to say, they sought in their study of groups and organizations to identify the emerging activities that expressed the trend toward democratic control and then to propose a reform of institutions so adapted to these activities as to enhance their operation. Thus, as capitalists and landlords showed their loss of function by not only failing to sustain the developing economic system but indeed by spreading waste and chaos throughout it, the rise of industrial democracy and consumer cooperation pointed toward new forms of popular control in the economy. The dysfunctional owners drop off, the eufunctional producers and consumers take over – with appropriate help from reform.

The Webbs' socialism, needless to say, was strongly ethical, but it was also buoyed up by an optimistic faith that the forces of history were moving strongly – they would sometimes say inevitably – toward their dual goal. Hence, they could feel safe in adopting this functionalist approach to social studies and reform.

The Syndicalist Challenge

But tendencies are hard to read and their ambivalences open the way to conflicting evaluations. A central problem facing the Webbs when writing the *Constitution* was what role to assign the economic power of organized labour. Disagreement over this question went far back into the history of the socialist and trade union movements. It had informed the conflict between the Marxists and anarchists in the First International. In the days of the Second International, the controversy became sharper as syndicalists pressed the case for 'direct action' in contrast to the political and parliamentary action favoured by social democrats.

The idea of direct action took many forms, ranging from the general strike as a means of proletarian revolution to the anti-political business unionism of American labour. In Britain the issue did not become serious until the years just before World War I. At this time the great oratorical battles of the Socialist Congresses over this question had subsided. But as syndicalist ideas found growing support in Britain, the industrial context gave them exceptional menace – or promise. For in these years and extending into the war, organized labour in Britain was gripped by a wave of militancy, often syndicalist in rhetoric, that led to a series of massive strikes, sometimes leading to violent confrontations with public authorities. Moreover, after the war, the trade union movement, now embracing a huge new membership, continued to be strongly affected by syndicalist ideas, and the tactic of direct action won notable victories in dictating public policy, such as its defeat of Lloyd George's Polish plans. The later decline of syndicalism should not be permitted to obscure the peak of influence achieved by it in Britain during the postwar years and the urgency of its challenge in the year the Webbs wrote the *Constitution*.

This clash of men and ideas within the British labour and socialist movements could not fail to be echoed within the Fabian Society. There the state socialism of the Webbs was challenged by the new doctrine of guild socialism, whose leading advocate was the young G. D. H. Cole. State socialism had been the orthodoxy not only of the Fabians, but also of British socialists generally. Its emphasis was sometimes centralist, as in the demands for 'nationalization' voted by the TUC from the nineties on, or decentralist, as in the Webbs' advocacy of 'municipalisation'. For both schools, the ultimate control of the socialist economy would rest with a representative body chosen by voters generally. In contrast the guild socialists would have each industry owned and controlled by a guild consisting of the workers engaged in the industry. As for general government, Cole proposed that the autonomous guilds send representatives to a national assembly, which, however, would have no power to decide questions by majority vote or in any way to exercise coercion, but would trust to the free consent of its members and their constituent bodies to produce consensus and compliance. The programme of this agitation, conducted by Cole's foundation, the National Guilds League (1915–25), was given a culminating formulation in his *Guild Socialism*, published the same year as the Webbs' *Constitution*.

These conflicts within British society and within the socialist movement shaped what the Webbs wrote in the *Constitution* and did much to impel them to write it. The polemical purpose of the book is obvious: to offset the influence of syndicalism in general and guild socialism in particular. But it would be wrong to conclude that they were interested in a merely polemical victory. On the contrary, it was far from absurd for them to believe that the war had dealt capitalism a blow from which it could not recover, and to see in their book, as their confident Preface suggests, a guide to 'the changes in the British Constitution and in the social and economic structure of the nation' that a socialist government might soon be called upon to make.

The principal challenge from within the socialist movement to which the Webbs were responding, it must be emphasized, was syndicalist not Communist or Leninist. The Webbs were acutely aware of the Russian Revolution and saw it as one more instance in the mounting evidence of socialist advance. But they were intensely hostile to Leninism because of its violent and undemocratic methods. Only in the next few years as Soviet Russia proved its ability to survive and the Third International with its affiliated Communist parties established a separate existence from the Second International did Leninism take the place of syndicalism as the main rival of democratic socialism on the Left.

The Conservative Challenge

Before looking more closely at the book, we must consider one other major influence, coming from a very different quarter. The socialist, Clifford Sharp was, referring to one of its major themes when he spoke of the 'decay of Parliament'. Yet the broad criticism of British institutions of which I am thinking, with its stress on political rather than economic analysis, was not socialist in inspiration. Nor did it express liberal and democratic premises, but rather a severe questioning of the institutions and expectations flowing from those premises. To some of the critics in this vein, the 'decay of Parliament' meant that the voters in Britain's new mass democracy did not and indeed could not control government in any significant sense. To others the problem was that MPs had little voice in making policy or supervising administration because of the congestion of business and the dominance of the cabinet. The Webbs themselves summarized much of the analysis in an uncharacteristically succinct sentence:

The great mass of government today is the work of an able and honest but secretive bureaucracy, tempered by the ever-present apprehension of the revolt of powerful sectional interests, and mitigated by the spasmodic interventions of imperfectly comprehending Ministers (p. 69).

With its stress on irrationalism and elitism, on leadership and expertise, and its general recognition of the stubborn roots of human conflict, this line of thought can most accurately be called conservative. Although often given utterance by liberals and socialists trying to cope with the problems that it revealed, it reflected a painful rediscovery of what Tories had always claimed to know.

This harsh view of British government had become prominent only in recent years. In 1908 Professor A. Lawrence Lowell of Harvard had been able to write:

The typical Englishman believes that his government is incomparably the best in the world. It is the thing above all others that he is proud of. He does not, of course, always agree with the course of policy pursued . . . but he is certain that the general form of government is well-nigh perfect.[1]

Graham Wallas' sceptical and disillusioned *Human Nature in Politics*, published in the same year as Lowell's book, was a better sign of the doubts of parliamentary democracy that rose and spread during the following years, along with economic unrest and the surge of revolutionary syndicalism constituting part of the malaise that suddenly assailed Liberal England just before World War I.

During the war this current of political criticism was further strengthened by reformers who, urged on by the Government for the sake of the war effort, worked up proposals for 'reconstruction'. To this developing critique Beatrice Webb contributed as a member of the famous Haldane Committee (the Machinery of Government Committee of the Ministry of Reconstruction) on the organization of the cabinet and the departments of the central government. Many of the Webbs' suggestions were accepted by the committee – so many, indeed, that the extent to which its proposals have been put into practice since that time is a good indication of their influence on the development of central government organization in Britain. Its more particular proposals, as W. J. M. Mackenzie has observed, were 'linked and harmonised by the great principle that the functions of Government should be organised according to the service to be rendered, not according to the clients to be served'.[2] The same idea had been expressed in the Webbs' old proposal for the break-up of the Poor Law. It was natural that in the *Constitution* they should refer to the Haldane report as stating authoritatively the correct principles of organization of Britain's growing bureaucracy.

These two currents of thought – one socialist, the other conservative in inspiration, one stressing economic and the other political analysis – seem to me to be the two main influences of the time upon the Webbs' book. Writing in this context, they sought to accomplish a 'summing up' of their life work, utilizing the outlook developed in the early years of their partnership to cope with the new problems raised by the second decade of the century. That they should address these problems was appropriate since these problems arose largely from developments on which the Webbs had looked with great favour: the spread of democracy, the growth of government activity, the rise of expertise, the organization of sectional interests. In trying to deal with the resulting difficulties, the Webbs were, so to speak, confronting some of the unanticipated political consequences of their own approved scheme of historical evolution.

The Webbs' response

With regard to the system of representation proposed for the new socialist commonwealth, liberal democracy (and indeed the still older concept of the state) win out with no significant concession to syndicalism or guild socialism. For both parliaments and for local government, representation is not vocational, but territorial, being based on groupings of 'citizens', not on organizations of 'producers' or 'consumers'. Yet the parliamentary arrangements have distinct syndicalist overtones. The identification of the functions divided between the two houses is, as the Webbs observe, taken from the Haldane proposals. The Political Parliament gets three functions – defence, external affairs and justice – straight off the Haldane list of the ten main government functions, while the jurisdiction assigned the Social Parliament coincides fairly well with the remaining seven. Neither syndicalist nor guildsman should disagree with the rationale of the Social Parliament. This is that government will acquire a whole new set of economic and social functions when it takes over the tasks formerly performed by the market under what the Webbs call 'the Dictatorship of the Capitalist '– the economic task of allocating resources and the social task of distributing the product.

The Social Parliament, moreover, dispensing both with a cabinet and with ministerial responsibility, will conduct its business through a series of specialized committees, each of which, although not representing a distinct vocation, will be concerned with an executive department defined by the skill and technique common to its members. While vocationally defined, these departments, which in some cases will consist of nationalized industries, will still be quite safe from workers' control. On the national board by which each will be administered, workers will be represented by 'nominees of the vocational organisations' (p. 178). These, however, will be overwhelmingly outnumbered by representatives of managers, consumers and other industries. At all levels, in short, the institutions of state socialism are too strong to permit us to take very seriously the Webbs' claim that they have based the regime on a tripartite partnership of citizens, consumers and producers.

What must interest the student of present-day British government is how far the Webbs successfully identified the tendencies of their times and proposed reasonable means of coping with them. As they foresaw, the rise of the welfare state and managed economy has added to British government a whole new complex of interrelated functions. This development, moreover, has created a set of relations between polity and economy that constitutes in effect a new system of functional representation alongside the old system of parliamentary representation. The basis of this new system is vocational, in the sense that it consists of contacts between government departments and the representatives of producers' groups, such as trade unions, professional organizations, trade associations and large firms. While these contacts usually consist of informal, day-to-day, bi-lateral relations between a producers' organization and a department, attempts have been made to organize them at very high levels, as in those recent ambitious experiments, the National Economic Development Council and the National Board for Prices and Incomes. At this level the con-sultations among the various parties constitute a kind of bargaining between central government and sectional interests concerning such vital matters as an export drive, productivity, and not least prices and wages. This bargaining may lead to decisions of sufficient moment to be regarded as extra-parliamentary legislation.

The Webbs were right in seeing that the new activities of the state would require new institutions and that these would include a dual system of representation, one side of which would be concerned with the new economic functions. In contrast with the Webbs, however, the guildsmen had a better grasp of the nature and thrust of economic power. For the new system of functional representation has risen up on a base consisting of the economic power of disaggregated groups of producers, not the political power of comprehensive groups of voters. When a producers' group bargains with government, its power varies not so much with the votes it represents as with its command over a specialized function.

Yet while right in recognizing the distinctive character of economic power, the guildsmen were surely wrong in supposing they could constitute from its representatives a public, decision-making body. The various economic and social councils that were tried during the interwar years showed empirically that such a scheme would not work. Nor have any of the high-level planning boards operated successfully as a 'parliament of industry'. Economic power inherently, it seems, tends to act from a narrow rather than a broad vocational base, to produce bi-lateral bargaining rather than multi-lateral negotiation and, most emphatically, to operate in private rather than in public.

Such relationships are not absent from the traditional parliament. But as the Webbs clearly saw, parliaments also express another kind of purpose. This is the purpose of people as citizens, in contrast with their purposes as this or that kind of producer or consumer. When people pursue purposes of this sort they create a distinctive kind of power which may properly be called 'political' because it groups their efforts according to general conceptions of the polity. Purpose so founded has the potential of aggregating many sectional interests and reflecting some view of the common interest and, because it is about things that are shared, tends to conduct its business in public. The Webbs were quite right in insisting that the ultimate governance of the new economic and social functions, as much as the more traditional functions, should be based on a system representing this sort of citizens' purpose and power. Indeed, they were so bent on asserting this truism of liberal democracy that they failed to provide a sufficient arena in the polity for the inevitable play of economic power.

This is not to say that the corporatistic arrangements of present-day Britain have successfully solved the problem of how to cope with economic power. The welfare state and managed economy cannot be run without the cooperation of managers, professionals and organized workers – the heads of nationalized industries, physicians in the Health Service, and the dockers of London and the other ports. Management of the economy entails the making of bargains between government and producer groups that will be kept. This means that there must be coherent and authoritative leadership within the producer organizations. Yet in spite of their comprehensive formal membership, these organizations in Britain are weak and fragmented. This is the case not only with the peak organizations, but also with the constituent bodies affiliated to them. Within organized labour, as when the Webbs looked at the subject eighty years ago, sectional interests are still overpowering. The same is true of organized business. So while action within the peak associations can be concerted around demands that affect all in a similar way (such as a reduction of profits tax for business, or a general increase in wages for labour) the highly differentiated and selective programmes necessarily entailed by economic management and social equity arouse acute and chaotic dissension.

·   ·   ·

With regard to what I have called the conservative critique of British institutions, the Webbs also made some sensible and prescient suggestions. Today the House of Commons still complains of being over-burdened. But this is nothing compared to what its plight would be if the new system of functional representation had not, as was expected of the Social Parliament, diverted from the parliamentary arena a great mass of decision-making. The separation of policy from administration which is stressed in the *Constitution* (e.g., p. 169) has been embodied in the current procedures of parliamentary control of the nationalized industries and, although the separation has proved hard to define and maintain, the effort has undoubtedly saved the time of the House by recognizing that there are spheres of government into which MPs cannot usefully intrude. The recent upgrading of the position of the trained specialist in the civil service as a result of the Fulton report expresses a Webbian regard for expertise. Current efforts to set up systems of 'output budgeting' and to introduce cost-benefit analysis are highly reminiscent of the proposals for measurement and control set forth in the *Constitution*, where some pages read like an early prospectus for PPBS (Planning Programming Budgeting System). Recent regroupings of government departments clearly show that the Haldane principle of organization according to function, not clientele, still has strong champions in Whitehall. The Webbs' stress on decentralization also has a contemporary ring. Rejecting the Liberal proposal of devolution on the sensible grounds that Britain had become far too interdependent to make feasible such a fragmentation of political power, they looked to local government to continue to perform 'the greater part of British public administration' (p. 203).

Yet in the light of Britain's later experience with collectivism, their book has no more glaring fault than

its total lack of appreciation of the ancient Tory principle of 'strong government'. When one considers the
fact that a major task of the Social Parliament would be
to control the economy, it is staggering to realize that
the Webbs provided this assembly with virtually no
agency for central direction and coordination. Explicitly
modelling its structure upon the London County
Council, where Sidney had served long and successfully, they proposed that the Social Parliament's many
specialized committees act as the centres of 'continuous
oversight' of the administration of the socialized economy, subject only to the assembly's decisions on 'the
great issues of policy'. The Webbs seemed to have no
inkling of the nearly intractable problem confronting present-day governments of achieving concerted
action by the complex plurality constituting the contemporary system of production. Leadership and
authority have no role in their theory of politics.

The Webbs take up this question under the heading
of 'The Transformation of Authority' and their answer
is exactly what you would expect. Under socialism, the
'old autocracy' will vanish while a 'steadily increasing
sphere will . . . be found for consultation . . . out of which
will emerge judgments and decisions arrived at, very
largely, by common consent' (p. 196). Price-fixing will
be readily accepted and strikes in the socialized sector
while continuing to be legal, will tend to die out. Their
concluding pages (written by Beatrice) again set forth
that ancient article of the socialist faith: Capitalism
fosters 'the passion for riches', while socialism will
substitute 'the motive of public service' for 'the motive
of self-enrichment' (p. 351). Given this transformation
of motives, rational persuasion will take the place of
authority in social relations, and science will reign as the
real directing force in govermnent. In a sentence that
could come straight out of Robert Owen or Edward
Bellamy, they conclude: 'It is to a free Democracy,

inspired by the spirit of social service, and illumined by ever-increasing knowledge, that we dedicate this book.'

This is not to say that Mr Atkins was right after all and that 'self-enrichment' is bound to remain a more powerful motive than 'social service'. For the empirical record does support the Webbs' contention that men and women can come increasingly to be motivated by social ideals. The rapid spread of professionalism – to which the Webbs continually refer to illustrate what they mean by the 'social service' motive – supports their conception of incentives. As many observers have pointed out, the managers of big businesses today are not moved so much by the prospect of personal material gain as by their identification with the success of an enterprise far transcending their personal interests. Indeed, this knowledge of their own selfless commitment to professional standards or organizational objectives is one reason why government finds it difficult to deal with those in command of specialized functions. The public-spirited head of a nationalized industry can cause as much distortion of the economic plan as any old-fashioned capitalist oligarch. Both the record of the mixed economy and of bureaucratic socialism show, on the one hand (contrary to Mr Atkins' belief) that people do respond to the appeal of 'social service' and, on the other, that their conversion to such a basis of motivation does little to remove the roots of human conflict. For this reason it has not been nearly as important to get rid of the capitalist as the Webbs thought it would be, nor as helpful to substitute for him a government manager. For this reason the Webbs underestimated the possibilities of a mixed economy and overestimated the possibilities of bureaucratic socialism.

THE IDEOLOGY OF THE WEBBS

Paradoxically, Beatrice Webb was sensitively aware

of such complexities of human motivation, but some block prevented this awareness from intruding into her books. I am thinking of that extraordinary contrast between her *Diaries* and her published writings, between her private insight and her public analysis, a contrast so gaping in style and substance as to make the reader wonder how a single personality could embrace two such opposed systems of response. The *Diaries* are vivid, concrete, personally warm, acute in their analysis of critical events and excelling in their pen portraits of individuals. The books are just the opposite: bland, impersonal, aloof, stressing general trends and sociological analysis and excelling as institutional history. At no time does this contrast appear more sharply than when one compares the *Constitution for a Socialist Commonwealth* with the *Diaries* for 1920. On the one hand, the book exudes a facile optimism, as when, for instance, the 'inevitability' of democracy is asserted. On the other hand, for the Beatrice Webb of the *Diaries*, the 'senseless cruelty of men and races of men, one towards the other, today vividly exposed in Russia, Central Europe, and Ireland . . . forms a dark background to the shortness and ineffectiveness of one's own life and the lives of those one loves'. Nor was it just men in great masses who showed these tragic propensities. Beatrice Webb also saw the corruption of individuals around her – the sneering Snowden, the vain MacDonald, the ranting Lansbury – among civil servants, professional men and trade union leaders, as well as capitalists and landlords and people 'living by owning'.

Without going into psychological causes, one can readily identify the barrier that blocked off Beatrice Webb's common sense from her social science. That barrier was a theory of man and society. An optimistic faith put forward during the Enlightenment and influencing not only the utopian socialists, but also many other political and social thinkers of the nineteenth century, its essence was the notion that conflict among men derives from corrupting institutions (certainly not from human nature) and can be eliminated by institutional reform. One variation of this broad theme added to its ethical imperative a philosophy of history showing how certain mechanisms of social development would bring about the desired institutional transformation. This doctrine of progress adopted and developed many of the ideas of the school of evolutionary sociology, which has remained a power in the world of social science from Comte to Durkheim to Parsons.

In late nineteenth-century Britain, the leading exponent of evolutionary sociology was Herbert Spencer, the personal confidant and intellectual mentor of the young Beatrice Potter. Spencer's influence on Beatrice is usually assumed to be slight because of the polar opposition between her collectivism and his rugged individualism. When, however, one looks at the general framework of thought on to which Spencer attempted (with great difficulty) to graft his archaic liberalism, the similarities with the Webbian outlook are fundamental. Both entertained a utopian expectation that the state as a coercive and authoritative agent would decline and vanish. In both utopias, the individualist and the collectivist, reason would become the dominant regulator of human relations and destructive conflict would be left behind in the earlier ages of man. Moreover, for both Spencer and the Webbs the model of historical development is evolutionary. Although Beatrice had worked with Charles Booth, she rejected his statistical method, which presented an 'instantaneous image' of social reality, in favour of an historical approach. This approach was rationalist in the sense that it looked for a gradual development of institutions largely through the influence of growing knowledge, and especially science. A principal theme of social evolution for the Webbs was the increasing functional organization of society which resulted from the vocational specialization produced by advancing knowledge. Like Spencer, the Webbs looked on the society so produced as an organism consisting of an increasingly complex system in which each specialized vocation and trained person would have its functional role.

My concern is not to argue that these ideas, shared by the Webbs with Herbert Spencer, were passed on to them through his influence. Such themes were part of the climate of opinion of the late nineteenth century from which they could have been imbibed by any educated person. The comparison with Spencer is intended not to show influence, but to bring out the element of ideology in the mind of the Webbs.

To see the Webbs as sociologists of the school of evolutionary rationalism is to reveal sources of strength as well as weakness. Thanks to this approach they were better able to appreciate the advance of functional organization. At the same time, the shallow rationalism of this way of looking at things gravely impaired their ability to understand the demonic century into which they survived.

Notes

1 *The Government of England*, 2 vols (Macmillan, New York; 1903), vol. 2, p. 507.
2 'The Structure of Central Administration' in Campion (ed.), *British Government Since 1918* (Allen & Unwin, London; 1950), p. 58.
I wish to thank Miss Vivien Hart for her help with the research for this Introduction

Short Bibliography

Samuel H. Beer, *Modern British Politics: a study of parties and pressure groups.* 2nd edn. (Faber & Faber, London; 1969).
Gilbert Campion (ed.), *British Government since 1918* (Allen & Unwin, London; 1950).

G. D. H. Cole, *A History of Socialist Thought*, Volume III, Part I, *The Socialist International, 1889–1914* (Macmillan, London; 1963).

G. D. H. Cole, *Guild Socialism: A Plan for Economic Democracy* (Stokes, New York; 1920).

Margaret Cole, *Beatrice Webb* (Harcourt Brace, New York; 1946).

Margaret Cole, 'The Webbs and social theory', *British Journal of Sociology*, vol. 12 (2) (June 1961), 93–105.

Margaret Cole (ed.), *Beatrice Webb's Diaries, 1912–1924* (Longmans, London; 1952).

Margaret Cole (ed.), *The Webbs and their Work* (Harvester Press, Brighton; 1975).

Maurice Cowling, *The Impact of Labour, 1920–1924: the beginning of modern British politics* (Cambridge University Press, Cambridge, England; 1971).

Herman Finer, *Representative Government and a Parliament for Industry* (Allen & Unwin, London; 1923).

Gertrude Himmelfarb, 'The Intellectual in Politics: the case of the Webbs', *Journal of Contemporary History*, vol. 6 (3) (1971), 3–11.

Gordon K. Lewis, 'Fabian Socialism: some aspects of theory and practice', *Journal of Politics*, vol. 14 (3) (August 1952), 442–70.

A. M. McBriar, *Fabian Socialism and English Politics, 1884–1914* (Cambridge University Press, Cambridge, England; 1962).

Ministry of Reconstruction. *Report of the Machinery of Government Committee* (Haldane Committee), cd. 9230 (H.M.S.O., London; 1918).

T. S. Simey, 'The Contribution of Sidney and Beatrice Webb to Sociology', *British Journal of Sociology*, no. 2 (June 1961), 106–19.

Trevor Smith, *Economic Planning and Democratic Government in Britain* (Allen & Unwin, London; 1974).

John Strachey, 'The Intellectuals and the Labour Movement: Sidney and Beatrice Webb', *Listener*, vol. 64, no. 1646 (13 October 1960), 617–19.

Adam Ulam, *Philosophical Foundations of British Socialism* (Harvard University Press, Cambridge, Mass.; 1951).

Graham Wallas, *The Great Society: A Psychological Analysis* (Macmillan, New York; 1914).

PREFACE

THIS book had its origin in a request transmitted by M. Camille Huysmans, the accomplished Secretary of the International Socialist Bureau, to all the constituent bodies of the International Socialist Congress, that they should furnish, for submission to the Congress, reports upon the " socialisation " of industries and services, and upon the constitution that should be adopted by any nation desirous of organising its life upon Socialist principles.

Great changes are everywhere at hand. Whilst every nation of advanced industrialism has been, in the present century, finding itself increasingly driven to measures of Socialist character, over a large part of Europe definitely Socialist administrations are actually in office, and the principles of Socialism are avowedly accepted as the basis of social and economic reconstruction. Open-minded students in every nation are watching the projects and the experiments of the other nations, in order to learn what is likely to be successful in their own. It behoves those who take part in the Labour and Socialist Movements of the various countries to think out, in some detail, the shape which their proposals should assume.

In response to the request of M. Huysmans the scheme set forth in this volume was prepared for submission to the Fabian Society. What seemed likely to be most useful, alike in this country and to the International Socialist Congress, was not any brief statement of abstract principles or vague generalisations, supposed to be of universal application, but a definite and concrete proposal, worked out in some detail, for one country only : naturally, the one about which the authors were best informed.

Such a draft, as will readily be understood, makes no pretence of expressing anything but our own opinions, or of giving anything more than a provisional judgment even on our own account. Those who wish to know what is the authoritative programme of the British Labour Party will find it stated, in considerable detail, in the pamphlet entitled *Labour and the New Social Order*, to be obtained, price 3d. post free, from the Labour Party, 33 Eccleston Square, London, S.W.1.

Naturally, no one is likely to agree with all our detailed proposals. Possibly some may dismiss them as unworthy of consideration. Nevertheless, we think that it may be of service to formulate, with sufficient precision to enable them to be understood, the changes in the British Constitution and in the social and economic structure of the nation, that seem to us such as a Socialist Ministry, supported by a Socialist Majority in Parliament and among the electorate, would probably be led to propose.

SIDNEY AND BEATRICE WEBB.

41 GROSVENOR ROAD,
WESTMINSTER, LONDON, S.W.1,
July 1920.

INTRODUCTION

WE do not seek in this book to attempt any indictment of what is commonly known as the Capitalist System. The situation which has to be faced is that, at the present moment, that system, as a coherent whole, has demonstrably broken down. From one end of the civilised world to the other it has, at least among the young generation that is growing up, lost its moral authority. Whole nations have avowedly rejected it as the basis of their social and economic structure; and, in all countries of advanced industrialism, great masses of people are increasingly refusing to accept it as a permanent institution. Among Socialists of all schools of thought, in all nations, there is no difference of opinion as to the purpose of the economic, social and political reconstruction that they recognise as Socialism. Under the Capitalist System the government of industry is vested in the hands of a relatively small fraction of the community, namely, the private owners of the instruments of production.

THE DICTATORSHIP OF THE CAPITALIST

This Dictatorship of the Capitalist is directed fundamentally to one end — the extraction of the largest attainable income for the owners of the land and capital in the form of interest, profit and rent. The economic result in Great Britain — and we believe that much the same is true of other countries of advanced industrialism—is a great waste of productive power through misdirection and internecine competition ; and also an inequality so gross that the manual-working wage-earners, comprising two-thirds of the population, obtain for their maintenance much less than half the community's net product annually, most of them living, accordingly, in chronic penury and insecurity. Nine-tenths of all the accumulated wealth belongs to one-tenth of the population. The continued existence of the functionless rich—of persons who deliberately live by owning instead of by working, and whose futile occupations, often licentious pleasures and inherently insolent manners, undermine the intellectual and moral standards of the community—adds insult to injury. This may seem a harsh condemnation ; but how many of the healthy adults who " live by owning " work as continuously, consume as little of the product of the labour of others, and bear themselves as modestly towards the community, as the common run of professional men and women ?

But the central wrong of the Capitalist System is neither the poverty of the poor nor the riches of the rich : it is the power which the mere ownership of the instruments of production gives to a relatively small section of the community over the actions of their fellow - citizens and over the mental and physical environment of successive generations. Under such a system personal freedom becomes, for large masses of the people, little better than a mockery. The tiny minority of rich men enjoy, not personal freedom only, but also personal power over the lives of other people ; whilst the underlying mass of poor men find their personal freedom restricted to the choice between obeying the orders of irresponsible masters intent on their own pleasure or their own gain, or remaining without the means of subsistence for themselves and

their families. At the same time this inequality in
power between a wealthy class and the mass of the
community corrupts also the political organisation of
the community and the newspaper press, and makes
it impossible for the National Government and even
the Municipality or other form of Local Government
(with their twin functions of defence against aggression
and the promotion of the permanent interests of the
community, and especially of the particular type of
civilisation that it desires) to be or to become genuine
Democracies.

What the Socialist aims at is the substitution, for
this Dictatorship of the Capitalist, of government of
the people by the people and for the people, in all
the industries and services by which the people live.
Only in this way can either the genuine participation
of the whole body of the people in the administration
of its own affairs, and the people's effective consciousness of consent to what is done in its name, ever be
realised. This application of Democracy to industry,
though it has its own inherent value as an unique
educational force, is in the eyes of the Socialist also
a means to an end, namely, a more equitable sharing
of the national product among all members of the
community, in order that there should be available
for all the members of the community the largest
attainable measure of personal freedom. Hence the
purpose of Socialism is twofold : the application of
Democracy to industry and the adoption by this Social
Democracy of the principle of maximising equality in
" life, liberty and the pursuit of happiness."

The Manifold Character of Democracy

What do we mean by the application of Democracy
to the industries and services by which the community lives ? To the nineteenth-century Socialist this

question did not occur. He accepted from the Victorian democrats their idea of the equality of voting power. Like them, he assumed that human beings in society needed only to be represented as human beings. Socialists in fact, like mere democrats, took it for granted, that Democracy was one and undivided ; that it was based on the equal and identical rights of all adult persons to take part, either directly or through their representatives, in the management of all the collective business of the community. There were, of course, controversies about such questions as the relative validity of mass meetings and representative assemblies ; the best method of voting ; the Referendum, the Initiative and the Recall ; the number and size of electoral or administrative units, the different ways of constituting the local authorities and the supreme executive of the State. There might be a division of powers between federal and state governments, or even a hierarchy of authorities from the village commune to a national legislature. But all these forms of Democracy assumed the individual citizen as a human being, having at all times and seasons, and in all the relations of life, an identical complex of desires and purposes.[1]

In the first years of the twentieth century the world has become aware of a new and more fundamental cleavage of opinion—due to a revolution in thought with regard to the nature of Democracy. It came to be realised that the democratic organisation of a community involved the acceptance of the representation, not of man as man, but of man in the leading aspects of his life in society : man as a producer, man as a consumer, man as a citizen concerned

---

[1] In all the nineteenth-century controversies about democratic institutions we find no specifically Socialist view. Socialists differed among themselves as to the advantage of this or that piece of constitutional machinery, just as did the members of other political parties, but without acute controversy.

with the continued existence and independence of his race or community, or with the character of the civilisation that he desires ; possibly also man as a seeker after knowledge, or man as a religious believer.[1] An organisation by functional grouping appeared to be the rival of an organisation based on mere inhabitancy of a particular geographical area. The issue became acute in relation to livelihood. In the modern State every person during his whole life consumes a great variety of commodities and services which he cannot produce, whilst men and women, occupied in production, habitually produce a single commodity or service for other persons to consume. Their desires, material interests and aspirations as producers, and as producers of a single commodity or service, are not identical with the desires, material interests and aspirations of these same people as consumers of many different commodities and services — just as their desires, material interests and aspirations as members of a race which they wish to continue in independent existence, and as citizens of a community with a particular type of civilisation, are not necessarily identical with what they are conscious of either as producers or as consumers. This new conception of Democracy sprang in fact from observation of the living tissue of society. Whilst metaphysical philosophers had been debating what was the nature of the State—by which they always meant the sovereign Political State—the sovereignty, and even the moral authority of the State itself, in the sense of the political government, were being, silently and almost unwittingly, undermined by the growth of new forms of

---

[1] We see this forcibly brought out by Mr. G. D. H. Cole : " It is impossible to represent human beings as selves or centres of consciousness ; it is quite possible to represent, though with an inevitable element of distortion which must always be recognised, as much of human beings as they themselves put into associated effort for a specific purpose. . . . What is represented is never man, the individual, but always certain purposes common to groups of individuals " (*Social Theory*, 1920, p. 106).

Democracy. Those who looked at society itself, and not merely at its verbal definitions, could not but realise that there had arisen in the second half of the nineteenth century, alongside the political Democracies, democratic organisations of producers and democratic organisations of consumers, wielding in fact great power, each of which believed itself to possess the only genuine form of industrial self-government. So long as the Capitalist System, working under the protection of the Political State, was unchallenged, the fundamental difference and the cleavage of interest between these two types of industrial Democracy was not apparent. The Trade Union Movement— the most extensive of all Democracies of Producers— was regarded as an organ of revolt against the Dictatorship of the Capitalist, and was by many Socialists deemed only a temporary palliative in a passing order of society. But with the advent of national and municipal Socialism, and the growth of the consumers' Co-operative Movement, the rival claims of associations of producers and associations of consumers to assume the ownership and direction of industries or services become a matter of heated controversy. Shall the mines be owned and managed by the representatives of the producers of coal, whether manual workers or brain workers ; or by the consumers of coal, as consumers, whether for domestic or industrial consumption ; or by the whole community, as citizens, interested in the conservation of the national resources for future generations ? Shall the service of education be directed by the representatives of the teachers of all grades, together with other persons engaged in the work ; or by the representatives of the pupils or of their parents, who may be regarded as the consumers ; or by the representatives of the whole community responsible for the mental development of the present and also of future generations ?

In the early stages of this controversy each of the parties tended to state its position in the most extreme form ; and to claim in fact that the only genuine Democracy was one that accepted, exclusively, the basis of Man as Producer, or Man as Consumer, or Man as Citizen, respectively. In fact, we had a repetition of the very fallacy against which all the parties were in revolt, namely, that Democracy must be one and indivisible. We may, we think, say that, in Great Britain at any rate, this controversy has now resulted in a large measure of agreement. It is, in fact, now recognised by all Socialist thinkers that, if we are to secure the largest attainable measure of personal freedom for the whole aggregate of individuals, together with the greatest net product in commodities and services in relation to the efforts and sacrifices involved ; if, moreover, we are to provide for the community of the future as well as for the present generation of citizens, the democratic organisation of society must not be based exclusively on the human being as such, but must spring from at least three, or as we think four, separate and distinct foundations, namely, man as the producer of a particular commodity or service ; man as a consumer of a whole range of commodities and services ; and man as a citizen in a twofold aspect : on the one hand concerned with national defence and internal order—that is to say, with protection against aggression from without or within — and on the other concerned with the promotion of the type of civilisation that he desires, expressed in the individual well-being of all members of the community (including the non-adults, the sick and infirm, and the superannuated) ; and with the non-material as well as the material interests of the future, in contrast with those of the present generation.

It might be expected that at this point we should

expound an ideal scheme for the reconstitution of society. We have no such object. We propose no more than a sketch of the developments of the British Constitution most urgently needed in order to extend Democracy to industry. But each society can only reconstruct itself on the lines of its own past development, and out of the social materials that are, for the time being, available. In order to make intelligible the several changes to be proposed we must therefore examine where the existing constitution falls short, and survey the organisations that have come into existence, with their various excellences and shortcomings. It is with these forms of democratic structure, moulded to fulfil the new requirements and rearranged so as to express the Socialist purpose, that reformers have, in Great Britain, necessarily to build.

PART I

A SURVEY OF THE GROUND

CHAPTER I

DEMOCRACIES OF CONSUMERS

THE rise of Democracies of Consumers, that is, of associations of men and women for the supply of their own needs, was one of the distinguishing features of the nineteenth century. Of these Democracies of Consumers there are two main species : (1) voluntary associations of consumers initiated and developed for the express and exclusive purpose of supplying specific commodities and services desired by the members, and (2) obligatory associations of the inhabitants within a given geographical area, organised primarily as Democracies of Citizens in the various Municipalities, and subsequently developing departments for the supply of commodities and services according to the will of the majority of the inhabitants. The distinguishing feature of all these Democracies of Consumers, voluntary or obligatory, is that all their activities start, not from a desire or capacity of the producer to produce, but from the recognition or ascertainment of the need or the desire of the consumer to consume—not from the factory or the workshop, but from the home or the market-place. During the last hundred years, and especially during the last two or three decades, these associations of consumers, both voluntary and obligatory, have made great strides in Britain, as in other countries. If rapid growth at the expense of the capitalist organisa-

3

tion of industry be the test of fitness to survive, the Democracies of Consumers have proved themselves, as owners and organisers of the instruments of production, in one service after another, actually superior to the Capitalist System.

VOLUNTARY DEMOCRACIES OF CONSUMERS

We need not seek to give any complete account of the innumerable varieties of voluntary associations of consumers which have sprung up and prospered in Great Britain during the last 150 years. We may, however, recall some of the leading types. There is the network of friendly societies, a couple of centuries old, with a present membership running into six or seven millions, for the co-operative supply of sick, funeral and other benefits. There is the great federation of nearly 2000 working men's clubs with a total membership exceeding half a million, owning or renting land and buildings and managing thousands of premises as social clubs, with reading rooms and circulating libraries, billiard tables and drinking bars, not to mention some convalescent homes. There are several thousands of building societies, many of them democratically organised mutual associations, which enable their members to buy sites and houses, or to erect homes for their own use. But by far the most important and most significant voluntary association of consumers is the working-class consumers' Co-operative Movement for the importation, manufacture and retailing of all kinds and varieties of household requisites, from the mining of coal and the growing of wheat to the weaving of cloth and the making of boots, from tea and sugar to furniture and houses, from newspapers and books to banking and insurance, for a constituency of four million families—meaning a population of fifteen million persons—from Caithness to Penzance and from Glasgow to Brighton.[1] The constitution of this most typical of consumers' democracies is well known. Perhaps the leading characteristic of the British Co-operative Movement— certainly if we compare it in constitutional structure with such associations of producers as the Trade Unions and the Professional Associations of brain-workers—is its pristine simplicity and automatic uniformity of type. The unit of administration and representation is the autonomous and self-governing local store, a group of men and women, of any size, from a few score to a hundred thousand, who choose to join the local society, at any time and for any period. Each adult member has one vote and one vote only, and is free to take part in all the decisions of the members' meetings, in the election of a managing committee and, through this committee, in the appointment of representatives to any federal organisation for the carrying on of the business of the Movement as a whole. These autonomous local Democracies are united in various federal bodies for special purposes, the largest and most powerful of them being, on the one hand, the Co-operative Wholesale Societies of England and Scotland respectively, which are linked together by a joint committee, and, on the other, the Co-operative Union, extending over the whole United Kingdom, for research, educational, propagandist and political purposes. The economic basis of this form of association of consumers is as simple

---

[1] For particulars of the Co-operative Movement—the continual progress of which makes all statistics immediately obsolete—the enquirer should refer to the publications of the Co-operative Union, Holyoake House, Manchester, or to the current issue of *The People's Year Book*, published annually. We may cite also *Co-operation and the Future of Industry*, by L. S. Woolf, 1919 ; *The Co-operative Movement in Great Britain*, by Beatrice Potter—a descriptive analysis of the Movement, in its meaning and purpose ; and "The Co-operative Movement," being a Report prepared for the Labour Research Department, by S. and B. Webb upon the then existing position and development of the Movement (published as a *New Statesman* Supplement, May 30, 1914).

as its constitutional structure. It rests exclusively on consumption and the elimination of profit on price. This is secured by the ingenious and now celebrated economic invention — made, it must be remembered, not by a capitalist *entrepreneur* or a professional economist, but by a simple-minded Lancashire weaver—of distributing the inevitable surpluses as " dividend on purchase." Through this device all profit, in the sense in which the capitalist uses that word, is eliminated. All commodities are taken by the members at conventional prices, usually approximating to the contemporary market price of the capitalist trader; and any margin which, in the event, may be proved to exist between the cost of production and the price charged, is returned to the members, so far as regards a bare five per cent, in proportion to their several not very unequal holdings of shares, but as regards by far the greater part, in the form of a quarterly " dividend " (virtually a rebate or discount) in proportion to each member's purchases. The 1500 co-operative societies in the United Kingdom have an annual turnover of a couple of hundred million pounds, whilst the two Co-operative Wholesale Societies have themselves a goods turnover of more than half this sum, and a banking turnover of no less than five hundred millions sterling. The greater part of this enterprise is importing and wholesale and retail trading by the two wholesale societies and the individual stores; but the two wholesale societies, together with many of the larger stores, turn out some sixty million pounds' worth of commodities annually from their manufacturing establishments. Thus, the co-operators have not only their own dairy farms and coal-mines, and the largest flour mills and boot factories in the United Kingdom, but also their own tea plantations in Ceylon, their own wheat farms in Canada, as well as their own steamers for the importation of goods, and their own steam trawlers for catching fish for their own consumption.[1] It remains to be added that the British wholesale societies have entered into exporting and importing arrangements with the Co-operative Wholesale Societies of foreign countries, for the exchange of their respective products ; thus actually demonstrating how foreign trade can be carried on on a basis of reciprocal imports, without any intervention of the capitalist, or any need for his profit.

The outstanding feature about the British Co-operative Movement, based on the association of consumers, is its great and continued success, extending over three-quarters of a century, alike in manufacture and in wholesale and retail distribution. It remains in its prosperity, as it has always been, an enterprise essentially of the manual workers. The management of its vast business enterprises is, and has always been, conducted by committees of manual workers, and by officials almost universally of working-class extraction. The members, almost entirely wage earners, have supplied, by combining their individual savings—largely by accumulating the " dividends " due to them on their purchases—all the capital that their enterprises have required, without borrowing from banks, discounting bills or raising money by debentures or shares on the Stock Exchange. They have thus proved that there is no need of " credit," or for the intervention of the capitalist, or of the payment of any toll of profit to any one outside the association, in the whole range of their great and varied enterprises.[2]

---

[1] *The Story of the C.W.S., being the Jubilee History of the Co-operative Wholesale Society, Limited, 1863-1913*, by Percy Redfern, 1914.

[2] In the present year the English Co-operative Wholesale Society is, for the first time, seeking by public advertisement to raise an additional £5,000,000 of capital on five or ten year bonds. This offer, however, is being addressed, in the main, to the constituent societies and to their individual members, and it is they who are taking up the bonds as an alternative to increasing their deposits or shares.

Obligatory Associations of Consumers

But the association of consumers is not always a voluntary organisation, which members may join and leave at their pleasure. The municipalities, or other forms of Local Government, which are based on the obligatory membership of all persons residing or occupying premises within a defined area, may also supply the needs of their members ; and in Great Britain, as in most other countries of advanced industrialism, they nowadays do so, for an ever-growing number of commodities and services, to at least as great an amount in money value as do the voluntary associations of consumers.[1] We do not, it is true, usually think of the Municipality as an association of consumers.[2] But when a Town Council provides the schools and teachers that the community requires, or the drainage, paving, cleansing and lighting without which the inhabitants of the city could not live in health ; when it supplies the water, gas, electricity and tramways which elsewhere are profitable enterprises of the capitalist ; when it provides houses, and

---

[1] It is interesting to trace the origin of some of the most important of the services administered by English Municipalities, not to the old Municipal Corporations connected with the Mediaeval Guilds, and reformed in 1835, mainly with " police powers," but to voluntary associations of the " principal inhabitants " in each area, who, during the eighteenth century, combined in order to supply for their common use the services of paving and cleansing, lighting and watching the thoroughfares. Subsequently, fortified by Local Acts of Parliament, these voluntary associations of consumers became statutory bodies of Improvement, Lighting or Police Commissioners, and as such sometimes supplied water, markets and even gas for the common benefit. Not until the middle of the 19th century were they usually merged in the Town Councils, which then took on the character of obligatory associations of consumers which has since been so greatly developed. (See *Municipal Origins*, by F. H. Spencer.)

[2] The extent, variety and range of the commodities and services supplied by municipalities and other Local Government organisations, in Great Britain as in all other civilised countries, and the steady increase in these activities year by year, are seldom realised. We may refer to *The Municipal Yearbook* (British annual) and the *Handbook of Local Government* published by the Labour Research Department, 1920 ; " State and Municipal Enterprise," by S. and B. Webb (*New Statesman* Supplement of May 8, 1915) ; *The Collectivist State in the Making*, by A. E. Davies, revised edition, 1920.

sometimes even hotels and restaurants ; when it organises (as it does in various cities or for various sections of the people), the distribution of milk and various foodstuffs, coal, drugs, and other commodities ; when it maintains hospitals and divers institutions for the sick and infirm, and organises the services of doctors and nurses, all these enterprises being carried on, not for the sake of profit, or with the object of enriching any capitalist, but for the accommodation and service of the inhabitants for whom it is an agent —it is clearly acting as an association of consumers. The Municipality, or other form of Local Governing Authority, has, at the same time, another character which we must not forget. It is simultaneously not only an association of the local consumers, but also an agent of the community as a whole, as represented by the National Government ; and as such it is concerned not merely for the provision of commodities and services, but also with carrying out the prescriptions of Parliament and the Home Office in the prevention of aggression by criminals and in the maintenance of order ; and not only for the desires and interests of the present generation, but also for those of the future inhabitants of its area.

The Municipality (or other form of Local Governing Authority) is, nowadays, in Great Britain, as in most other countries, governed by a council elected on a suffrage which approaches ever more closely to universality, nearly every adult man and a large proportion of the adult women resident within the area being now entitled to one vote, and to one only. The elected council, by the machinery of standing committees supervising the several branches of municipal work, appoints, pays, directs and controls the officials by whom its various enterprises are carried on. It also decides the policy to be pursued, subject to more or less limitation by the law, or by the executive government, which has to carry out the decisions of the national legislature. Thus the Municipality, as an association of consumers, is not wholly autonomous, as the ultimate control is shared between the local electors resident within its area and the electorate of the nation as a whole. The limitations on its freedom fall, usually, under one of three heads. It is subject, in the first place, to a not always clearly expressed " Policy of the National Minimum," according to which—in Great Britain—it is required in some matters (such as the supply of elementary schools, elementary sanitation, the institutional provision for certain kinds of sick, infirm, or destitute persons, and the maintenance of a police force) to come up to a standard of efficiency prescribed in the interests of the nation as a whole, and of future generations. In all these matters the Municipality is usually free to do as much above the minimum, and in what manner, as it chooses. A second restriction is that on the purposes for which a Local Authority may incur expense and the powers that it may exercise. These are limited to those that have been definitely entrusted to the Local Authority, either by general law or by special statute. Thus a Local Authority can only start such enterprises, and satisfy such desires of its inhabitants, and may only levy taxation in such forms as it has statutory authority for. Finally, there is a third class of restrictions imposed by law or the executive government in the interests of financial accuracy and solvency. A Local Authority is free to spend what it pleases for any of the enterprises or services that it is authorised to undertake, so long as it provides the funds annually from the authorised forms of taxation of its inhabitants. But it is required to keep accurate accounts, and to publish them, and to have them audited in the prescribed way ; whilst any borrowing of money, or running into debt is subject to limitations of amount, purpose and conditions (including an annual sinking fund or provision for gradual repayment) prescribed in the interests of the community as a whole and of future generations.

Within the range thus permitted to them, a range which is widened every year, the municipalities and other Local Authorities of Great Britain, acting as associations of consumers, now provide the inhabitants within their several areas with an enormous and steadily increasing amount and variety of commodities and services, requiring the daily work (in 1911) of 700,000 persons in Local Government employ—a staff of teachers, doctors, nurses and institutional attendants ; of workers in water, gas, electricity and tramways ; of lawyers, accountants, architects, engineers, surveyors, draughtsmen and clerks ; of artisans and labourers of every kind, that now probably exceeds a million. The salaries and wages bill of the British Local Authorities must now exceed two hundred millions sterling, or approximately one-tenth of that for the whole of the capitalist enterprises of the United Kingdom. Taking the value of all the commodities and services provided by the Local Authorities as no more than their cost, we may fairly reckon the total at as much as the aggregate expenditure of these Authorities (including materials) which now apparently exceeds 300 millions a year.

The product of this vast and diversified municipal enterprise—a considerable proportion of the whole national income—is enjoyed by the local inhabitants under a variety of conditions. Usually consumption or use is optional, but in some cases and in certain circumstances (as with elementary schools and isolation hospitals), it is legally compulsory. Sometimes no payment is exacted, and the principle of distribution adopted is that of Communism. Every one, for instance, is free to make as much use as he likes, without payment, so long as other regulations are conformed with, of the drainage system ; the paving, lighting and cleansing of the streets ; the varied amenities of the parks, public libraries and icture galleries ; the elementary schools ; and usually the infectious disease hospitals, the sanitary service and the public provision for the destitute. In the case of some services, like the water supply, a separate charge is usually made, but one based not on the quantity supplied, but on an assumed measure of affluence, the inhabitant then using as much water as he pleases. In other cases such as the tramway service, the public baths and wash-houses and the public cemeteries, there is a fixed scale of charges for each occasion of use, but the scale has little reference to the actual cost of each item of service. In yet other cases (such as the supply of gas and electricity) payment has to be made according to consumption ; but the practice varies from town to town, from charging only enough to cover cost up to levying in this way a large proportion of net revenue. What the Local Authority does with its surpluses is, unlike the Co-operative Society, not to return them as " dividends on purchase," in proportion to consumption, but to apply them to part - maintenance of the unremunerative services ; and then, in order to make up the balance, to levy on the occupiers of land and houses within its area the well-known rate, or local tax, being an equal percentage of the annual rental value of their premises, which is taken to be an index, though a very imperfect one, of the respective " ability to pay " of the several occupiers. Thus it is not unfair to say that the dominant principle of distribution supposed to be adopted in most cases by the Local Authority for the commodities and services which, as an association of consumers, it supplies is " to each according to his needs, and from each according to his ability." [1]

The question arises how far we ought to include in our class of obligatory associations of consumers the organisation by which the national Government supplies certain services, either to the citizens individually or for the use of the community. We do not usually think of our elaborately constituted national Government, with its King, Lords and Commons, its judiciary, and its great Civil Service, as being the complex organ of a nation-wide association of consumers. Yet, when the central Government organises for us such services as post, telegraph, telephone, banking, insurance, railway and canal transport, public works, medical treatment, education, and what not, together with incidental manufacturing and trading of every kind for the service of its several departments, it is engaging in industry essentially as an association of consumers, producing not for profit but for use— not with the object of deriving the utmost money income from the capital invested, but of being as helpful as possible to the users or consumers of the commodities or services in question. In so doing, the State has silently changed the character of its authority. What was originally wholly what the Germans call *Verwaltung*, and the French *autorité régalienne* or police power, has become increasingly *Wirtschaft*, *gestion*, or administration of public services—in fact, merely housekeeping on a national scale. The Government has passed from being an *Obrigkeitsstaat*, an autocratic monarch, whether a person, a class, or an

---

[1] Mention should be made of the system of Grants in Aid, by which the National Government helps the Local Government by annual subventions, intended (*a*) to effect a certain equalisation of the burden as between poor localities and rich ; (*b*) to enable the National Executive to enforce, in the least invidious way, its " Policy of the National Minimum," by which the prescribed minimum of efficiency is, in the national interests, secured ; and (*c*) to give weight to the counsel and criticism, inspection and audit of the National Executive. (See *Grants in Aid*, by Sidney Webb.)

official hierarchy, to whom we owe loyalty and obedience; and has become, in these departments of its
work, a busy housekeeper, whose object is to serve
the citizens, and to whom we owe only such adherence
to the common rules and such mutual consideration
as will permit the civic household to be comfortable.

It can hardly be suggested that there has yet been
any deliberate adoption of nationalisation as a principle;
but the advantages of production on a scale exactly
commensurate with the community for which the
work is done—of production for use instead of production for profit—have been found, in certain departments,
so great and so demonstrable that, notwithstanding all
drawbacks, national enterprise in the provision of
commodities and services has in this, as in all other
civilised countries, been for half a century increasing
by leaps and bounds. It is indeed difficult to give,
in any brief summary, an adequate idea of its extent
and variety. Confining ourselves to Great Britain,
we may point out that the Postmaster-General is the
most extensive banker, and the principal agent for
internal remittances, as well as the conductor of the
most gigantic monopoly in the conveyance of letters
and messages. The Minister of Health provides
insurance for a far greater number of persons than all
the insurance companies put together, and is, in effect,
the organiser and paymaster of the largest staff of
medical practitioners in the world. The largest
shipbuilder in the kingdom, though we often forget
it, is the First Lord of the Admiralty, whilst the
Controller of the Stationery Office is the most extensive
of publishers, who is now beginning to be not only his
own bookseller but also his own printer. There is no
tailoring firm making as many suits of clothes, even
in peace times, as the Minister of War. We need not
pursue the list. How extensive will be the aggregate
value of commodities and services annually supplied

by the Government when matters have settled down after the war it is hard to compute. But even before the war the total, reckoned at mere cost, can hardly have been much less than the aggregate provided by the Local Authorities.

But although in this economic analysis the national Government appears, in certain growing sections of its functions, as an association of consumers, it is useless to pretend that, in its constitution and political characteristics, it is anything like a Democracy of Consumers. The individual users or consumers of the services or commodities supplied by the national Government do not feel that, as users or consumers, they can control either the quality or the quantity or the price of what is provided for them ; nor can they effectively do so. These users or consumers are scattered far and wide ; they are not even aggregated, as is the case with some of the producers of these commodities, in particular geographical constituencies, an aggregation which enables these roducers to bring pressure to bear, at least, on one or two Members of Parliament. An occasional question may be asked in the House of Commons, but there is no skilled representative of the consumers' interests present to challenge the evasive reply of the Minister. When a General Election comes, other and more sensational issues are before the electorate, and the shortcomings of the Post Office or the telephone service, and the defects in guns and battleships, have little chance of being considered or explained by electors or candidates, or of securing their attention. It is to this ill-considered attempt to make shift with the machinery devised for the political Democracy for fulfilling the functions of a nation-wide Democracy of Consumers—employing for the provision of commodities and services the same organisation, the same kind of governmental structure and the same hierarchical discipline as were devised

for the fulfilment of the older State functions of
national defence, the maintenance of order and the
execution of justice — that is to be attributed much
of the present disillusionment with Parliamentary
government. To this hypertrophy of the functions
of the organisation of our national Government we
shall recur in our section on Political Democracy.

The Relative Advantages of Voluntary and Obligatory Associations of Consumers

We cannot in this book deal adequately with the
relative advantages of voluntary and obligatory associations of consumers. But experience seems to indicate
certain general conclusions. The first need of a
Democracy is to have a practicable constituency, that
is to say, a sufficiently stable and clearly defined body
of members who are able to exercise continuous control
over their executive organ ; and this, not only with
respect to policy in the abstract, but also with respect
to the application of the policy from time to time prescribed by the electorate. Experience proves that
the consumers of household requisites, within a given
neighbourhood—the housekeepers who day by day
are in and out of the Co-operative Society, who hour
by hour are testing, by personal consumption, the
quality of the goods supplied, who are able to attend
the members' meetings and become acquainted with
the candidates for representation on the governing
bodies of the store and of the federal organisations—
form such a practicable constituency. On the other
hand, it can hardly be suggested that the millions of
persons who send letters and telegrams or who travel
or consign goods and parcels by a nationalised railway
system could be marshalled into an effective Democracy
for controlling the management of the post office and
railway service. Similarly, the hundreds of thousands

of separate individuals who travel on the tramway service of London or any other great city, would be an impossible electoral unit for the constitution of a tramway authority. Further, many municipal services, like education and medical treatment, are actually used at any one time by only a small minority of any community, but are necessarily paid for by the community as a whole, whilst the interdependence of all the municipal services one with the other—of education with public health, of drainage with the water supply, of housing with transit and parks, of roads with the building regulations—would make a number of separate *ad hoc* bodies for the management of each service a cumbrous, if not impossible, form of Democracy. Finally, there is the question of the monopoly value of certain factors, such as land or coal ; and that of the common enjoyment of others, such as the air and the supplies of pure water. Each of these entails the consideration of other interests besides those of any existing body of local consumers of particular products. For all these reasons it seems that whilst the appropriate sphere of voluntary associations of consumers may be of great importance, it has its limits. We have had, in fact, to fall back for the remainder of the work on the obligatory associations of the inhabitants of particular geographical areas.

For the control of the supply of commodities and services for the consumption or use of the inhabitants of particular areas, in those branches of production for which the voluntary association of consumers does not afford a practicable constituency, resort has been had, all over the world, increasingly to the Municipality, or other form of Local Government. This, as we may note, has the advantage over the Co-operative Society of being provided with a definitely prescribed and known electorate. It has also a legally determined and stable area of operations, so that no inhabitant can be under any doubt or uncertainty as to which unit he belongs to—a fixity which is economically advantageous in some respects, but disadvantageous in others. The fixed geographical unit is advantageous for the election of representatives and the levying of taxation. On the other hand, it is a drawback to a municipal authority that its area may not havé been defined with any consideration of what is the most efficient unit of administration, and that there is great difficulty in getting it altered, whilst the fact that the same area has to be adopted for all the services of each Municipality almost necessarily involves the unit of administration being relatively inefficient with regard to some of the services. The voluntary association of consumers, like the private capitalist, is free to extend in whatever direction it finds customers.

THE ECONOMIC AND SOCIAL FUNCTIONS OF ASSOCIATIONS OF CONSUMERS

What are the economic and social advantages and disadvantages of Democracies of Consumers, first as an alternative to the present capitalist system, and secondly as a way of fulfilling the purposes of socialisation already defined. We note, first, that Democracies of Consumers are practicable. The fact that they afford a successful alternative to the capitalist ownership and organisation of the instruments of production, is demonstrated by their steadily increasing prevalence in all civilised countries. This success, in marked contrast with the uniform failure of the " self-governing workshop " to which we shall presently refer, is to be ascribed, we think, fundamentally, to their characteristic habit of governing all their activities by the preliminary ascertainment of the needs or desires of the consumers, rather than by

the wishes or capacities of the producers. As against
the capitalist trader, the success of associations of
consumers is to be ascribed to the security that they
afford against the exaction of anything in the nature
of profit, over and above the bare cost of conducting
the enterprise. In so far as the association of consumers is, as is usually the case, the owner of the
land and capital with which it works, its very constitution ensures the distribution among all the
members of the surplus that the economists know as
rent, which would otherwise become the landlord's
tribute. Thus, the association of consumers, in
such cases, does not leave to any individual the
appropriation and enjoyment of those advantages
of superior sites and soils, and other differential
factors in production, which ought to be, economically
and ethically, taken only by the community as a whole.
From all this it follows that there is, in a Democracy
of Consumers, no danger of private monopoly ; no
opportunity for particular groups of producers to
make corners in raw materials, to get monopoly
prices for commodities in times of scarcity, or to
resist legitimate improvements in machinery or processes merely because these would interfere with the
vested interests of the persons owning particular
instruments of production or possessing a particular
kind of skill. Further, management by associations
of consumers, whether obligatory or voluntary, gives
one practical solution to the problem of fixing prices
without competition among producers. This solution has been found in the practice of remunerating
each grade of producers, whether by hand or by brain,
according to an agreed standard rate, whilst prices
can be fixed just over cost, the whole eventual surplus
being either returned to the purchasers in a rebate
(or discount on purchases) called " dividend " ; or
else otherwise appropriated for the benefit and by

direction of the consumers themselves. Indeed, under a democratic system of production for use the prices charged to the user or consumer of particular services or commodities need have no relation to their actual cost of production, but may be fixed according to the relative desirability of encouraging the consumption or use of one commodity or service over another. A Democracy of Consumers, whether voluntary or obligatory, may decide to give some services or commodities, such as medical attendance in sickness, or education, or libraries, or the use of open spaces or roads, free of any charge, whilst charging for other services far more than they cost, as is often done in the case of gas, electricity or tramways, and as might be done with municipal theatres or cinemas, as an alternative to making up the deficiency by taxation. In short, the conduct of industries and services by Democracies of Consumers realises the Socialist principle of production for use and not for exchange, with all its manifold advantages. To us, it seems that the most significant of these superiorities of production for use over production for exchange is its inevitable effect on the structure and working of Democracy. Seeing that the larger the output the smaller the burden of overhead charges—or, to put it in another way, the greater the membership the more advantageous the enterprise — associations of consumers are not tempted to close their ranks. This kind of Democracy automatically remains always open to newcomers ; and, as has been repeatedly pointed out by Co-operative enthusiasts, if the whole population of any nation were to become included in the network of associations of consumers, themselves owning the land and the other instruments of production—it might even be the whole population of all the civilised nations of the world—rent would cease to be a tribute levied by a landlord class, the whole aggregate of what would otherwise have gone to the individual owners of land being, under a universal co-operative system, by the device of " dividend on purchase " automatically distributed among the entire community proportionately to the several expenditures of the various households.

Exactly the same may be said about the tribute of interest on capital in all its various forms. At present most Co-operative Societies choose to distribute a small part of their surplus among their members proportionately, not to the members' purchases, but the amount of the shares or loans or deposits standing to the members' credit, at a fixed rate per cent, irrespective of the amount of the surplus or " profit." This they call interest on capital. In so far as the shares or loans or deposits of the several members differ, relatively among themselves, from the relation between the purchases of these same members, this division of a fixed rate of interest in proportion to the several capital holdings differs from the distribution that would be made if the members decided not to recognise interest on capital. As a matter of fact, there are no large shareholders in the Co-operative Movement—holdings are often legally limited in amount—and the inequality among members is relatively small. It would, moreover, at any time be open to an association of consumers—and some small ones have done so—to decide to distribute the whole surplus or profit among their members in the form of " dividend on purchases," without distributing any part of it proportionately to the members' several holdings of shares, loans or deposits. In that case what has just been said of rent would be true of interest in all its forms. There would be no longer a tribute levied by share-holders, debenture-holders, mortgagees or capitalists of any kind, the whole excess of price over cost being automatically distributed among the whole community in proportion to the expenditure of the several households. All kinds of Surplus Value would have ceased to exist. The economic advantages offered by the form of associations of consumers are therefore great.

But the Democracy based on associations of consumers, as exemplified particularly in the Co-operative Movement, reveals certain shortcomings and defects, some transient and resulting only from the existing Capitalism, and others needing the remedy of a complementary Democracy of Producers. So long as we have a society characterised by gross inequalities of income, it is inevitable that the conduct of industries and services by associations of consumers should be even more advantageous to the rich than to the poor, and of little or no use to those who are destitute. The same trail of a capitalist environment affects also the conditions of employment. The Co-operative Society cannot practically depart far from the normal conditions of the rest of the community ; and thus avails little to raise the wage-rates of the manual working class. If, however, the associations of consumers were co-extensive with the community, they would themselves fix the standard. But there are defects inherent in Democracies of Consumers, defects which by their very nature would outlast the blighting influence of an environment of capitalist enterprise. The Democracy of Consumers, in Co-operative Society, Municipality or nation—however wide may be the franchise, however effective may be the machinery of representation, and however much the elected executive is brought under constituency control—has the outstanding drawback to the manual working producer that, so far as his own working life is concerned, he does not feel it to be Democracy at all ! The management, it is complained, is always " government from above." There is even a deeper and more serious defect in a Democracy of Consumers. It is, as all experience shows, a soulless constituency ; it lives by bread alone ; it judges all things by the quantity, quality and price of the commodities presented for its consumption. This fundamental fact in itself makes the representative of the consumers an impartial and alert judge, alike of persons and of qualifications for employment, of plant and of processes, regarded from the standpoint of economical and efficient production. But it makes him á biassed and incompetent judge, alike of the mechanical factors in production and of the methods of selecting, training, organising and promoting the workers concerned in any other respect than in quantity, quality and price of the product. Especially is he disqualified if our main purpose be not to live, but to live well—to attain among the whole community of producers by hand and by brain the maximum development of character, intelligence and free initiative.

These advantages and shortcomings of the voluntary associations of consumers, manifested in the British Co-operative Movement, characterise also, in varying degree, the other types of associations of consumers, notably the obligatory associations of local and national government in their capacity of providers of services and commodities. All of them, in so far as they become owners of land and capital, exceeding in value their corporate indebtedness, to the extent of that net ownership emancipate the community from its tribute to the landlord and capitalist class ; and to that extent place the surplus value, which would otherwise go in rent and interest, at the disposal of the community. But the Local Authorities and the Government departments do not distribute their surpluses of price over cost as dividend on purchases. As is done also to a small extent by British Co-operative Societies, and very largely by those of Belgium, the distribution takes the form of common services, which are placed gratuitously at the disposal of those who need or desire them. Thus we have Co-operative

Societies maintaining libraries and educational classes —in Belgium also providing medical attendance and nursing, orphanages and old age pensions, theatrical and musical performances. The Municipalities provide parks and museums, libraries and art galleries, schools and colleges of every kind, hospitals and sanatoria and what not. The national Government itself distributes vast sums annually, not in dividends on purchases, but in maintenance for its citizens when sick, unemployed or superannuated. It is evident that a national Government or Municipality that was as effectively democratised as a Co-operative Society is would find no difficulty in multiplying its common services ; and thus distributing what it possessed of the nature of rent and interest substantially in proportion to needs. But this very distribution by Municipalities and the national Government, as obligatory associations of consumers, of their surpluses in the maintenance of common services, essentially in proportion to needs, brings, in a capitalist society, its own difficulties. We have seen that, in the Co-operative Society distributing its surpluses by the device of dividend on purchases, in a community in which there are differences of income, even merely in the form of considerable inequality in wage-rates, it is the members with the largest incomes who benefit most, whilst the very poorest benefit least. Exactly the reverse is true of the common services by which the obligatory associations of consumers, whether Municipalities or national Governments, distribute their services. In a community of unequal incomes, especially where the inequality is aggravated by the individual ownership of land and capital, it is the poor citizens who get most benefit from the schools and hospitals, the parks and public libraries, maintained at the public expense, whilst it is the richer citizens who in one or other way control the public administra-

tion. This produces tension and conflict. The difficulty is aggravated by the fact that, owing to the small
amount of land and capital in public ownership, the
Municipality and the national Government at present
always levy taxes to make up their deficits, and find
themselves levying these taxes increasingly on the
wealthier citizens in proportion to their wealth or
" ability to pay." There is at once a conflict of interest
between those citizens who find themselves contribut-
ing from their income for common services of which
they do not themselves take advantage, and the•mass
of indigent people who take advantage of the common
services and would like more of them. The Municipality and the national Government are dominated
by the payers of direct taxation and the capitalist
press. Hence the common services are increased only
with great difficulty ; and are always more or less
subject in their administration to the *sabotage* of the
elected councillors and officials. The Municipality
and the national Government are therefore, even in
professedly democratised communities, always finding
their operation to a great extent frustrated, with the
result of financial waste, by the inevitable effects of
the division of the community into the rich and the
poor. This difficulty, like the analogous but contrary
difficulty in a Co-operative Society, would disappear
with an approximation to equality of incomes.

In the twentieth century, Municipalities and national
Governments (because they are, simultaneously, also
Democracies of Citizens, concerned as such not merely
with present consumption but also with the future
of the community and of the race) are, in their action,
not quite as soulless as a voluntary association of
consumers—recognising in these days rather more
responsibility for the provision of free communal
services for the humblest and poorest of their citizens.
On the other hand, they are still influenced, even in

the most democratic nations, by the capitalist assumption that the manual workers and the minor brain workers should be paid as little as possible, whilst certain kinds of superior brain workers and managers ought to be paid high salaries, more or less commensurate, not with the actual needs of their households, not even with the social utility of their services, but with the incomes enjoyed by the owners and organisers of the instruments of production for private profit, being the social class to which most of these superior brain° workers have hitherto belonged. Finally, the obligatory associations of consumers in Municipality or national Government are, for similar reasons, even more characterised than is the Co-operative Movement by what we have called the spirit of "government from above," so that those who are employed in their service often declare that, in respect of personal freedom and the opportunity for individual initiative, State and Municipal employment, even in professedly democratic communities, has hitherto in no way differed from the "wage slavery" of commercial Capitalism.

We see, therefore, that associations of consumers, great as are the tangible advantages that they offer in carrying out the Socialist principle of production, not for exchange, but for use, and considerable as is or might be their success in solving the economic problems presented by rent and interest, or surplus value in its various forms, do not, in themselves, as a formula of socialisation, give us all that Industrial Democracy requires.

CHAPTER II

DEMOCRACIES OF PRODUCERS

WE are, however, not restricted in our constitution-making to Democracies of Consumers. We also have at our disposal the various forms of Democracies of Producers, which have, by their survival and steadily increasing development, proved their practicability within their own sphere. The difficulty of surveying this branch of social experience is, indeed, both the antiquity and the ubiquitous variety of associations of producers by hand or by brain. Associations of consumers are, in the world's story, of quite recent origin;[1] associations of producers are as old as history itself, ranging from the immemorial castes of India and the guilds of China to the modern Trade Union of labourers and the perennial and ubiquitous organisations of lawyers, priests and doctors. Further, the associations of consumers, born almost contemporaneously with political Democracy, tend to be uniform and stable in their constitution. Associations of producers, on the contrary, are characterised by the utmost diversity and instability of constitutional

[1] We suggest that associations of consumers for the purpose of supplying themselves with commodities or services—apart from Democracies of Citizens for the primitive functions of the political State—are scarcely to be found, even in their municipal guise, prior to the end of the seventeenth century. We have here the emergence of a new form, which has in the course of a couple of centuries won its place in rivalry with the once ubiquitous associations of producers and the rising Capitalist System. See *Towards Social Democracy?*, by Sidney Webb.

structure. Who can tell us, for instance, whether the mediaeval guild was a democracy or an oligarchy ; or exactly at what periods the London College of Physicians or College of Surgeons was governed from above by a privileged section of the vocation or from below by all those workers subject to its jurisdiction ? We find the same baffling uncertainty when we pass from the constitutional to the economic aspect. Are we dealing in the mediaeval guild with an association of individual owners and organisers of the instruments of production, dictating to different grades of wage-earners the conditions of employment ; or with an association of working craftsmen super-intending, as fathers of families and master craftsmen, the co-operative production of youthful or less accom-plished fellow-workers ? And it is not only in the history books that we find this ambiguity of structure and function. When we seek to examine the innumer-able attempts made during the last three-quarters of a century in Great Britain alone by groups of manual workers to establish self-governing workshops in which they would " call no man master," we discover them struggling with kaleidoscopic constitutions, now granting, now taking away the right of self-determina-tion from the working members ; becoming in times of good trade associations of small capitalists exploiting non-members at wages ; in bad trade either selling out to their own managers, or, more usually, agreeing to hand over their concerns to the powerful consumers' Co-operative Movement. And if we look at the other end of the scale we may sometimes trace the origin of a great capitalist enterprise, now owned by thousands of functionless shareholders and managed by a hier-archy of salaried brain workers, in a genuine association of producers, composed of a few relations or friends, as penniless and as insignificant as the twenty-eight flannel-weavers of Rochdale who started in 1844 the British consumers' Co-operative Movement—the difference being that it is the brothers and friends composing the association of producers who have founded families, purchased landed estates, and procured titles, whilst the Rochdale flannel-weavers enriched neither themselves nor their descendants, but created an organisation now greater and wielding more wealth than even the greatest capitalist enterprise in the kingdom—the whole surplus of price above cost being shared among the three or four million working-class families by "dividend on purchase." The upshot is that, in the Britain of to-day, there exist few, if any, Democracies of Producers owning or organising the instruments of production by which they work. All such associations of producers that start as alternatives to the Capitalist System either fail or cease to be Democracies of Producers.[1]

But this does not mean that there are to-day no democratically organised associations of producers at all. It is one of the paradoxes of the present political and industrial situation that Democracies of Producers are, alike in the economic and in the political sphere, the most powerfully organised force in the kingdom. It is safe to say that the consumers' Co-operative Movement and the Municipalities, in spite of their very great success in organising and owning the instruments of production, are, in their political and industrial power, insignificant compared with the Trade Union Movement of manual working wage-earners, to which we must now add the nascent professional organisations of the brain workers. We hazard the opinion that the British Trade Union Movement, by its discovery and application of the methods of Mutual Insurance and Collective Bargaining, and its device of the Common Rule, worked out

---

[1] "Co-operative Production and Profit-sharing" (*New Statesman* Supplement of February 14, 1914), by S. and B. Webb.

in the Standard Rate and the Normal Day, has done more to raise the Standard of Life and to enlarge the personal freedom of the eighty per cent of the population who are manual-working wage-earners than any other one agency, not excluding either the churches or the House of Commons itself. And we cannot imagine a political party, based on the members of the Co-operative Movement as such, nor one based on the ratepayers of the municipal authorities, putting forth a claim to be, in the House of Commons, " His Majesty's Opposition " to-day, and, as public opinion now accepts, " His Majesty's Government " to-morrow. But this, by common consent, is the position of the organised Labour Party, with its three or four million membership, made up, for the most part, of the members of Trade Unions, and, to the extent of a small fraction, of the members of the professional organisations of the brain workers.

The Trade Union Movement, in fact, owes its very existence, not as in the case of the Co-operative and Municipal movements, to its being the owner and organiser of the instruments of production, but to the exactly contrary fact of the divorce of its members from that ownership and organisation. Originating as a movement of revolt against the Dictatorship of the Capitalist, the Trade Union Movement has in the course of a couple of centuries won its way to an acknowledged but strictly limited participation, not in the ownership of the instruments of production, but in the management of the nation's industries and services, whether these be conducted by capitalist *entrepreneurs* or by Democracies of Consumers. Meanwhile we have an analogous movement arising among the brain workers, whether medical men or teachers, civil servants or scientific workers, in the claim of these brain workers to take part, through their organisations, in the conduct of their services. This movement towards the control of industries and services by the workers concerned has received a great impetus from that necessary imperfection in the consumers' Co-operative and Municipal enterprise which, as we have seen, is very largely due to the environment of the modern Capitalist State, with its capitalist government and bureaucracy, its capitalist press, its capitalist degradation of the manual workers' livelihood, and its capitalist determination to hamper communal enterprise in the interests of private profit-making. Under the spell of disillusionment, largely created by those who are hostile to the purposes of Socialism, a new school of revolutionary Socialists has latterly turned against Democracies of Consumers, and has proposed, as the really effective alternative to the Dictatorship of the Capitalist, an exclusive reliance on a development of Democracies of Producers for the conduct of industries and services. The Trade Union Movement, it is suggested, might be developed so that the whole conduct of the nation's industries and services should be undertaken by their several vocational associations. Before we examine how far this claim on behalf of vocational Democracies of Producers may be justified, let us consider briefly the extent, constitution and working of the Trade Unions of manual workers and the Professional Associations of brain workers, out of which it is suggested that the new vocational administration should be developed.

The Trade Union Movement

We note first that among the Trade Unions (as distinguished from some professional organisations) there are no legally obligatory associations of producers. Whatever may be the pressure, social and economic, put upon individuals to join Unions, they are not at present required to do so by statute. The

Trade Union Movement in Great Britain, as is well known, consists to-day of seven millions of men and women organised in fifty main bodies, though a small proportion of the membership is dispersed among about 1000 separate autonomous societies.[1] These organisations are grouped in many different federal organisations for special purposes of uniting allied crafts or industries. But there are three federal systems which stand out as specially representative —the British Trade Union Congress (membership $6\frac{1}{4}$ millions) with its annually elected Parliamentary Committee ; the federations of local Trade Unions and local branches of national Trade Unions in the five or six hundred local Trades Councils ; and the Labour Party, with its Trade Union membership of three or four millions (including also Socialist and Co-operative Societies with an aggregate membership of fewer than 100,000). These three main federal systems are loosely organised and have restricted functions. What counts in the Trade Union Movement is not these loosely constituted and limited federal bodies, but the more closely knit separate autonomous Unions and their alliances and industrial federations among themselves. The constitutions of the separate societies are varied and constantly changing. Some Trade Unions restrict their membership to male workers only, and some to such workers who have received a specific training, whilst others take in any wage-earner who chooses to join. There are some Trade Unions, like those of the engineers, carpenters and clerks, and some of those of the general labourers, which have been recruited on the principle of combining in one organisation all the persons working at the particular craft, or belonging to a

---

[1] *The History of Trade Unionism* (new edition, extended to 1920), by S. and B. Webb, 1920 ; *Industrial Democracy*, by the same ; *An Introduction to Trade Unionism*, by G. D. H. Cole, 1918 ; *Trade Unionism*, by C. M. Lloyd, 1915.

particular industrial grade, irrespective of the industry in which they may be temporarily or permanently working ; there are other Unions, like those of the railwaymen and the miners, which have been deliberately formed on the principle of combining in one organisation all the persons, whatever their particular industrial grade or special vocation, who are for the time being engaged in the same industry or working for the same combination or category of employers. There are yet other Unions, and some of the largest and most active, who refuse to be tied by any principle except that of sweeping in members whenever and wherever they can, even at the expense of other Unions. This lack of any one agreed basis of organisation has produced confusion and internecine strife within the Trade Union world, one Union sometimes refusing to work with the members of another. A similar but less disastrous variety is shown in the innumerable ways adopted by the different Unions of providing for the government of the organisation, in the use made of the referendum and the initiative, in the establishment of periodical delegate meetings on the one hand, or of a permanent and " whole time " executive council on the other ; and in the varied character of the relationship between the executive committee and its officers, and of both of these to the representative conferences and the members at large. Perhaps the most important of the vexed questions of Trade Union structure—certainly the one bearing most directly on the efficient working of Trade Unionism—is the amount of autonomy accorded to local branches or divisions, and the relation of this autonomy to localised or centralised contributions and accumulated funds. It is, in fact, difficult for any student of Trade Union structure to-day to decide whether some of the organisations ought to be classed as a federation of autonomous constituent societies, each of which retains a general right to take independent action ; or as an amalgamated Union having branches or divisions enjoying much local autonomy, but subordinate to the decisions of the central executive council, the delegate meeting or the vote of the entire membership — an uncertainty as to status which has, before now, led on the one hand to local strikes in disregard of central decisions, and, on the other, to the suspension or suppression of recalcitrant local branches and divisional representative committees. Yet another complication is the extent of the representation accorded to minorities having distinct and in some cases conflicting interests, in order to persuade these minorities to come within the organisation. Compared with the constitution of the consumers' Co-operative Movement, or even with that of our Municipalities, the internal structure of the Trade Union world is a maze of difficult and in some cases almost insoluble problems.

Professional Associations of Brain Workers

The complexity and confusion of constitutions and powers among the Professional Associations of brain workers transcends even that of the Trade Union Movement. We note, in the first place, that whilst many of them are newly formed, others are of immemorial antiquity, reaching back in the Middle Ages, if not, indeed, to the Roman Empire and the beginnings of the Holy Catholic Church. It is doubtless an outcome of this immemorial antiquity that we find the organisations of lawyers and physicians and surgeons —not to mention those of the priests within what have become established churches—enjoy certain legal rights and privileges, including, in some cases, a statutory power to enforce membership on all who practise the vocation, to determine what shall be professional

qualifications, to make regulations governing professional conduct, and to compel obedience under
penalty of expulsion from the profession. A lawyer
or doctor will often be found declaiming against the
pretensions of Trade Unions of workmen to regulate
their own vocation, whilst entirely forgetting how
strictly his own professional corporation maintains its
monopolistic privileges. These ancient professional
associations often retain an oligarchical form, the rank
and file of the profession having no direct influence in
the government. But there has been, during the past
generation, a great tendency not only to democratise the
ancient professional corporations, but also to form
avowedly democratic associations of particular professions or sections of professions, which have taken
on essentially the Trade Union spirit.[1] In these
hundreds of professional associations of modern origin
we find the same difficult problems of organisation as
among the Trade Unions, the same uncertainty and inconsistency of basis, leading to the same competition for
members and the same internecine struggles between
rival societies. It is clear that it is not merely a lack
of education, a deficiency of culture or any failing in
mental capacity that has prevented the solution of
these recurring problems of democratic organisation
among all these different grades and sections of producers. As we shall presently explain, they seem to

---

[1] This tendency has been more apparent in the medical than in the legal
profession. The Royal College of Physicians has become democratic, at
least in form ; whilst the members of the Royal College of Surgeons can now
vote for its governing body, though only the superior class of fellows are
eligible for election to it. The supreme governing body of the profession,
the General Medical Council, established by statute in 1858, is now
partially elected, to the extent of six members, by all the registered practitioners. Meanwhile, the British Medical Association, and other voluntary
societies among members of the profession, have been instituted on a
completely democratic basis. For the organisation of these and other
brain-working professions, see *New Statesman* Supplements of September 25
and October 2, 1915, and April 21 and 28, 1917, entitled " British Teachers
and their Professional Associations," and " Professional Associations "
(each in 2 Parts), by S. and B. Webb.

us to be connected with the very nature of associations of producers.

There is, however, one conspicuous feature in which the Professional Associations of brain workers, for all their likeness to the Trade Unions, differ fundamentally from them. There is nothing among the brain workers—nothing even among the two or three hundred thousand of them who are joined together in Professional Associations—to correspond with the Trade Union Movement. There is not even an annual congress of Professional Associations as such, equivalent to the Trades Union Congress. There may be loose and ephemeral combination among different sections of a profession, or even, for particular purposes, among associations representing cognate professions. But there is no sense of solidarity among brain workers as such, and therefore no combined movement of Professional Associations to maintain or achieve anything. On the contrary, there is visible a fissiparous tendency, breaking up all the professions into specialities' or other sections, together with a marked inclination on the part of some of the grades and sections to ally themselves with the Trade Unions in the Trades Union Congress or in the Labour Party, whilst other grades and sections, sometimes under pretext of remaining exclusively scientific societies, exhibit a disposition to ally themselves, openly or covertly, with the organisations of landlords and capitalists among whom their clients are found.

The Relative Advantages and Disadvantages of Obligatory and Voluntary Associations of Producers

We have seen that, in the sphere of Democracies of Consumers, some are voluntary and some are obligatory ; and that the voluntary association of con-

sumers has succeeded best in organising and owning
the instruments of production with regard to the
common supplies of the household, whilst an obligatory association of all the consumers resident within
a prescribed area seems to be required, alike for
constitutional and for functional reasons, in the
organisation of such services, among others, as public
sanitation and public systems of transport. Moreover,
there is, with regard to voluntary associations of consumers, usually a genuine option as to the use or consumption of the collectively organised service. Every
person is effectively free to seek or to refrain from
seeking membership of a consumers' Co-operative
Society, a Friendly Society, a Building Society or a
social club.

In the sphere of Democracies of Producers there is no
such clear distinction between voluntary and obligatory
associations. It is true that the Trade Unions among
the manual working wage-earners began, in all cases,
as voluntary associations, and that membership remains,
to this day, nominally optional. But it is part of the
aspiration of every Trade Union to become co-extensive
with its occupation, craft or industry; and as soon
as a Trade Union comes to include, in any locality,
the bulk of those engaged in the work, the obligation
of membership becomes, in that locality, practically
even more effective on all who wish to exercise the
vocation. Where the work is done in common, this
follows simply from the recognised right of each
individual to enter or not to enter into a contract of
service. When the bulk of the workers exercise their
freedom to refuse to work alongside non-Unionists
there comes to be an effective obligation, even if non-
statutory, on all the workers to join the Union. Nor
is the sanction of the State now always withheld from
this compulsory association. We may note, to begin
with, that many " Working Rules," formulated by the

Trade Unions, and often agreed to by Employers' Associations, are made obligatory in the contracts of public authorities, and are deemed by County Court Judges to be implied terms of the contract of service, so that they become, in fact, universal in the industry for particular localities, and are thus practically enforced on all who wish to obtain employment. A further step is taken when, in some arbitration proceedings, the authoritative awards, obtained at the instance of the Trade Union, are actually made applicable throughout the industry, on Unionists and non-Unionists alike. We see a further development in the Whitley Councils, composed exclusively of the nominees of Trade Unions and Employers' Associations, and set up to make what will be, in effect, laws for their trades. The check-weigher clause in the Mines Regulation Act compels every miner to pay his share of the check-weigher's salary, when such an appointment is voted by a majority of the persons employed—virtually by the Trade Union—whether or not he has agreed to his appointment or to his wage. Thus, so far as concerns subjection to the regulations, and even to payment of a share in the necessary expense, there may often be no real liberty to the dissentient individual who wishes to abstain from combination. Even membership of the Trade Union may become explicitly obligatory, as when the employers accept the Trade Union requirement that no non-Unionist shall be engaged. To this obligation of actual membership social sanction is now coming to be given, as in the staffs of many Co-operative Societies ; and, in the South Wales coal-mines, since 1916, even the sanction of Government itself—the Coal Controller, under his statutory powers, explicitly agreeing to require that no person should be employed in or about the mines who is not a member either of the South Wales Miners' Federation, the Colliery Enginemen and Firemen's Association or the Colliery Mechanics' Union.

Among the professional associations of the brain workers there is even less distinction than among the Trade Unions between obligatory and voluntary association. The whole medical profession, including the dentists, is required by law to conform to the regulations as to admission, training, qualifications and professional conduct imposed by such exclusively professional bodies as the General Medical Council, the Medical Colleges, and the Medical Faculties of the teaching bodies. In other professions, such as engineering, architecture and accountancy, membership of the professional body is still optional, but many of the regulations that it makes become virtually obligatory on members and non-members alike, through being embodied in specifications and contracts; and even membership is made obligatory by sections of Acts of Parliament and regulations of public authorities requiring it as a condition of eligibility for whole classes of appointments. In the case of pharmacists or druggists actual membership of the Pharmaceutical Society is enjoined by statute.

Thus, alike among the Trade Unions and the Professional Associations of brain workers, there is an assumption that membership ought to be obligatory; and that every person engaging in the vocation ought to be required, in one or other way, to conform to the regulations made for the vocation by the vocational association concerned, and to bear his part of the expense.

What has not yet been enforced on associations of manual working producers, even where they have become effectively obligatory, is any formal or prescribed constitution. Where the associations of consumers is obligatory, as in the Municipality, exact provisions are made as to the conditions of citizenship, voting, the assessment of contributions and the rights of the individual. Even in a Co-operative Society statutory provision is made that there shall be a certain code of rules, and the model constitution is, in effect, prescribed subject to minor variations. This has not been done with regard to Trade Unions, even where they are accorded statutory functions, such as nomination to public bodies, the dispensing of millions of pounds under the regulations of the National Insurance Act, the appointment of such essentially public officers as check-weighers, and the constitution of half of each of the Whitley Councils. Unlike a Co-operative, a Friendly or a Building Society, a Trade Union need have no constitution authoritatively recorded, and the Courts are loth to interfere in mere quarrels among its members. When, in 1913, a group of members raided the head office of the Amalgamated Society of Engineers, forcibly ejected the duly elected executive council, installed themselves in office, and proceeded to take a ballot of the entire membership for the election of a new executive council, arbitrarily excluding from the ballot papers the names of the dispossessed executive councillors, the law courts decided that they had no power of interference, and that the new-comers must be left to be dealt with by the retaliatory " Direct Action " of any other group, or to the inevitable compromise characteristic of all British rebellions. When it is realised how seriously the result of a ballot of the membership of a Trade Union, or the decision of its elected council, may affect the whole life of the community, as in a stoppage of the railways or the mines, or in a dispute between rival Unions, the case for some authoritative definition as to who is to be entitled to vote and how the vote shall be taken appears strong. To the leaders of the Trade Union Movement, on the other hand, it seems imperative that, as an organ of revolt against the Capitalist System,

Trade Unionism must keep its organisation elastic and entirely in its own hands.

There is a like lack of authoritative decision as to the spheres and constitutions of particular bodies among the Professional Associations of Brain Workers. The trouble does not here take quite the same form as among the Trade Unions. It is to be noted that, in respect to associations of brain workers, wherever Parliament has given statutory powers over any vocation to a Professional Association, this has nearly always been conditional on the acceptance of a pre-scribed constitution, as in the case of the General Medical Council and the Teachers' Registration Council. But these statutory constitutions rest on a shifting basis, which leaves their obligatory character indeterminate. In deference to the demand for the self-government of the profession we find the existing voluntary Professional Associations adopted by Parliament as the electoral units for the statutory council. These Professional Associations, like the Trade Unions, have ever-shifting constitutions, liable to be changed at the will of the members for the time being. The associations themselves wax and wane in membership, so that it is by no means certain that this somewhat arbitrarily selected electorate does at any particular time represent even a majority of the vocation over which authority is exercised. Meanwhile, new associations arise, treading on the heels of the old organisations, and clamouring for a share in the government of the profession. To this lack of any agreed basis of organisation we attribute the atmosphere of intrigue and rivalry of principles, which at present impairs the credit of the organisations of the professional classes.

The Economic and Social Functions of Associations of Producers

(i.) *Trade Unions*

Whatever may have been the aspirations of British Trade Unionists during the revolutionary period of 1830–48, and however much the claims of Labour may have been broadened and deepened in recent years, the practical achievements of Trade Unionism have been so far limited to the maintenance and improvement of the conditions of the wage-earners' working life. No Trade Union in Great Britain owns the instruments of production on which its members work; or plays any positive part in the direction of business enterprise. Whenever the Trade Union representative or official finds himself actually negotiating the terms of an agreement with capitalist employers, government departments, Local Authorities or Co-operative Societies, he claims only to participate in arranging with the management, singly or in association, the conditions of the contract of employment. But few persons realise the wide range of the questions thereby covered. It includes not only all the elaborate technique of the Standard Rate and the Normal Day, but also the innumerable circumstances of the wage-earners' life as they might be affected by the will of the employer, whether inside the factory or the mine, the office or the shop, the ship or the warehouse, or during the hours of leisure; from the conditions of apprenticeship and the insistence on certain qualifications for employment, to the personal character and manners of the manager and foreman; from the workers' right to inspect, through their own representatives, the plant, the machinery and the material with which they are expected to work, up to the right to think and say what they like within the work-place as well as outside it; from the enjoyment of absolute freedom to live where they like, to buy from any one they choose, to conform to any religion they believe in, to spend their leisure in any amusements or in any propaganda they prefer, up to the exercise in any way of their rights or obligations of voting, of belonging to political parties, of sitting on local bodies or even of standing for Parliament against their own employers—without danger of dismissal or loss of promotion so long as they do the work for which they are paid. In the achievement of this dominant purpose of preserving the personal freedom and raising the standard of comfort of the manual workers' life, the British Trade Union Movement has been markedly successful. Trade Unionism, by its methods of Mutual Insurance and Collective Bargaining, has demonstrably raised wages and shortened the hours of toil ; by its influence upon the legislature and its activities in the law courts it has not only secured for all the workers compensation for accidents and industrial diseases, but also obtained a large measure of costly precautions to ensure the safety, alike from accident and from disease, of the factory and the mine. How much all this represents to the wage-earning community in money and in health no one can compute. An advance of even one penny per hour in the Standard Rate for all the wage-earning population of Great Britain amounts to more than a hundred and fifty million pounds a year. But Trade Unionism has done much more than prevent accidents, shorten the hours of work, and make wages higher than they would otherwise have been by one or more pennies per hour. What has been won for the workers is a large measure of emancipation from wage-slavery. Without combination, under the Capitalist System the common run of men and women find themselves, it is safe to say, not merely economically on the very margin of subsistence, and having to work " all the hours that God made," but also at the mercy of the practically unchecked authority of employer or foreman, liable to summary dismissal with or without cause, compelled to do or to abstain from doing anything outside the workshop on which the employer chooses to insist. The Trade Unions have, in short, compelled the owners and organisers of industry, whether they represent functionless shareholders or voluntary or obligatory associations of consumers, to grant to their workers a constitution.   Under this constitution, which, in our British way, is not formulated in any written code, the management of each enterprise, in case of any dispute about the conditions of employment of even the humblest employee, has to abide by the Common Rules agreed to by the Democracies of Producers, or else to get these Common Rules altered in negotiation with the authorised representatives of the various grades of workers by hand and by brain within the vocation as a whole.

So far there is substantial agreement and identity of aim among all the manual working Democracies of Producers.   But with regard to the amount of the incomes to be insisted on in return for the workers' toil there is, as yet, in the British Trade Union Movement, no settled philosophy or common agreement. There is, for instance, no assumption in the Trade Union Movement that there should be equality of income.   Without taking into account any abnormally high or exceptionally low earnings, due to temporary or unusual circumstances, the standard wages that are simultaneously being demanded and obtained by different sections of the organised manual workers in Great Britain vary as widely as from one to twenty pounds a week.

Now this lack of any clear idea as to the right

remuneration for different classes of labour by hand and by brain, is becoming every day a more conspicuous defect of the World of Labour. So long as the Trade Union is regarded merely as an organ of revolt against the Dictatorship of the Capitalist, so long as the battle is between the four-fifths of the community who live by working with their hands, and the one-fifth who either live by owning or by organising the instruments of production, almost any claim made on behalf of this or that section of workers seems justified compared to the enormous incomes in rent, profit or interest, paid out to a fraction of the community, many of whom " toil not neither do they spin." But it is obvious that the further we go in the socialisation of industry, the more completely we are able to eliminate the landlord and the capitalist, and to absorb for the use, in one way or another, of present and future generations of workers, that portion of the national product now paid in rent, interest and profit to the owners and organisers of the instruments of production (over and above the necessary salaries of management), the more acute will become the controversy as to the amount to be paid to each section of workers in return for their services.

Hence we must inquire what principles, if any, have hitherto guided Trade Unionists, and what machinery the Trade Union movement can supply for an equitable division of the available national product among all classes of workers after provision has been made for the other needs of the community.

We discern on this point, in the course of the nineteenth century, three separate and conflicting views of justice, or of social expediency, by which British Trade Unionism has been inspired with regard to the sum of wages or earnings to be insisted on. There is first the doctrine of the vested interest in a particular occupation—a doctrine inherited by the skilled craftsmen from the mediaeval organisation of industry. This doctrine of a vested interest assumes certain customary standards of living for those who exercise particular crafts—standards of living admittedly superior to that enjoyed by the common run of labouring people. This view of social expediency has a direct effect on the devices used for the maintenance and improvement of the standard rate. Thus, we find that section of the Trade Union Movement which is dominated by the principle of a vested interest in a trade, attempting to secure to themselves a privileged position by a rigid restriction of the persons entitled to practise the craft, through apprenticeship regulations, the exclusion of women, and, in some cases, the restriction of the trade to the children of existing craftsmen. The second doctrine has been termed the principle of Supply and Demand ; it is an adaptation of the axiom of the classic political economists that it is the right and even the duty of each individual (and therefore of each group of individuals) to exact at all times the highest possible remuneration that can be obtained, quite irrespective of what other individuals or classes are getting for their labour or paying for their commodities. This principle has led some powerfully organised Trade Unions to adopt any device that seemed likely for the moment to increase their earnings ; sometimes being in favour of restricting apprentices, sometimes promoting an extensive use of boy labour in order to increase their own output, sometimes holding up whole industries in order to compel employers to accord their terms, sometimes entering into arrangements with their employers with a view to eliminating commercial competition, or to obtaining, by a Customs Tariff, protection against foreign competitors. But with the better organisation of the labourers and the women during the last decades, we see emerging quite another and perhaps a more defensible doctrine for the determination of Standard Rates, that is, the principle of a living wage. This doctrine is now increasingly accepted. It is not only embodied in the Standard Rates laid down by Parliament or by government tribunals, but is also manifested in a steadily increasing tendency in the Trade Union world to agree to a progressive levelling up of the lower wage rates, in an endeavour to ensure to all alike, whatever their strategic position, at least a common minimum at a full standard of life, even at the cost of not securing the highest possible rates for the minority of relatively highly-paid grades.

We must count it as a further shortcoming of the Trade Union world that it has been unable to come to any clear or consistent view as to where it would wish the authority, or the power to give decisions in the factory or the mine, ultimately vested. The uncontrolled Dictatorship of the Capitalist is universally objected to. In the preceding analysis of the voluntary and obligatory associations of consumers, by which the rule of the profit-making capitalist has actually been superseded, it was noted that, to the workers employed in the enterprises concerned, it seemed as if there was the same objectionable " government from above " as in private Capitalism. But among the aspirations and desires of the workers themselves we find no clear or identical alternative scheme of direction and discipline. The first idea, as the recorded history reveals, is always to assume that the workers in a particular factory should themselves collectively direct the administration, decide the policy, and enforce the discipline, by appointing and controlling the manager and the foremen, and ratifying or reversing their decisions (the " self-governing workshop "). Apart, however, from the uniform failure of such an organisation,[1] it quickly becomes apparent that no such industrial autonomy is practicable in any such industry as the railway and canal service, or a line of steamships ; and that, even in the manufacturing industry, the individual factory cannot in the circumstances of modern times be an entirely self-governing industrial unit. This is easily apprehended by the experienced Trade Unionist, who has seen the " self-governing workshop " in his own industry, started with such high hopes, sometimes actually by the Trade Union itself, needing to be sharply watched to prevent it, in its eagerness for business, from submitting to less than the Standard Rate, from working longer than the Normal Day, and from foregoing advantages which the Trade Union was successfully enforcing on the common run of employers. The first discovery of the " self-governing workshop " is that it cannot, for the safety of Trade Union conditions themselves, be allowed to be completely autonomous. Whatever these particular members of the trade may desire, they cannot be permitted to depart from the rules laid down in the interest of the whole ; and to that extent at least they must find themselves submitting

[1] An examination of the experience of the large number of experiments in " self-governing workshops " in all sorts of industries in England and France makes it clear that the principal and almost invariable cause of their failure has been the inability to maintain, either the necessary workshop discipline, or any continuity of industrial or commercial policy, by a management that is chosen and controlled by those to whom it has to give orders. Over and over again the manager or foreman has been chosen, not because he was efficient in producing results, but because he maintained a government conducive to the ease and agreeable to the feelings of those whom he had to direct. The position of a manager or foreman, who is subjected to the control and direction of a committee elected by the very workers whom he has to control and direct, is always found to be an impossible one (" Co-operative Production and Profit Sharing," by S. and B. Webb, *New Statesman* Supplement of February 14, 1914).

This applies, it should be noted, to management and discipline. Systems of " Collective Piecework," where a whole workshop takes joint responsibility for mere output of an exactly prescribed article, and then chooses its own foreman or ganger, are not open to the same criticism. They have, however, been found to be open to very serious criticism from the Trade Union standpoint, as failing to maintain the standard conditions.

to an external authority. But in many other matters than in the conditions of employment—in the procuring of supplies and in the marketing of the product, in the arrangements for transport and the rate of delivery, in the quantity, the kind, and the quality of what is to be produced, and above all in the price or exchange value to be credited to the producers—the direction and control has to be exercised, in any industry or service more highly evolved than that of the village blacksmith, not factory by factory, but for the industry as a whole. If it is then realised that each industry or service must be organised as a whole, on a national scale—the mines, the manufacture of woollen cloth, the production of steel, shipbuilding, the railway system, the steamship lines, banking and insurance, and what not—it becomes evident that the policy will have to be determined, and that the administration will have to be directed, from a national centre, by an authority which, however constituted, will have to be national in its character and scope. Each factory or mine, like each railway station or steamship, has then necessarily to conform to the rules, and to obey the orders emanating, not from the particular workers concerned, but from a distant superior, transmitted through a hierarchy of managers and foremen—with the inevitable result that these rules and orders will seem, to the workers, very much the same " government from above " as that to which they are now subjected in the Capitalist System, or (to take a closer analogy) in the Democracy of Consumers known as the Co-operative Movement. We shall attempt to show, in a subsequent section of this volume, the manner and the extent to which this problem of authority can be solved. Meanwhile the divergence of views between those who still vaguely aspire to the ideal of the " self-governing workshop," and those who rest their hopes on a centralised administration by a " Guild " in each industry or service (to be composed of all the various grades of " producers," including manual workers, the clerks, the technicians and the managerial or directing officials)—between those who wish each industry or service to be, as a whole, completely autonomous, and those who realise that the consumers will have something to say as to quantity, quality, process and price—not to mention those who recognise the necessity of safeguarding the interests of the community as a whole and of the consumers of other commodities and services, and of maintaining and promoting the interests, not of the present generation alone, but also those of the future of the particular type of civilisation and of the particular race—weakens the intellectual influence of the British Trade Union World.

It will be apparent from this cursory survey of the conflicting assumptions current among Trade Unionists with regard to a just system of remuneration of labour and the character of the discipline to be maintained that the Trade Union Movement suffers, like State, Municipal and Co-operative enterprise, from the influence of its present capitalist environment. But it suffers in an exactly opposite way. The representative of a Democracy of Consumers finds himself compelled, in order to hold his own within a predominantly Capitalist System, to resist the demands of the workers for better conditions of employment, and for a larger measure of control over their own working lives, even when these are fully justified and, it may be, urgently necessary, if these conditions are markedly superior to those obtained in competing private enterprise. The official of a powerful Trade Union finds himself compelled, by the public opinion of the members of his Union, to insist on conditions of employment which may secure to a particular occupation or craft a position of virtual monopoly and a far larger share of the national product than is accorded to any other class of workers, merely because these advantages seem to be obtained at the expense of profit-makers, rent receivers and functionless shareholders. In like manner a powerful Trade Union will sometimes support a strike to secure " reinstatement " of a man dismissed, or to enforce the removal of an obnoxious foreman, even where the justice of the case is, to put it moderately, open to doubt. And these demands will, at the time they are made, not be overtly resented by the great body of Trade Unionists, who will always side in any struggle with the workers against the capitalists. This does not prevent a state of irritation within the Trade Union movement at constantly rising prices, or at perpetual demarcation disputes between one privileged craft and another, or between the skilled craftsmen and the newly organised labourers and women. Nor is there at present any central body in the World of Labour sufficiently powerful and authoritative to adjust this antagonism of interest between one section and another. The very considerable shortcoming in industrial efficiency resulting from these differences remains unremedied.

(ii.) *Professional Associations*

What are the economic and social functions fulfilled, in the Britain of to-day, by the Professional Associations of brain workers compared with those of the Trade Unions of manual workers ? Owing to the tangle of multifarious bodies, some of ancient origin, others only just emerging into life, it is difficult to sum up concisely the character of their activities.

Regarded as a method of protecting the Standard of Life and the personal freedom of the whole community of brain workers, Professional Association can hardly be said to have started on its task. There is, as yet, no feeling of brotherhood among brain workers as such. We see, for instance, no attempt, on the part of the ancient organisations of the legal and medical professions, or even on the part of the more modern organisations of engineers, architects, or accountants, to secure for all professional brain workers either a living wage or freedom from personal tyranny. The powerful Trade Union of steel smelters will subscribe large sums in aid of a strike of women match-makers or agricultural labourers. We have yet to see the Benchers of the Middle Temple voting their corporate funds in support of the claim of women teachers in the elementary schools, or of the under-paid ushers of the secondary schools, to a decent live-lihood. Moreover, even within any one profession, and still more, as between different sections of pro-fessional brain workers, there is even less tendency than in the Trade Union world to a concerted demand for equality of remuneration. Professional life, in the Britain of to-day, exhibits even within the same section of a single profession an enormous range of incomes, from the scanty fees of a junior barrister or the exiguous earnings of a slum doctor up to the tens of thousands of pounds a year of a leading K.C. or of a Harley Street expert. And if we pass from one pro-fession to another, from the Law Courts and the Colleges of Physicians and Surgeons to the elementary and secondary schools, and even to the lecture halls and laboratories of famous universities, we find whole categories of brain workers of high intellectual attain-ments and prolonged training earning, not merely a small fraction of what is obtainable by men of equal standing in the legal, medical and engineering pro-fessions, but actually less than the wages of a carman or a coal-hewer. There is, in short, no feeling of solidarity between one group of brain workers and another ; and no provision for fighting a common enemy. On the contrary, each profession tends to segregate itself from other professions, and tries its hardest to ring round its position of privilege with impassable barriers, against the claims of other professionals or the adventurous inroads of unrecognised practitioners. The doctrine of the vested interest in a " mystery " or a craft, reigns supreme in determining the relations between one profession and all other sections of the community, tempered only, within the profession, by the feeling that the luckiest or the most gifted men are quite justified in taking, not a standard or customary livelihood, but the maximum income which they are able to extract from clients anxious to obtain, when life or property is at stake, the services of the best man in the market.

In some respects, however, Professional Associations of brain workers are both more privileged and, we think, superior in function to the manual-working Trade Unions. The organisations of the older learned professions, such as the barristers, the solicitors, the physicians and the surgeons, not to mention the Church, have retained from mediaeval times certain powers of self-government not yet accorded to any other class of workers. The two branches of the law, for instance, exercise, in Great Britain, complete self-government in respect of the qualifications for employment and the admission of recruits, whilst the General Medical Council, though nominally dependent on the approval of the Privy Council, exercises similar authority over the medical and dental professions—a like position having been granted, in respect of pharmacists or druggists, to the Pharmaceutical Society. This means, that in respect of certain classes of brain workers the professional organisations have been allowed, in effect, to undertake the task of determining the qualifications to be required from future generations of professionals by prescribing the education of all the incoming members. Moreover, the older professions have secured the power of striking practitioners off the register, and thus preventing them from continuing in the profession, not merely for crime, but even for " unprofessional " conduct. The result is that we have in the world of professional organisation, in marked distinction to the world of manual labour, the gradual evolution, at the hands of the professionals themselves, of a code of morals special to each profession, a code which dictates the conduct of the professional not only in relation to his fellow professionals, but also in his relation to those to whom he renders his services, and to the community as a whole.

One of the most valuable characteristics of the brain-working professions in Great Britain, and generally throughout the Anglo-Saxon world, is the claim which they have maintained to intellectual freedom in the exercise of their several vocations.[1] This is at present secured by the remuneration of the professional " consultant " not by salary, but by fees from a series of different clients ; or, in the case of workers in science, and to some small extent in art and letters, by the permanent tenure of university and similar appointments unconnected with government or capitalist enterprise. The existence in the professions of law, medicine, accountancy, architecture and

---

[1] It is difficult to exaggerate the difference that is produced between social evolution in Great Britain (and, speaking generally, Anglo-Saxon countries) and the nations of Continental Europe, resulting from this one cause. The fact that in France, Germany and other countries, the legal, medical, engineering, architectural and other professions are, to such a considerable extent, connected with the government service by their place and method of training, their professional apprenticeship, the engagement of so large a proportion of them in a hierarchical salaried service, and their aspirations to professional promotion, gives, we suggest, a character to these professions markedly different from that of their British or American or Australian colleagues. The slow extension, outside Anglo-Saxon lands, of the profession of the independent public accountant is significant. As will be seen in a subsequent chapter, there will be scope in the Socialist Commonwealth for a great development of the independent professional, remunerated by a series of fees from a succession of clients.

engineering of a whole class of independent experts, not in the service of any person or corporate body, but ready to give responsible advice and assistance to a succession of clients, affords to the community the advantage of an independent check on the necessarily considerable influence of the secretarial bureaucracy and its own salaried technicians, whether in the service of the national and Local Government, or in that of the Co-operative Movement or of joint-stock Capitalism. This does not mean that a part of each profession may not be definitely in the employment of particular government departments, Municipalities or Co-operative Societies, which need the full-time salaried service of many lawyers, doctors, engineers, architects, accountants, chemists and what not. But it has been of the greatest value in Great Britain that the other members of each profession have continued in the position of unsalaried, independent consultants, called in only for specific purposes as required, and rendering their services in return for separate fees. We shall see, in subsequent chapters, that it will be quite possible, in a Socialist Commonwealth, for these independent consultants to continue to be called in by any one of the thousands of separate government departments and boards, town or district or county councils, port and harbour authorities, universities and other educational bodies and voluntary associations of producers and consumers in different parts of the country, among whom the work of administration must necessarily be distributed. This independence of professional status, and the free exercise of professional opinion is promoted by, if not dependent on, the existence of strong Professional Associations with certain powers of self-government ; and on the inclusion, in one and the same association, of both the salaried and the independent practitioners, who are thereby enabled to afford to each other the support necessary to uphold the dignity and freedom of the brain worker against the powers of both corporate authorities or private capitalists. It is a calamity of no mean gravity that the journalists, who ought to constitute one of the most powerful and responsible of professions, as they do constitute one of the most influential, should be without the status and the support, and therefore most frequently without the security and the intellectual independence, which might be attained if their profession could be put on the footing of law, medicine or accountancy. In a lesser degree the same may be said of the teaching profession, in so far as it is outside the protection of university endowments and university autonomy.

There is, to-day, another distinction between the Professional Associations of brain workers and the manual-working Trade Unions, which we may hope will not be a permanent one. Owing largely to the independence and self-government of the professions, and partly to the very nature of their function, professional brain workers easily develop or help to develop associations for the improvement of their technique and the enlargement of their knowledge. These " Subject Associations," or scientific societies, have, in some cases, become, to a great extent, dominant in determining the nature of the service to be given or the commodity to be made by all those engaged in turning out the product, whether manual workers or brain workers. For instance, the Engineering Standards Committee,[1] now the British Engineering

[1] The Engineering Standards Committee, established in 1901 and incorporated in 1918 as the British Engineering Standards Association, represents an interesting example of a Joint Committee of the experts of production and the experts of consumption, designed for the purpose of determining what shall be the processes of industry. * It was initiated by the Institution of Civil Engineers, and now has the support of the representatives of the five great technical societies of the engineering industry—the Institutions of Civil Engineers, Mechanical Engineers, Naval Architects and

Standards Association, with its innumerable sub-committees, is very largely controlled by the various Institutes of Engineers, supplemented by the expert representatives of industrial and other consumers of engineering products ; and it is this organisation which, in innumerable cases, virtually decides what methods and processes shall be adopted, in connection

---

Electrical Engineers respectively, together with the Iron and Steel Institute and latterly also the Federation of British Industries. Owing to the value and importance of its work, which is supported mainly by subscriptions of the principal manufacturing firms and railway companies together with some Local Authorities, it has received from the British Government and from those of India and the Dominions, a series of Grants in Aid, and it has on its innumerable sub-committees representatives of those Government Departments and Local Authorities who are large purchasers and users of the articles dealt with. But other bodies of consumers are represented, and also the principal manufacturers and technical societies. For instance, on the " Sectional Committee on Automobile Parts " we find representatives of the War Office, General Post Office, the Crown Agents for the Colonies, Royal Automobile Club, the Automobile Association and the Motor Union, the Society of Motor Manufacturers and Traders, the Commercial Motor Users Association, and the Institute of British Carriage Manufacturers. During the twenty years of its existence there have been no fewer than 250 sub-committees and sectional committees, investigating and determining the processes, the materials, the forms, the measurements of every imaginable type of component from angle iron to locomotive engines, from carbon filament glow lamps to salt glaze ware pipes, from structural steel for bridges to field coils of electrical machines. It is impossible to over-rate the importance, in the control of industry, of this silent but all-pervading determination of processes, materials and products. In nearly every contract of importance, whether carried out by a public authority or by a railway company, at home or abroad, whether enforced by the purchaser or by a bank or an insurance office, we find insisted on these standard specifications with regard to materials, processes and product. Hence, though the British Engineering Standards Association has no legislative or other authority, and is in no way empowered to make rules for the trade, every manufacturer finds himself in fact constrained to make use of specified materials of specified shape, size and weight, put together in a specified way. Although every purchaser remains nominally free to order what he likes, in the vast majority of cases he finds himself equally obliged to accept what has thus, by the mere weight of expert agreement, been authoritatively recommended. It follows that, although every workman, and every Trade Union remains nominally free to bargain as to the contract of service, they are virtually compelled to work according to the processes thus determined. This essentially expert control exercised over industry without any democratic control—conducive, we may admit, to its technical efficiency and to the satisfaction of the community of consumers—cannot fail to have its effect on the cost of the articles to the purchasers, as well as upon profits and wages. (See *Thirteenth Report on Work Accomplished*, 1917–19 ; previous Annual Reports ; over 100 reports on particular articles ; and 280 Standard Specifications, all published by the British Engineering Standards Association, 28 Victoria Street, Westminster.)

with the specific articles that it "standardises," throughout all the wide range of engineering, machinery of every kind, the materials and components of railway equipment, ships, buildings, electrical apparatus, automobiles, and air-craft. In like manner the scientific societies of the medical profession, and the "Subject Associations" of the educational world, with their continual discoveries of new facts and their constant evolution of improved methods of treatment and education, exercise an ever-increasing influence on medical practice and on pedagogy.

In short, whether we consider professional training or professional qualification, professional etiquette or professional technique, we see the Professional Associations of brain workers developing activities unknown to the Trade Union world, and exercising far-reaching authority, not only over the working lives of their respective members, and incidentally over those of the manual workers associated with their operations, but also over the nature and character of the services or commodities to be enjoyed by the community of consumers, or citizens. There is, as will be described in the constructive portion of this book, good reason to hope that the Trade Unions of manual workers, once they are freed from the incessant struggle to defend the economic position of their members against encroachment, will develop, within each vocation, or in combination with allied vocations, similar "Subject Associations" or scientific societies for the development of a professional ethic and for the advancement of the science and art of their particular service to the community.

CHAPTER III

THE POLITICAL DEMOCRACY

WHEN we turn, in the Britain of to-day, from the existing Democracies of Consumers and Democracies of Producers to the present political Democracy, which is assumed to be a Democracy of Citizens, we are struck by the extreme imperfection of its organisation, and by the very small degree of correspondence between the institution and the work that it has to perform. The institution, in fact, was not made for the job. Political Democracy arose, not as a method of government, but as an organised revolt against government by the king and his warriors, or the Church and its priests, compelling these autocrats to " grant a constitution " limiting their dictatorship. Further, in every case, political Democracy has begun as the struggle, not of all the inhabitants of a country but of a privileged layer of them claiming the right of self-determination for themselves alone. In the elder civilisations of Europe the so-called representatives of " The People " were for centuries the representatives only of the propertied, the professional, or the employing class, the rest of the people being kept out of all share in the " self-government " that was gained ; whilst the enfranchisement of half the race —of the women—has only just been accomplished, and that not completely and only in some States. In spite of the fact that political Democracy has hitherto been thus imperfect in its adoption of the principle of self-determination, we may take it that, when we speak of political Democracy to-day, we mean the association of all the adult inhabitants, within a given area, claiming and exercising the rights and powers of political self-government.

But there is another qualification to political Democracy as we know it to-day. The political Democracy of Great Britain, of France, and to a lesser extent of some other countries, exercises jurisdiction not only over its own electors, but also, in Colonies and Dependencies of different kinds, over masses of other persons, usually of a different colour, who are denied, like the British woman of a few years ago, any part in national self-determination. Hence the political Democracy of the modern " World-State " is often an autocracy, or an oligarchy in respect of an actual majority of those coming under its jurisdiction. This qualification is, of course, patent and acknowledged. But there is a more insidious ambiguity in the constitution of existing democratic States. The majority of the electors within a political Democracy, having one type of religious, economic and social culture, may, by insistence on a pedantic uniformity where differentiation is practicable, deny any effective self-determination in matters essentially bound up with the religious, economic or social culture to a minority interspersed among the majority, even whilst admitting that minority to the electoral roll, in such a way as to outrage the strongest and most deep-seated of human feelings. The issue becomes at once most acute and least excusable when the oppressed minority is fortified in its sense of difference by racial, religious, or historic separateness, and is segregated in a geographical unit, within which it constitutes a considerable majority of the inhabitants. It is, in fact, this ambiguity in the meaning of political

Democracy that has caused many of the tragedies and wars in modern history. To bring this fact home to our readers we need only mention Ireland.

THE STRUCTURE OF BRITISH POLITICAL DEMOCRACY

We need not enquire too curiously about the historical anomalies of the British Constitution, with its ostensible vesting of the supreme government of the British Empire in " King, Lords and Commons." Nor shall we deal with the constitutional relations between the congeries of nations that we still style the British Empire. We confine ourselves, indeed, to the organisation of Great Britain.

(a) The King

It is an essential feature of the British Constitution that our sovereign king reigns but does not rule, and that he holds his title, not by any religious or metaphysical right, but by an Act of Parliament, which has been more than once amended and which, admittedly, can be repealed like any other statute ; and thus, in effect, by the continued assent of the British people. In fact, the contract of service between the British king and the British people may be legally and rightfully terminated at any time by the will of either party ; we cannot force any member of the Royal Family to serve us as king, any more than he can compel us to continue him in office as the first official of the State. And if we pass from the constitutional theory of the text-books to the facts as we see them to-day, what we have to note is that the particular function of the British monarch—his duty as king—is not the exercise of governmental power in any of its aspects, but something quite different, namely, the performance of a whole series of rites and ceremonies, which lend the charm of historic continuity to the political institutions of the British race, and which go far, under present conditions, to maintain the bond of union between the races and creeds of the Commonwealth of Nations that still styles itself the British Empire. This function could not be fulfilled to the satisfaction of either king or people, unless the tie of mutual sentiment between citizen and sovereign remained real and, vital. If ever this breaks, the institution of monarchy, in Britain or elsewhere, would almost automatically come to an end—we venture to think, by common consent of king and people.

(b) The House of Lords

The House of Lords, with its five hundred or so peers by inheritance, forty-four representatives of the peerages of Scotland and Ireland, a hundred and fifty newly created peers, twenty-six bishops, and half a dozen Law Lords, stands in a more critical position. No party in the State defends this institution ; and every leading statesman proposes either to end or to amend it. It is indeed an extreme case of misfit. Historically, the House of Lords is not a Second Chamber, charged with suspensory and revising functions, but an Estate of the Realm—or rather, by its inclusion of the bishops—two Estates of the Realm, just as much entitled as the Commons to express their own judgment on all matters of legislation, and to give or withhold their own assent to all measures of taxation. The trouble is that no one in the kingdom is prepared to allow them these rights, and for ninety years at least the House of Lords has survived only on the assumption that, misfit as it palpably is, it nevertheless fulfils fairly well the quite different functions of a Second Chamber. Unfortunately, its members cannot wholly rid themselves of the feeling that they are not a Second Chamber, having only the duties of technical revision of what the House of Commons enacts, and of temporary suspension of any legislation that it too hastily adopts, but an Estate of the Realm, a co-ordinate legislative organ entitled to have an opinion of its own on the substance and the merits of any enactment of the House of Commons. The not inconsiderable section of peers and bishops which from time to time breaks out in this way, to the scandal of democrats, can of course claim to be historically and technically justified in thus acting as independent legislators, but constitutionally they are out of date ; and each of their periodical outbursts, which occasionally cause serious public inconvenience, brings the nation nearer to their summary abolition. Perhaps of greater import than the periodical petulance of the House of Lords is its steady failure to act efficiently as a revising and suspensory Second Chamber. Its decisions are vitiated by its composition—it is the worst representative assembly ever created, in that it contains absolutely no members of the manual working class ; none of the great classes of shopkeepers, clerks and teachers ; none of the half of all the citizens who are of the female sex ; and practically none of religious nonconformity, of art, science or literature. Accordingly it cannot be relied on to revise or suspend, and scarce y even to criticise, anything brought forward by a Conservative Cabinet, whilst obstructing and often defeating everything proposed by a Radical Cabinet.

Yet discontent with the House of Commons and its executive—the Cabinet—is to-day a more active ferment than resentment at the House of Lords. The Upper Chamber may from time to time delay and obstruct ; but it cannot make or unmake governments ; and it cannot, in the long run, defy the House of Commons whenever that assembly is determined. To clear away this archaic structure will only make

more manifest and indisputable the failure of the
House of Commons to meet the present requirements.

(c) *The House of Commons and the Cabinet*

The House of Commons consists of 707 members
representing the United Kingdom, who are, with few
exceptions, elected by single-member constituencies,
having populations averaging about 70,000 each. The
franchise is practically universal for men over 21,
though not yet so for women (who must be over
30, and themselves independent occupiers, or else
the wives of electors); women, like men, being eligible
for election at 21. Of the functions of the House of
Commons the principal is not itself to govern but
to create a government, no Cabinet being able to
remain in office or to rule without its continued
acquiescence. But we must not overstate the freedom
of the House of Commons to select its own executive.
In this respect it finds itself far more restricted, alike
in theory and in practice, than are the Trade Unions,
Co-operative Societies and municipal authorities.
The members of a Trade Union or Co-operative
Society always elect their committee or executive
council, person by person, either by vote of the
members or by vote of their elected representative
assembly : a municipal council elects its Mayor and
its committees as it thinks fit. No such power is
enjoyed by the House of Commons. Ostensibly it is
the prerogative of the King to send for any one he
likes to be his Prime Minister, and to form a new
government, when the existing one has forfeited the
support of the House of Commons. We may admit
that this power of choice by the King is more nominal
than real ; indeed, the King has almost invariably no
choice, seeing that he must take as Premier the statesman who is able to form a government which will
in fact be continued in office by a majority of the

House of Commons. But it is an incident of this involved procedure that the House of Commons, having got the Prime Minister that it desires, finds itself constrained to accept as Ministers such colleagues as are selected by the Prime Minister, who forms his own judgment of the acceptability of the Cabinet as a whole. The House of Commons cannot exercise any choice in the selection of Ministers, still less assign particular men to particular offices. We need not come to any conclusion here as to whether this delegation to the Premier of the power to choose all departmental heads is a good or a bad device. On the one hand, it is asserted that by this device, and by this device only, can we secure a responsible Cabinet having a common policy by which it stands or falls. On the other hand, the favouritism and arbitrariness exercised in the selection of men to fill responsible posts, and more especially the defiant disregard of the opinion of the House of Commons in some appointments—a disregard which has latterly gone the length of taking men who are unknown to the public, without experience in governmental administration, and not even Members of Parliament, has brought out the weak points in the system. Still more flagrant is the inability of the House of Commons under this system to get rid of any Minister who proves himself incompetent or who disregards the will of the House.

Owing to the very imperfect procedure of the House of Commons, which does not get mended, and to the failure of the House to organise itself in standing committees responsible for the several branches of its work, the Cabinet, once installed in office, has complete control of the time and business of the assembly. Thus, in practice, though the House of Commons may cause the alteration, and even the abandonment, of measures proposed by the

Government, it cannot pass legislation or come to any important decision without the active concurrence of the Ministry. Unlike a municipal council, with its standing committees supervising the day - to - day work of the official staff, the House of Commons finds itself unable to exercise any control over the current administration of the national government, whether at home or abroad ; and owing to the traditions of secrecy and the alleged impossibility of divulging present or past dealings with foreign Powers, and past and present communications with the governors of our Dependencies, the House of Commons has practically no power to control foreign and imperial policy, otherwise than by tardy approval or disapproval after the event. The elected representatives of the British Democracy are in fact to - day practically limited to the function of making and unmaking a government and of criticising, obstructing or amending any legislative projects brought forward by the Government, and of offering a belated criticism on any administrative policy which has involved expenditure. So long as the House of Commons does not choose to dismiss the Government and set up another, it has in fact to abide by the collective decisions and individual vagaries of the Cabinet and its members, except in so far as these may be influenced by a general sense of the " feeling of the House."

But are we governed by the twenty or more gentlemen who form the British Cabinet ? Is it they who collectively determine how the work of the Government shall actually be carried on ? For instance, is it the Cabinet that settles what shall be our foreign relations—shall they make for peace or war—what shall be the spirit and purpose of our rule in India, Ireland and Egypt ? Is it the Cabinet that decides whether or not our system of taxation shall tend to increase or to decrease the present inequalities of life :

what sort of education shall be given to the vast bulk of British citizens ; how exactly medical treatment can be so specialised and distributed that it shall actually raise the common standard of health ? Is it the Cabinet that decides whether the Post Office shall or shall not become the bank and life assurance office of the poor, and whether unemployment shall be prevented or allowed to occur and then merely relieved ? We think that if any ex-Cabinet Minister were to be compelled to tell the truth, the whole truth and nothing but the truth, about his own participation in the gradual shaping of policy on such vital questions during his term of office, he would tell us that he hardly remembered any Cabinet decision being formally taken on general policy, unless legislation of a controversial kind had to be introduced into Parliament, unless some dramatic decision had to be taken, or unless the administration of a particular Department had offended some powerful outside interest or had become a public scandal. Even in his own Department he would plead that, what with the attendance at the House of Commons, periodical appearances in his constituency and on other public platforms, he getting up of the Party's case in some vividly topical controversy, often an issue of little real importance, he had no time or energy left with which to supervise the day-by-day administration of the public service over which he presided. The government of Great Britain is in fact carried on, not by the Cabinet, nor even by the individual Ministers, but by the Civil Service, the Parliamentary Chief of each Department seldom actively intervening, except when the point at issue is likely to become acutely political. It has been the supreme good fortune of Great Britain that she has, during the past century, developed a Civil Service of exceptional capacity and integrity ; but, like other men, the

Permanent Heads of the several Government Departments desire the amenity of a quiet life and the opportunity for getting through with some measure of
efficiency the immense amount of technical detail
involved. The easiest way to secure this condition
of smooth working is so to transact the Government
business that its doings are unnoticed in Parliament,
and rarely come up for Cabinet decision. It might
almost be said that the supreme test of the perfect
efficiency of a Government Department—in the eyes
of its Parliamentary Head and of the Cabinet—is that
it should never be mentioned either in the House of
Commons or in the press. Hence it happens that
the special skill in a civil servant which is most
appreciated by his Parliamentary Chief and by his
colleagues in the Civil Service is not initiative or
statesmanship, and not even the capacity to plan and
to explain the departmental projects, but either to avoid
questions in the House, or, if these are asked, to furnish
answers which allay without satisfying the curiosity
of the enquirers. And in pursuing this ideal of being
neither seen nor heard the great civil servant has
an excellent justification. He knows by bitter experience that a Member of Parliament, unless he be a man
of encyclopaedic knowledge and tireless energy, has,
owing to the multifarious issues raised in the many
departments of national government, neither the
capacity nor the opportunity of becoming really con-
versant with the subjects to be considered. He can
cavil, but he can seldom offer useful criticism of a
constructive kind. As a matter of fact, the only
questions upon which the Member of Parliament
becomes even superficially versed are those which
are being pushed by some vigorous group of persons
outside the House of Commons, sometimes phil-
anthropists, reformers or the adherents of particular
religious creeds ; sometimes the professional repre-

sentatives of great capitalists, or of technical or labour organisations. Hence the able civil servant and the expert Minister are always trying to placate these little groups of outsiders and to make arrangements with those who really understand and are interested in the issues involved in new legislative or administrative work, so as to prevent these issues being raised in Parliament. In short, the real government of Great Britain is nowadays carried on, not in the House of Commons at all, nor even in the Cabinet, but in private conferences between Ministers, with their principal officials, and the representatives of the persons specially affected by any proposed legislation or by any action on the part of the administration. The great mass of government to-day is the work of an able and honest but secretive bureaucracy, tempered by the ever-present apprehension of the revolt of powerful sectional interests, and mitigated by the spasmodic interventions of imperfectly comprehending Ministers.

When we pass from the control exercised over the Civil Service by the Ministers and over the Ministers by the House of Commons, to the control exercised over them all by the electorate itself, without which there can be no true Democracy, we come to a land of still deeper shadow. The House of Commons can at any rate unmake a Cabinet to-day and set up another to-morrow. The Cabinet can maroon a leading civil servant of whose action it disapproves, or transfer him to another Department. But the electorate is bound for five years to put up with the representatives that it has sent to Westminster, whatever may be their action or inaction. And this helplessness on the part of the electorate to control its representative assembly is immensely aggravated by the fact that a Parliament elected predominantly on one issue or group of issues may proceed, and must inevitably proceed, to determine other issues or groups of issues of equal importance to the community—issues which may have ever even been mentioned in the election manifestos of rival political leaders. For instance, a Parliament elected to carry through a war to a successful conclusion may find itself completely transforming the educational system of the country. Another Parliament elected to reform or abolish the House of Lords may find itself acquiescing in the conclusion by the Cabinet of secret agreements with foreign Powers involving the country in immense financial and military responsibilities, whilst we might see another Parliament elected to nationalise the mines and railways, and to enforce legal minimum wages and maximum prices, confronted with a crisis in the British Empire which would entail a radical change in its constitution, or even its supersession by a League of Nations. The House of Commons in fact, if it happened not to be resisted either by the King or by the House of Lords, might make itself, or the Cabinet for the time being, the ostensible dictator in home and foreign affairs, leaving to the bureaucracy, in consultation with powerful outside interests, the task of actual management of public business. Already we see it habitually supporting and not controlling the Prime Minister of its choice in carrying on any kind of administration or any kind of foreign or imperial policy. Hence the Cabinet might, under the same conditions, even abolish the British Constitution, restrict the franchise, and sweep away all democratic institutions, including the House of Commons itself. It might set up a new House of Lords with unlimited legal power to thwart a future House of Commons. It might reintroduce industrial conscription, or even chattel slavery, or exterminate by tanks and bombing aeroplanes any recalcitrant mining village or factory population. We have been in the habit of saying that such things " do not happen " in Great Britain. If they did there

might be a " revolution " in which even the police and
the army would participate. But such a revolution,
which might be bloodless, would be effected not by
anything that could be termed a political Democracy,
as we have defined it ; it would be a case of " Direct
Action " not contemplated in the British Constitution.
It would be civil war.

CABINET DICTATORSHIP

We pause to recollect how silently, and yet how
completely, the British Constitution has been changed
by the gradual effacement of the House of Lords,
culminating in the Parliament Act of 1911, and by
the submergence of the House of Commons in the
flood of government activity. In eighteenth-century
Britain the Constitution provided for a " balance of
power " exercised by different social forces : the power
of the Crown and the personal favourites of the
monarch for the time being ; the power inside Parliament and outside of the great hereditary landlords
and of the Church ; the power of the county
constituencies of freeholders and the independent
members whom they sent to Westminster ; the power
of the Municipal Corporations more or less rooted in
vocational associations, or wielded by their wealthy
proprietors. Even after the Reform Act of 1832 the
authority of the House of Commons continued to be
effectually qualified by the customary influence of the
Crown on the one hand, and by the very real concurrent legislative powers of the House of Lords on the
other. Moreover, the limited and differentiated franchise of 1832–85, not then exposed to the extreme
tendenciousness and suggestiveness of the newspaper
press of the present day, habitually produced a House
of Commons more heterogeneous in its character,
less liable to be chosen on waves of electoral passion,

and, in the limited range of subjects to which it commonly restricted itself, less amenable to any other influences than the spontaneous instincts of the electorate of property owners. There was thus, right down to the end of the nineteenth century, a real balance of power between different vested interests and an active control of the executive government by Parliament. To-day practically all the functions of political government and all the powers of the State, enormously widened in penetration and scope, are concentrated in the House of Commons and the executive that it is assumed to create. Further, owing to the obsolete internal machinery of the House of Commons and to the immense variety and complexity of the issues with which it nowadays purports to deal, the power which it is incapable of exercising has been virtually transferred to the Prime Minister and his co-opted group of colleagues in the Cabinet, and by them to the Civil Service acting in conjunction with the powerful outside interests. The result is that, under the guise of government by a majority of the people acting through its elected representatives, we have now the dictatorship of one man, or of a small group of men, exercised through a subservient party majority of more or less tied members, and an obedient official hierarchy of unparalleled magnitude —a dictatorship tempered, on the one hand, by a continual watchfulness against explosions of popular feeling, and on the other by the necessity of privately securing the acquiescence, or at least preventing the revolt, of powerful capitalist or other interests.

HYPERTROPHY

What has contributed more than anything else to this transformation of the British Constitution has been the extraordinary hypertrophy of its political institutions. The national government of a hundred years ago—whether we take it as King, Lords and Commons, or as a Cabinet of Ministers directing an administrative hierarchy—was occupied almost exclusively with national defence and foreign affairs, the maintenance of order and the administration of justice, together with the taxation that these functions necessitated. The military and naval establishments, and even the Post Office, were inconsiderable, and the Civil Service had scarcely begun to exist. There was, we may fairly say, no thought of consciously promoting, or even of deliberately maintaining, the interests of the community in future generations, or of developing the type of civilisation that the nation preferred. There was not even any serious consideration of how best to utilise the nation's natural resources for the ·satisfaction of the desires of the contemporary citizens, or of organising industries and services to the greatest advantage. All this work, it was assumed, was a matter for individual enterprise, stimulated by the desire for profit, and with it the Government had no concern. The political organs of the State were charged exclusively with the older or, as we may say, the primary political functions.

Nowadays we find not only that these primary political functions are greatly swollen in volume, but also that a whole array of new duties have been thrown on the political machinery, from the organisation of an extensive service of public health, including most elaborate provision for the sick and infirm of all kinds, the infants and the aged, up to the direction of such industries as coal-mining and transport ; from education of every grade and kind to the promotion of invention and research, and actually to the planting of timber and the manufacture of sugar ; from the insurance of two-thirds of all the population and their deposit banking on a gigantic scale, up to the provision of houses for them to live in and the regulation of their daily supplies of food and clothing ; from the determination of wages to the fixing of prices and rents. In short, the Government now finds itself not only, when required, conducting on a gigantic scale the operations of war, but also at all times implicated on an equally gigantic scale in the control and administration of the operations of peace. All the new functions, as well as all the old, have been simply heaped upon the former political machinery of King, Lords and Commons at Westminster and a Cabinet of responsible Ministers in Whitehall.

It was often assumed, a generation ago, that the bulk of the new work of government would fall, not to Parliament and the Cabinet, but to the local governing bodies, and that the expansion of the functions of these Local Authorities would relieve the congestion of public business at Westminster. The Local Authorities have indeed grown by leaps and bounds, until they have to-day in Great Britain alone nearly a million households directly on their pay - rolls ; but their expansion has effected nothing in relief of the national government. A considerable part of the increase in volume and variety of the governmental work is necessarily national in scope and centralised in administration (such as the supervision and control of factories, mines, shipping and railways, and all the developments of the Post Office). But what was less clearly foreseen was the correspondence in expansion between the activities of the Local Authorities and the work of the departments of the national government. The more numerous and extensive are the functions of the Municipality, the greater the number of points at which other interests are touched, the more frequent are the references to the government departments concerned, the more difficult becomes the adjustment of financial relations, the

heavier and more complex grow the Grants in Aid,
and the more intractable the problems presented to
the Cabinet for solution. Experience, in fact, far
from promising from the development of local institutions any relief in the burden of national government, teaches an exactly contrary lesson. Every new
service undertaken by the Local Authorities (such
as public education, or the provision for maternity
and infancy, or the erection of dwelling-houses) has
involved up to now at least a proportionate addition,
not only to the calls upon the time and understanding
of Members of Parliament, but also to the work of
the Ministers and Departments concerned, and, be
it added, as things are now arranged, at least an
equivalent new drain on the national exchequer.

A Vicious Mixture of Functions

But it is not only the hypertrophy of business in
the House of Commons and Cabinet that we have
to complain of. The heterogeneity of the functions
inconsiderately heaped upon the political institutions
is itself a factor not only in the bewilderment of the
legislator, but also in the growing inefficiency of the
institutions themselves. At present we make shift with
one and the same social machinery for the primary
functions of defence, police and justice ; for the
very different administration of public services and
nationalised industries ; and for yet other duties
involved in taking thought for the future, the promotion of the particular form of civilisation desired by
the community, and the safeguarding of the interests
of the generations to come. All three sets of responsibilities may be equally duties of the national authority,
but it does not follow that they need be equally
associated with the social influence of the Crown,
the sanctions of the Courts of Justice and the impera-

tive authority of the military forces. The national authority, as wielding all the power of the nation for defence against aggression and for the maintenance of order, inevitably assumes a highly disciplined hierarchical form, pushes to an extreme its supremacy over the individual citizen, and tends to exact an unquestioning obedience to commands merely as commands—all of which may be as necessary to efficiency in the domain of army and police as they are certainly incompatible with the highest accomplishments in social and industrial administration ; and also, as we should suggest, with any scientific anticipation of the future. The most obvious danger from this combination, in one and the same national executive and legislature, of the community as power and the community as social and industrial administration is seen whenever a great industrial dispute arises, or is threatened, in such an essentially national industry as the railway service or coal-mining. The threat to use the whole organised forces of the community in protection of the interests of " the consumers " as against the interests of " the producers " is regarded by so large a proportion of the population as illegitimate that, if it were actually carried out, it might easily bring the nation to the verge of civil war. It is commonly felt that, in any dispute; the business of the Government as an organ of power is to " hold the ring," to confine itself to the maintenance of order, and not to intervene, except to prevent attacks on life and property. To use the military and police force, not merely to keep order but actually to conduct the service hitherto performed by the strikers, as has happened in more than one country, goes far to evoke a combination of physical violence with industrial action. It is often " touch and go " whether it may not lead to the rank and file of the army refusing to act as blacklegs, a refusal which, if an attempt was made to court-martial the men for disobedience, might easily be the beginning of revolution. Such an emergency may be occasional only, and the conflict between soldiers and officers—the soldiers objecting to act as blacklegs and the officers ordering them to do so — may never arise, given a prudent tendency to compromise before pushing matters too far. A more habitual disadvantage of the exercise of the two functions of government by one and the same official hierarchy is the undesirability of introducing the necessarily disciplinary character of military forces into other public services. It is ridiculous when letter carriers and postal sorters are accused of " disloyalty " because they exercise their legal right of withholding their labour in strict accord with their contracts of service, if they can get no redress of what they consider grievances. It is felt to be an act of tyranny when railway shunters and porters are summarily called up for military service, for which they are not required, merely in order that the Government as employer may be able to refuse to enter into negotiations with the railwaymen's Trade Union ; or for munition workers, even in war-time, to be arbitrarily sent to the front merely because they are complained of as guilty of " disobedience " to a foreman. On the other hand, it may well be incompatible with efficiency to extend to the army and navy the methods of administration and the attitude of discussion and criticism which, as we are now discovering, are required in industries and services, alike for the greatest efficiency and the utmost personal development, and, indeed, by Democracy itself. A more subtle objection to the union, in one and the same executive organ, of such a diversity of functions and services is the almost certain encroachment upon civic liberties to which it leads. The prestige of the Crown is used to cover the arbitrary decision of every official. The right of the citizen to appeal to the Courts of Justice against any unlawful decision is silently eaten away by every extension of the Royal Prerogative. The very growth of the government business, and the enormous multiplication of the number of persons directly in the government service makes almost inevitable—if every public service is administered by one and the same executive hierarchy—a development of that " Administrative Law " by means of which a bureaucracy entrenches itself against interference.

The Task of the M.P.

Here we may incidentally remark how absurd and unmerited is the abuse of the Member of Parliament for incapacity because he does not master the impossible task with which he is nominally charged—that he does not properly understand even a twentieth part of the multiplicity of different issues that are every day presented to him ; that he fails to keep himself informed of what is being done with his authority in a hundred different spheres of government at home and abroad ; and that he is incapable of bringing under control a Cabinet preoccupied with a thousand difficulties which are not even imparted to him ; that he has become the " fly on the wheel " of a powerful bureaucracy as to the extent, the functions, and the activities of which he has scarcely an inkling. It is not the shortcomings of the individual members, whether landlord or rentier, busy lawyer or journalist, active business man or Trade Union official, to whatever political parties they belong, that is bringing the House of Commons into contempt. The plain truth is that no one, however gifted and however single - minded, could possibly cope simultaneously with such numerous and heterogeneous issues.

The Failure of the Elector

Nor is it, we suggest, a sufficient answer to say that the people themselves are at fault in not arriving at definite decisions on public affairs ; and in not formulating explicitly any " General Will " that the legislators and administrators could confidently set themselves to carry out. We may, indeed, admit that the electorate of twenty-two million persons is at present very far from affording, to those who have to act on its behalf, any very definite mandate as to what should be done in its name. But can this ever be otherwise, so long as what is presented to the electors is an incongruous mixture of the most diverse issues ; itself the result of indiscriminately heaping upon a single popular assembly, administration, control and the making of law, on all sorts of subjects at once ? We ask the elector what is his will as a human being ; whereas he has, and never will have any definite will as a human being. When he is conscious of himself as a consumer, he has a will, which he can often express articulately enough. When he is conscious of himself as a producer, he has a will, very often a turbulent and determined will. When he is conscious of himself as a citizen, concerned with the administration of the national resources, and the physical and mental environment in which he and his family have to live, he has a will, though often needing, on the part of his representatives, patient study and expert interpretation, so as to secure, in the event, what he desires. When, finally, he is conscious of himself as a citizen concerned with the independence of his country, with the maintenance of personal liberty, and with defence against aggression from without or from within, he has a will, which may easily become so intense that, to attain his ends, he will go even to death. But when the twenty-two million electors are asked, in the vague, what is their will about all sorts of things at once, how can we wonder that any manifestation of a " General Will " is imperfect and indistinct ?

The Warping of Political Democracy by a Capitalist Environment

It has been observed that the machinery of political Democracy was devised by Rousseau and Jefferson for an essentially equalitarian community of independent producers. The results of the Industrial Revolution and the growth of the Capitalist System have been to give us a Democracy—to the extent of 80 or 90 per cent of the entire population—of " hired men " serving a privileged class of something like 10 per cent, in whom nine-tenths of the wealth of the community has become vested. We need not elaborate the innumerable ways in which the working of Democratic institutions is warped by their essentially capitalistic environment. In all countries the manipulation of elections, the selection of representatives and the pressure upon the Executive Government by the employing class and—what is no less sinister—by the functionless rich, is patent and notorious. The political parties, the influence of which on the working of the political Democracy is incessant and all-pervasive, become, almost inevitably, the instruments of those by whose subscriptions and payments for honours and place they are supported.

With an electorate numbered by tens of millions, a new peril has become manifest. In the highly developed newspaper press, playing incessantly on the minds of the electors with a stream of selected items of news, suggestively compiled descriptions of fact and deliberately persuasive incitements to this or that judgment or decision, the Party System has found

at once a tool and a rival.   The danger of an illegitimate
perversion of the popular voice has been aggravated
by the growing predominance in the community of
an immensely rich class of capitalist *entrepreneurs*,
operating on a world scale for purposes of profit.
Their command of the press is secured, not only by
their indispensable subsidies in the form of advertisements, but also, in recent years, by the development
of newspapers into gigantic capitalist enterprises,
each of them commanding millions of pounds of
capital, and attaining circulations of national extent,
with millions of daily readers.   We should be very
much surprised if Capitalism claimed a like influence
on the elementary schools of the nation, or upon its
universities.   If one great capitalist, in conjunction
with his co-adventurers and friends, made himself the
proprietor of all the schools in South London, and
another of all those of Manchester or Scotland ;   if
each of these became the employer of great groups
of teachers, and dictated the character of the instruction that was given to the pupils ;   if the mental
pabulum of whole sections of the community were in
this way controlled, and from time to time changed
according to the caprice or ambition or pecuniary self-
interest of irresponsible millionaires, we should at
once denounce such an exercise of the power of
wealth as an unendurable dictatorship.   But we permit
just as unwarrantable a control of the mental environment of the adult citizen to be exercised almost without
objection.

The warping influence of the capitalist environment
in which Democracy has become, almost unawares,
embedded, is seen not merely in its effect on the Liberal
and Conservative but also on the Labour Party.   The
very rise of such a party, based fundamentally on the
necessity for asserting and protecting the interests of
a class of " hired men," is itself a result of Capitalism ;

and to the extent that the " Rights of Labour " are asserted, as distinguished from the rights of all citizens, and from what is in the interests of the community as a whole, the effect is detrimental to the highest social welfare.

POLITICAL PARTIES

Once the electors become too numerous for a township meeting of neighbours, the most active-minded citizen who does not concert group action finds himself individually powerless ; and the organisation of parties becomes the only way in which the dominant streams of opinion can be discovered, formulated and made effective. There grows up accordingly, in every live Democracy, a series of voluntary associations of citizens undertaking this task ; and these organisations, although voluntary and without legal sanction, become in fact part of the machinery of the constitution.

The basis of all effective organisation in a Democracy is, we suggest, an authoritative register of the citizens. And it is not sufficient, as experience shows, that this register should be in use only for checking the right of the elector to deposit his voting-paper when he presents himself on election day. The electoral register has to be accessible, not merely to the authorities conducting the elections, but to those necessarily private citizens who undertake the grouping and marshalling of the electorate in such a way as to enable the majority to prevail. No small part of the gradually increasing effectiveness of Democracy in Great Britain is, we suggest, to be attributed to the institution in 1832 of an electoral register in each constituency, and to the successive changes in the law and practice which, after 1878, made this register easily obtainable.[1] The voluntary associations formed

---

[1] We cannot here explore to what extent the very different developments of political Democracy in America and on the European Continent, and

to see that no citizen was omitted from the register, and to organise the voting of electors of various opinions, grew in Great Britain into a network of local bodies, the most influential of which concerned themselves with securing the return to the House of Commons of candidates belonging to the Liberal or the Conservative Parties, though others from time to time promoted the return of candidates pledged to the support of particular measures. We need not attempt here to trace the development of these " extra-legal " political organisations, from the Chartist Movement and the Anti-Corn Law League, through the " Birmingham Caucus " of Joseph Chamberlain and the associations of the Irish Nationalists in Great Britain, down to the National Liberal Federation and the National Union of Conservative Associations of to-day. But the evolution of party organisation, necessary feature of Democracy though it may be, brings with it, in a world of busy, uninformed and apathetic citizens, its own distortions of the popular voice, not to be obviated by even the most scientific systems of marshalling the electors and counting their votes. The Liberal and Conservative party organisations, though they may at their best have come fairly near to representing the upper and middle class electorate, failed to incorporate the mass of wage-earning electors, to whom those in command were never willing to concede the influence that would have been warranted by their numbers. The effectiveness of the voluntary party organisations was, moreover, impaired, like the rest

---

latterly in Russia, have been influenced by the non-existence of a printed electoral register, authoritative, complete and obtainable by any applicant. This enquiry would be interesting. We do not find the point adequately dealt with in the principal works on Political Parties, such as *Democracy and the Organisation of Political Parties*, by M. Y. Ostragorski ; *Political Parties*, by Robert Michels ; *The American Commonwealth*, by Lord Bryce ; *Public Opinion and Popular Government* and *The Government of England*, both by A. Lawrence Lowell ; *History of the Relation between Law and Opinion in England*, by A. V. Dicey.

of the constitutional machinery, by the growing hypertrophy of the functions that we have already described
as being heaped upon the political Democracy during
the past half-century. In 1870 it was comparatively
easy to get a consensus of opinion from a whole mass
of electors, predominantly of the landlord or capitalist
or professional class, upon the narrow range of subjects
of political controversy. In 1920, so great is the
variety of issues and so wide the range of the questions
for which the Cabinet and the House of Commons
have to find answers that the marshalling of the enormously swollen electorate into masses in which anything like homogeneity of opinion prevails has become
ever more difficult.

THE LABOUR PARTY

It is interesting to see how the difficulty has been
met by the Labour Party, the newest and youngest
of these voluntary political associations. The basis of
the organisation of the Labour Party is fundamentally a
recognition of the solidarity of interest—and not only
of material interest—among the great mass of wage-
earning folk (together with the " black-coated salariat,"
in so far as this realises the fact), as against the divergent
interests of the landlord, rentier and capitalist-employer
class. With this goes a conviction that in the realm
of Social Reconstruction, as in that of what we have
called the primary functions of the State, the aspirations
and desires of the wage-earners and the salariat can
be formulated in a programme for legislation and public
administration that will command their general assent.
To ensure a continual correspondence between the
opinions of this portion of the electorate and the
programme and activities of the Party, this organisation, unlike any previous political party, is based on
a combination of vocational with constituency repre-

sentation. The Trade Unions, in which the bulk of the manual working wage-earners and an increasing proportion of the " black-coated salariat " are now enrolled, supply the greater part of the base on which the Labour Party stands, whilst the local constituency organisations complete its foundation. The Labour Party, in fact, is a federation of such Trade Unions, Trades Councils, Co-operative Societies, Socialist organisations and similar bodies as choose to affiliate to it, together with the Local Labour Parties formed in the various constituencies. Individual members, men or women, obtain admission by joining one or other of the federated bodies. In each constituency the Local Labour Party admits to affiliation any of the fifty or sixty thousand branches of the societies eligible for affiliation to the national Party that are within the constituency, and also enrols as members local residents of either sex who accept the basis and constitution of the Party. The Labour Party is thus based partly on the nationally affiliated membership of constituent associations and partly on the Local Labour Parties, which themselves include both individual members and affiliated groups of members. By a carefully devised system of representation, all the members and constituent bodies are enabled to elect local executive committees, and to send delegates to a national conference, electing a national executive, on which there must always sit representatives of the constituent associations and representatives of the Local Labour Parties, together with not less than four women taken from either section of the Party.

So far the Labour Party has achieved a great measure of success in welding into a homogeneous political force the aspirations and desires of its four million members—a number greatly exceeding the membership at any period enrolled by other political parties. At the same time the fact cannot be ignored that the vocational basis on which the Party is partly organised—useful as it has proved in surmounting the difficulty presented by the heterogeneous character of the subjects dealt with and the multiplicity of the issues raised in our hypertrophied political Democracy—has defects of its own. The predominance in the Labour Party of the vocational organisations, notably the great Trade Unions of miners, railwaymen, textile operatives, engineers, and general workers, and the paucity of funds available for the election expenses of other Parliamentary candidates, has led, down to the present, to the selection of candidates, in too many instances, on a vocational basis. Whatever may be urged in favour of the choice of a representative actually because he is a miner or a cotton spinner, to an assembly having to deal with mining or cotton spinning, it is plain that there is a loss when what is in question is the Democracy of Citizens—when the choice is of members of an assembly having to represent the interests of the community as a whole—if the members elected represent, not so much those aspirations and desires which the citizens have in common, as those peculiar to a particular industry. The place of the vocational representative is where the affairs of his vocation are dealt with.

The Success of Political Democracy in general, and of British Democracy in particular

It might be imagined, from the vigour with which we have criticised the machinery of political Democracy in Great Britain, that we shared in the reactionary opposition to democratic institutions which is, for the moment, common to plutocratic and academic circles. Quite the contrary. It is just because it is the object of this book to propose changes that would make British Democracy much more democratic that we have in the foregoing description stressed the defects and shortcomings of its organisation, emphasising always the features in which, as it seems to us, drastic alteration is required. But this criticism must not blind us either to the success of political Democracy throughout the world or to the particular advantages of the political institutions of the Democracy of Great Britain. To the political thinkers, leaders and parties who have, during the last ninety years, carried through the gradual democratisation of our community, so far as it has been achieved, the present generation owes an immense debt of gratitude. It can be said by every British Socialist of Fox and Grey, Cobden and Bright, Gladstone and Chamberlain, that, like all honest enthusiasts in the cause of liberty, they builded better than they knew. If they had realised that political Democracy would inevitably lead to industrial Democracy ; that the ideal of equality would not be fulfilled by even the widest suffrage, but would transform the factory and the mine, the school and the home ; they might have shrunk from the first step to a social order surpassing their limited conception of personal freedom. Fortunately, they not only suffered, like most Anglo-Saxons, from a beneficent short-sightedness—in itself a kind of wisdom—but they also enjoyed a stalwart faith in the essential common sense and fairmindedness of all classes of their countrymen.

The peculiar success of the British political Democracy is that—favoured by a comparatively homogeneous and closely knit population, century - long security against foreign invasion, and a growing predominance of industrial over rural occupations—it has managed to provide, in spite of the sinister influences of the Capitalist System, more universally and less imperfectly than in any other nation of the Old World, for an effective exercise, by the whole body of its adult citizens, of the powers of freely electing its

representatives. The first condition as it seems to
us of such exercise is that every citizen shall have a
genuinely free and equal opportunity for giving his vote;
and that this opportunity shall be completely protected,
not only by law but also by social institutions and public
opinion, against any direct interference by outside
influences, whether of powerful individuals or corporate groups. By its now fairly accurate and up-to-
date automatic registration of every elector ; by the
careful distribution of sufficiently numerous voting
places ; by the considerable though still inadequate
limitations imposed by the Corrupt Practices Act on
the perverting influences of wealth ; by the free trans-
mission by post to every elector of each candidate's
election manifesto ; by the elaborate secrecy, not only
as against his employer, but also as against his neighbours, his workmates and his family, in which the
elector is enabled to give his vote ; and above all, by
its system of direct election of the representatives by
the electors themselves, without any intermediary,
the British Constitution as it now stands, notwithstanding all its manifold imperfections (and the outstanding difficulty of extreme economic inequality)
has, in fact, secured a larger participation, a more
continuous interest and a more widespread influence
in Parliamentary elections than can be found in any
other great nation. It is at least to the credit of the
political Democracy of Great Britain, as compared
with the Democracies of Producers, whether Trade
Unions or Professional Associations, and with the
Democracies of Consumers in the Co-operative Movement, that it is habitually far more successful than any
of these, even in Britain itself, in getting the citizens to
take an interest in the questions involved and to record
their votes on the issues submitted to them.

The large measure of success thus achieved by the
institutions of British political Democracy has been

contributed to by the limits set by national habit, first to any improper interference with the elections by the Government or its officials—we are apt to forget how rare is the complete abstention from illicit government interference that the British electors enjoy—and secondly to any flagrant interference by corporate bodies, powerful individuals or the mob. The absence of " terrorism " is a necessary condition of any genuine Democracy. Freedom of speech, freedom of public meeting and freedom of the press secured by past generations of Radicals we take equally for granted, furiously resenting any occasional violation of these essentials of political liberty. And, to democratic government equally necessary with electoral freedom, not the least of the successes of the British political Democracy has been its gradual development of an absolutely honest, highly capable and habitually faithful Civil Service, which takes a pride in serving loyally any Ministry whom the House of Commons calls to power, and may always be counted on to carry out, to the greatest advantage, any decision come to by that Ministry. Fundamentally, however, the success of the British political Democracy is to be seen in the temper which it has bred in the British people themselves. All parties have come to accept, if not as ideally right at least as practically decisive, the arbitrament of the public judgment and the public conscience, as manifested, after a battle of wits in free discussion, and with the widest possible dissemination of information, by the majorities at the poll.

It is abundantly clear that what is wrong with the world to-day is not too much Democracy but too little, not too many thoroughly democratic institutions but too few. Alike for the primitive and for the more modern functions of society, we need the willing co-operation and the universal consciousness of consent brought about by the participation of all the citizens in the decisions to which they have necessarily all to submit and in the execution of which the whole community has to take part. No practical statesman or sane political thinker nowadays believes, for instance, that it is safe to leave the function of national defence, and therefore the decision to make war or peace, in the hands of one man or of a single caste of men, however astute or heroic they may be ; nor does he imagine that the liberties of individual citizens will permanently find adequate protection under a criminal law devised and administered by successive personal dictators, or by the dictatorship of one particular section of the community. Whatever may be the imperfections of the political Democracy with which we are familiar in Europe, America and Australia, it is now self-evident that no other form of political government has any chance against it. Judged by the test of survival, political Democracy has proved itself superior to political Autocracy or political Oligarchy, alike in the function of protecting the community against foreign aggression and in that of maintaining order at home. In the twentieth century, at least, men will fight better and longer for a community, endure more hardships on its behalf and more willingly accept its institutions, if they feel that they can, by concerting together, themselves direct its policy and themselves make the laws under which they have to work and live. And this consciousness of consent on the part of the inhabitants of a self-governing community, vital as it is for the successful fulfilment of the primitive functions of society, is even more necessary for success in the other and more complicated functions now entrusted to our political government. Little as we may consciously attend to it, there comes first the whole function of anticipating the future. Every nation has to provide for its own continuance in independent existence after all the

persons now living have passed away. Its future
maintenance in security and self-determination is as
important as its momentary affairs. Moreover, every
community has to administer its resources so as to
make provision not merely for the needs or desires
of the whole contemporary generation, but also for
the needs and desires of future generations, as far as
can usefully be foreseen. More and more it becomes
apparent that the supreme decision that the community
has year by year to make is how much of the annual
product of commodities and services should be appropriated to the immediate satisfaction of the desires
of the existing population, and how much to anticipation
of the future, whether this anticipation takes the form
of provision for childbirth and infancy, for education
and preventive hygiene or for scientific invention and
research, the improvement of land and other natural
resources and the construction of additional buildings
and machinery. But it is more than the mere amount
of the provision for the future that has to be decided
by society in each passing year. What has to be
decided, though it may not be explicitly formulated,
is what kind of social order, what sort of civilisation,
it is desired and intended that the community of the
future shall in this country enjoy. Do we prefer a
universally educated people closely approximating to
economic equality, or a society of grades and layers,
highly differentiated in degrees of culture and amounts
of wealth ; a predominantly urban or a predominantly
rural existence ; an overwhelmingly commercial or
a principally manufacturing population—even, if we
come to think of it, a population within this island
of fifty, seventy-five, or a hundred millions ? So
complicated are these issues, and so dependent are
they for successful solution on the willing co-operation
of the whole people, year in and year out, in all their
personal affairs, that it is even more essential to gain

their assent to what is proposed than it is to such emergency decisions as peace or war. The very fact that all the people affected by the institutions of the community in which they live can alter these institutions if a majority of them concur has, in itself, a great psychological influence in obtaining general acquiescence. This consciousness of consent and this feeling of security rest on the assumption that, if men and women have to live together, the convenience must be consulted, not of any minority, but of all of them ; that where there is a difference of opinion the minority must temporarily give way. Or, to put it in another way, there must be no inherently privileged class. Every individual must be deemed to be equal to every other individual in his right to " life, liberty and the pursuit of happiness."

Now, it is significant that, leaving aside for the moment the conduct of industries and services, for all the functions that have been entrusted to the political Democracy, whether they are the primitive functions of national defence and foreign relations, the maintenance of order and the execution of justice, or the more modern duties of anticipating the future, determining the character of the civilisation that we intend and providing for the material as well as for the social conditions under which subsequent generations will have to live, it is man as a citizen who is concerned, man as an inhabitant of a particular piece of the land surface, not man as a consumer, nor man as a producer of a particular commodity.

The Need for Constitutional Reform

Our conclusion is that, whatever may be done in the way of eliminating the warping influence of the Capitalist System, or of improving the education of the citizen—at present, in our view, certainly no less defective in clubs and college common rooms than in the workshop and the mine—and however widespread may become an intelligent and continuous interest in public affairs, the first requisite is so to amend our institutions as to sort out the issues. When what is wanted is a manifestation of a Common Will from the stand-point of the consumer, there must be a separate channel for it, unconnected with the manifestation of a Common Will that is equally required on some other issue from the standpoint of the producer ; and both must be distinct from the channel to be provided when the issue requires a manifestation of a Common Will from the standpoint of the citizen. The whole body of citizens, as we shall hereafter indi-cate, must have two channels—one through which they can express their will in the group of issues involved in the protection of the community and the individual against aggression, including the maintenance of personal liberty ; and the other through which they can exercise their creative impulse towards such a use of the national resources as will provide for them-selves a finer and fuller civilisation.

PART II

THE CO-OPERATIVE COMMONWEALTH OF TO-MORROW

INTRODUCTION

THE task that we have set ourselves in this book, under the circumstances stated in the preface, is that of describing, for the purpose of initiating discussion, such a reorganisation of the principal institutions of our own country as might serve, both to arrest the growing dissatisfaction with these institutions, especially with Parliamentary Government, and to permit of a progressive democratisation of industry.

There are many persons to whom any proposal for a change of social institutions, whether economic or political, is profoundly distasteful. To some, indeed, it seems almost impious to suggest that the institutions amid which they have grown up, and to which they have become accustomed, are other than eternal. But it is, of course, mere delusion to imagine that social institutions, however venerable, do not require perpetual adaptation to changing conditions ; or, indeed, to suppose that such institutions can escape perpetual change. No community remains, even for as long as a single generation, unchanged ; and in the so-called civilised nations of our own day the rate of change, compared with that of past ages, or of more primitive peoples, is amazingly rapid. The mere growth and mobility of population, the successive transformations of the methods of production and distribution, the speed with which ideas are now disseminated over the whole globe, the common accessibility of knowledge heretofore monopolised by small classes—all these conditions make the nation of to-day a very different entity from the nation of even thirty years ago. Social institutions which seemed, in the last generation, to fit fairly well, cannot possibly, in the very nature of things, fit so well to-day, and will be still greater misfits to-morrow. Painful as it must be to the essentially conservative mind, a perpetual adaptation of existing institutions becomes unavoidable. If social institutions are not changed, deliberately and successively, so as to fit the ever-moving conditions of the age, they will break, and then inevitably be changed, violently and abruptly, in revolutionary spasms. It is one great advantage of Democracy as the basis of social organisation that it permits of a continuous process of adaptation in all social institutions, so that these remain at all times in correspondence with the development of the minds of the people concerned.

Unfortunately, although change is inevitable, progress is not. Perpetual change, which doubtless always means adaptation to the environment, in no way implies what man calls progress. Even within the brief span of human experience recorded by history there have been centuries in which whole nations have quite obviously retrograded ; losing in a generation or two the painful accumulations of past ages in manners and morals, in arts and sciences and in productive capacity ; sometimes indeed, altogether succumbing to such non-human forces of Nature as famine and disease, or to such human forces as the superior penetrative capacity of lower races. Whole civilisations have in this way perished from off the earth, leaving progress to be begun again elsewhere, at a lower level, from which men start once more to climb the painful secular stages. Whether or not human society in Great Britain will continue to advance or will slip back to a lower level—whether, indeed,

European civilisation can even survive its present
difficulties—depends essentially on man's power to
control the environment to which he must, perforce,
become adapted or perish.   Unless he can and will,
by taking thought, so control the environment that
this adaptation means an advance in civilisation, and
not a retrogression — more life and fuller, in the
community, and not less—what is assured for future
generations is not progress but decay ; decay that
in these times of rapid change may be cataclysmic.
Now, of all that is summed up in the word environment, by far the most potent factor, at the stage in
evolution that has been reached by European man,
is not climate or famine, not the aggressions of wild
beasts or barbarian races, but the institutions which
each society generates, and by which the minds as
well as the bodies of its people are moulded.   And
because it is our social institutions that are the most
potent factors in the environment that determines
our evolution, the future of our civilisation is, very
largely, in our own hands.   For, within wide limitations, we can mould our institutions so that they may
produce the society that we desire.   What the statesman is doing when he constructs an educational
system or an institution for promoting research, a
new method of organising an industry, or of developing
local administration, a new plan of representative
government, or some device for otherwise expressing
the Common Will, is not—as is often foolishly imagined
—merely " changing machinery."   It is by such transformations of social institutions that man himself is
transformed.

Is it necessary to state explicitly that the desirability,
and indeed the inevitability, of Democracy is here
taken for granted ?   Whatever may be said in theory
in favour of government by a wise and benevolent
autocrat, or by a humane and well-meaning superior

class, it is the assumption of this book that what is
intended and desired by the people is self-government.
A constitution has to be devised which shall enable
the whole adult population of Great Britain to
share among all its members, without exclusions, the
legislation, the control and even the administration
affecting the life which this people has necessarily to
lead in common. And the object of Democracy is
not merely the negative one of excluding the alternative of legislation, control and administration being
exercised by individuals or classes contrary to the
desires of the people at large, but also the positive
one of obtaining for all the people, in the fullest degree
practicable, that development of personality, and that
enlargement of faculty and desire dependent on the
assumption of responsibility and the exercise of will.
To the community as a whole Democracy brings the
further gain of the increase of strength and stability
given by all its institutions and all its collective
activities being " broad based upon the people's will "
—rooted in a universal consciousness of common
consent. People have sometimes forgotten the
spiritual value of Democracy. The very necessity for
obtaining that consciousness of consent involves the
substitution of persuasion for force ; implies, therefore,
that those who are superior in will-power or intelligence
consent to forgo the use of this force to compel other
men to obey them and seek to convince the average
sensual man so that he too may exercise his intellect
and his will. The very consciousness of being engaged
in co-operative enterprise, determined on and directed
by common consent, is a stronger stimulus to self-
activity, imperfect though it may be, than the docility
of slavery. Hence there is, in all the armoury of
sociology, no such effective instrument of popular
education, no such potent means of calling forth the
latent powers of thought and feeling in the whole

mass of citizens, as Popular Government. It may be true—and in certain stages of development it certainly is true—that individual independence and personal self-determination is more successful in this evocation and stimulus than any joint action whatever. But in modern society, in densely crowded communities, with highly developed industrial enterprises of magnitude, and a closely integrated economic life, no such complete individualism is practicable, either politically or industrially. The problem to be solved is how to remould the social institutions that have come into existence in such a way as to evoke, in all men and women, and not merely in a favoured few, all their latent powers ; to stimulate the whole population, and not only the exceptionally gifted or the exceptionally energetic, to the utmost possible exercise of their faculties ; and at the same time to promote, throughout the whole mass and not alone in exceptionally altruistic or exceptionally enlightened individuals, the greatest attainable development of public spirit. It is the thesis of this book that, towards the attainment of these ends, the whole-hearted application to industry, as to political government, of a carefully co-ordinated Democracy offers the best expedient. At the same time, Democracy does not cover the whole of life. It is, in fact, one of its objects, and a large part of its justification, that it should set free the individual—not of any favoured social class but from one end of the community to the other—to work out his own mental or spiritual development, to " make a happy fireside clime to weans and wife," and to live his own life in literature, science, art and religion. The purpose of Democracy is, in fact, the maximum expansion of personality " in widest commonalty spread."

We desire to make clear, at the outset, that what we are attempting is not to frame a model constitution for an Utopian community. We aspire to nothing more ambitious than to put forward for discussion, so far as Great Britain is concerned, the suggestions that seem to accord with the trend of development towards a fully democratised community. If our suggestions are explained with some particularity, this is not because we imagine it to be possible for any one to plan in detail the constitution that is likely to be eventually adopted, but merely from a desire to free our meaning from the uncertainties and ambiguities that lurk in merely general propositions. The working out of the detailed application of our proposals should be regarded as no essential part of our recommendations. The analysis in Part I. has shown what, in fact, are the materials with which the constitution can be built. It has incidentally revealed, also, how unselfconscious and spontaneous has been the growth of these institutions, in response to different needs and for the achievement of particular ends. Any fully developed democratic community must take account of the fact that " government of the people, for the people, by the people," is not and cannot be made simple, homogeneous and indivisible, but must adapt itself to interests and purposes which are simultaneously diverse and varied, not only as among different sections of the people, but actually within each man or woman. It will have become clear from the preceding analysis that the General Will of the community, which Democracy seeks to discover, is not and cannot be found by attempting to represent, for all purposes, the whole varied complex of emotions and desires that are joined together in the individual elector. He or she has never one will or purpose, but several different wills or purposes, which have no identity, and often but little connection with each other. The description of the institutions already called into existence has revealed four such purposes, or spheres of will, in respect of each of which a Common Will of the community as a whole has to be discovered.

Thus, provision must be made for Democracies of Consumers, because men and women are concerned about the provision of all the commodities and services by which they live. Provision must equally be made, with regard to these same men and women, for Democracies of Producers, vitally interested, vocation by vocation, in the conditions in which they spend their working lives, and in the conduct and advancement of the craft or profession by which they serve the community. But it cannot be ignored that, whilst Democracies of Consumers are interested in the abundance and cheapness of the commodities and services that they severally desire, and whilst Democracies of Producers are at least equally interested, vocation by vocation, in upholding their social and industrial status, maintaining their own particular standards of life and conduct, and controlling the conditions of their own working lives, they are not concerned, either as consumers or as producers, for the well-being of the community as a whole. These very same consumers and producers are, however, interested in the corporate action of the community ; but it is as Democracies of Citizens that they seek to control what used to be regarded as the primary functions of a self-governing community, such as national defence and foreign relations, the development of law, the maintenance of order and the execution of justice, which have no necessary or direct connection with either the production or the consumption of commodities and services. And there is, as will more clearly appear in the next chapter, yet another, and quite distinct, aspect of the life of man in society in which every man and woman is concerned, again not as a producer or as a consumer, but as a citizen, in the management of the common economic life on which all production and distribution depend ; the equitable distribution of the national income ; the conservation and wise administration of the resources of the nation, for the advantage not only of the present but also of future generations ; the determination and the maintenance of the kind of civilisation that the community intends and desires ;[1] the hygiene of the race and the education of each successive generation, and the promotion of literature and art, no less than of scientific discovery and research. It will now be plain that, if our Democracy is to be effective, the constitution must take account of all these four fundamental aspects of social life, and must appropriately provide, in its organisation, for the discovery and execution of a Common Will, not only for one or two, but for all of them.

Moreover, constitution-making must have regard for historical development. The future of each community must spring from its own present, and cannot escape being conditioned by its own particular past. Everywhere there are institutions already in existence ; not, indeed, consciously directed towards the precise ends that the community now has in view, but moulded by its past and present needs, shaped by the historical development of which the present generation forms a part, and intertwined by many a subtle tie with its very being. There is, for instance, the organic structure of the Municipalities and other Local Governing Bodies, which already administer, in Great Britain alone, more than fifteen hundred million pounds' worth of our national capital. There are, as the nucleus of a Democracy of Producers, the

---

[1] We do not exclude those larger ideals and those wider sympathies which reach beyond the interests and desires of any one nation, and which take into account the welfare of humanity itself. But in so far as these ideals and sympathies get translated into corporate action beyond national boundaries, this is either coercive (as in the prohibition and suppression of the slave trade, or in the proposed activities of the League of Nations), and thus plainly within the sphere of the Political Parliament ; or else propagandist (like missionary enterprise), which would, if aided from public funds, fall within that of the Social Parliament.

couple of thousand separate Trade Unions and Professional Associations already extending, in their sixty thousand branches, to nearly every corner of the Kingdom, and already enrolling a considerable majority of those engaged in their various occupations. There is a scarcely less ubiquitous network of Democracies of Consumers, organised in the rapidly growing Co-operative Movement, with its couple of hundred million pounds a year of trade in all household supplies. Finally, there is, as an organ of the community as a whole, the national Parliament, hypertrophied in function, as yet very imperfectly organised, with its popularly elected House of Commons constantly checked and hampered by its hereditary and arbitrarily selected House of Lords, but assumed to control a Cabinet of Ministers which professes to carry out the people's will, and to direct in this sense the administration of the national government. If, as is now commonly accepted, the future must grow out of the present, it behoves us to consider, not a brand-new structure but how this social machinery can be changed, how the powers and functions of its several parts can be limited or extended, what must be added and what suppressed, in order to produce an efficiently working, genuinely democratic constitution for the community.

But the materials available for the constitution of a fully democratised community will not be rehandled to advantage, unless our minds escape from the domination of the old categories. No rooted prejudices or prepossessions must hamper our freedom to make the best use of the elements with which the building has to be constructed. Thus, no one can to-day take for granted the assumption—nowadays, in fact, scrutinised so severely—that, for all the purposes of government and administration, there must necessarily be one and the same geographical area, and one and the same sovereign authority. It must even be open to enquiry whether this does not hold equally when what is under consideration is the existence of self-contained autonomous sovereign states, as when discussing the bounds of municipalisation. It might be found, on the contrary, that each of the various functions of government requires, for its most efficient fulfilment, its own particular geographical area, and, most revolutionary of all, that some of these functions are better without any predetermined geographical limitation at all. For instance, one of the advantages of the Dictatorship of the Capitalist has been his freedom to ignore in his operations, not only Local Government areas, but also national boundaries, and to organise his business irrespective of race, colour or religion. Hence it might be found that for the essentially economic Democracies of Consumers and Producers respectively, some analogous internationalism may be the condition of the fullest efficiency and the largest measure of freedom. On the other hand, it may be discovered that for what is termed Political Democracy—that is, for fulfilling the functions of national defence, foreign relations and the maintenance of internal order — a larger geographical area is required than it is necessary or expedient to provide for the organs of Social Democracy which have, as their purpose, the organisation of the national resources, the deliberate maintenance of the mental and physical environment suitable to the persons of the same race, religion or culture, who happen to live within a particular geographical area, and the provision for their future.

In the same way, it is impossible to-day to assume as a matter of course that there must necessarily be in any given geographical area either a personal sovereign or one supreme organ of government in which will be embodied all the sovereignty of the people. It may be sufficient for the purpose of Democracy to postulate that the sovereignty of the people resides in the people themselves, and to provide that it should be manifested, not necessarily in any one organ of the community, but in various co-ordinate organs for different purposes, which may from time to time wax and wane in importance.

It may be added that the various changes that are here suggested need not necessarily be taken as a whole. The new constitution may easily be adopted only in part, or successively part by part. Nor is the change called for only by the demand for any extension of the nationalisation or municipalisation of industries and services. Even as matters stand in Great Britain to-day some such transformation of the constitution is plainly required if Democracy is to be made effective ; whilst any enlargement of the sphere of public administration, whatever may be its form, will render the changes proposed or some alternative alterations absolutely essential, if Democracy is to become more than an empty form. Our proposals are confined to the constitution of the Socialist Commonwealth in Great Britain : no attempt is made here to solve the problems raised by the growth of the self-governing Dominions into free nations, or by the dominance of British Democracy over other races within the British Empire.

CHAPTER I

THE most influential, and in many respects the most important, constitutional organ of the democratic State must be that by which the community, as a whole, formulates and declares its will in national affairs ; and it is in connection with this that our proposals are most novel. We shall first give the suggestions themselves, and subsequently adduce some arguments in their favour.

THE KING

The national organisation herein proposed does not involve the abolition of the ancient institution of an hereditary Monarch. The common decision that it is both necessary and desirable that the titular head of the State should not be charged with any part of the actual government or administration of the community may certainly be accepted in the Socialist Commonwealth. Especially for the British Commonwealth of Nations, of which we assume the continuance in a democratic form, is such a titular or ceremonial headship almost indispensable, and any union of this headship with government or administration quite impracticable. It does not seem necessary to propose any change in the system, to which the nation is accustomed, of this titular or ceremonial headship being vested—not by Divine Right or any independent title, but merely by virtue of a statute like any other statute, open to be repealed or amended at any time as any other law is repealed or amended, by decision of the popular Legislature—in a member, accurately designated according to heredity, of a particular family. In the circumstances of the British Commonwealth of Nations, including, as it must for a long time to come, communities of many different races, many different civilisations in many different stages of self-government, with institutions of many different grades of Democracy, there seem to be insuperable difficulties in providing for an elective headship.[1] Without

---

[1] We need not labour these difficulties. How hard it is to discover a man (or woman) sufficiently famous to get chosen, and to be acceptable, as the Ceremonial Head of a whole nation ; and yet devoid of desire to exercise personal power ; qualified to set the right tone by his influence, and unembarrassed by a circle of relations and adherents pressing for appointments and concessions, has been demonstrated by experience in France, the United States and other republics. With regard to our own problems, no one has yet been able to suggest any practicable way in which the congeries of races, religions and civilisations that we call the British Empire could either do without a titular head, or obtain one by popular election among 400 millions of people. The solution of the problem presented by (a) the restriction of the monarch to ceremonial duties ; (b) the deliberate selection of a particular family, having no pretence to " Divine Right " or hereditary title ; (c) the placing of the title to kingship entirely in a statute, which can be amended or repealed with no more formalities than any other Act of Parliament; and (d) the training of the heir apparent under the direction of the Cabinet responsible to Parliament, seems to have many political advantages. Its social disadvantages of (a) an intensification of the snobbishness to which the British are prone ; (b) the influence of certain archaic conventions relating to intercourse with " royalty " in maintaining an inequality of manners between human beings—which is only another name for bad manners—together with a servility offensive to the well-bred ; (c) the special association of the prestige of the Court with persons of title or wealth, including even persons of no occupation, as forming a superior class, instead of with persons of distinction in any vocation ; and particularly the social pre-eminence accorded to the " profession of arms " over occupations more conspicuously useful to the community, may or may not be promptly remediable in a predominantly Socialist Commonwealth. But unless " the Court " can acquire better manners, and a new sense of social values, it may be expected that the institution of monarchy, whatever its political advantages, will become unpopular ; and in that case it might very quickly disappear, probably by the voluntary resignation of the holder of the office for the time being, and the repeal of the Act of Settlement by common consent. Resort might then be had to the next-best expedient—possibly election of a supreme ceremonial officer for a term of years by the Imperial Conference representing, by that time, all the communities in the Commonwealth.

exaggerating the political advantages of an hereditary monarch of the British type—without ignoring, on the other hand, the social disadvantages by which it has hitherto been accompanied—it is suggested that the necessary titular and ceremonial headship of the State should be retained essentially in its present form.

THE HOUSE OF LORDS

There is, of course, in the Socialist Commonwealth, no place for the House of Lords,[1] which will simply cease to exist as a part of the Legislature. Whether the little group of " Law Lords," who are now made peers in order that they may form the Supreme Court of Appeal, should or should not continue, for this purely judicial purpose, to sit under the title, and with the archaic dignity of the House of Lords, does not seem material.

THE NATIONAL PARLIAMENT

With regard to the national assembly or Parliament, in any reorganisation of a completely democratised community, it seems vital to divide, and sharply to separate, what is strictly political government from

---

[1] It may be pointed out that the argument in favour of fixing by heredity the person to undertake the duties of the Ceremonial Headship cannot be invoked in favour of hereditary legislators, or of placing powers of veto or obstruction of the popular will in an hereditary caste. Even under the present British Constitution the Royal Office is ministerial only. The King, in the performance of his duties as Ceremonial Head, acts under the direction and supervision of the Cabinet responsible for its decisions to the elected representatives of the people. Moreover, the heir apparent to the Ceremonial Headship is specially educated and trained for the job, also under the direction and supervision of the Cabinet. In an hereditary peerage, on the other hand, sitting in the House of Lords, the claim is that a narrow caste, privileged by immense private riches, controlling its own environment, educating its children as it chooses, and acknowledging no obligation of public service, should exercise independent powers, to which the rest of the community is subjected. We refer elsewhere to the arrangements that may be made for the function of revision and possible temporary suspension of hasty legislation.

the control of social and industrial administration. To use an old slogan of Socialists, the government of men must be distinguished from the administration of things. Our conception of the State, which has become almost irretrievably associated with armies and navies, law and punishment, and even imperial autocracy, needs, in a democratised community, to be separated into two parts. What we shall call the Political Democracy, dealing with national defence, international relations and the administration of justice, needs to be set apart from what we propose to call the Social Democracy, to which is entrusted the national administration of the industries and services by and through which the community lives. The sphere of the one is *Verwaltung, autorité régalienne*, police power ; that of the other is *Wirtschaft, gestion,* housekeeping. The Co-operative Commonwealth of To-morrow must accordingly have, not one national assembly only, but two, each with its own sphere ; not, of course, without mutual relations, to be hereafter discovered, but coequal and independent, and neither of them first or last. We regard this splitting of the House of Commons, as regards powers and functions, into two co-ordinate national assemblies, one dealing with criminal law and political dominion and the other with economic and social administration, not merely as the only effective way of remedying the present congestion of Parliamentary business, but also as an essential condition of the progressive substitution, with any approach to completeness, of the community for the private capitalist.

The Political Parliament and its Executive

Within the sphere of the Political Parliament and its Executive there would fall, in the first place, all of what is called " Foreign Affairs." Whatever may lie in the future in the shape of the direction of all international relations by the Supernational Authority of a League of Peoples, having its own organs for world legislation and world administration, it is plain that no such League and no such Supernational Authority exists, or has more than begun to be established. Each community has therefore, at the outset, to deal with its own foreign affairs. The same considerations compel the provisional maintenance of defensive armaments on one or other scale of magnitude. Further, so long as the British Commonwealth remains charged with the government of other races or peoples — even if all imperialistic or capitalistic elements were eliminated from that dominion, and if it became merely a temporary guardianship of non-adult communities — the supervision of this charge, and the gradual working-out of self-government must long remain part of the functions of the Political Democracy of Great Britain. Within the community too, as well as in its relations with other communities, our lives and liberties have to be protected from aggression by those abnormal citizens whom we stigmatise as criminals ; and controversies between individual citizens and the State as well as those among citizens have to be authoritatively adjusted. The maintenance of order and of the Courts of Justice would, therefore, also fall within the sphere of the Political Democracy. The Political Parliament of the Democracy will need, accordingly, as its chief executive officers, not only a Premier as its responsible general executant, but also a Minister for Foreign Affairs ; one or more Ministers for the Dominions, India, the Crown Colonies and the Dependencies ; one or more Ministers of National Defence ; and a Minister of Justice. It would, in short, correspond in sphere very closely with the whole State as Marx in his young days knew it, and as pictured by the Benthamites and the Manchester School.

We do not pretend to be able to foresee the extent to which the work of the Political Parliament and its Executive may grow, nor exactly how it will develop. The need for armaments may pass away with the increasing authority of the League of Nations ; and with armies and navies surviving merely as police forces, much of the most characteristic features of State governments of previous centuries will disappear. Future generations, abandoning projects of domination over other races and subject peoples, may carry through to completeness the evolution of the British Empire into an Alliance of Free Nations. It was in view of both these aspirations that Socialists of a past generation contemplated a shrinking of what they called the State, and its supersession by merely administrative organs of the Democracy. Even assuming the greatest possible development in these two directions, the process will take a long time ; and in the meanwhile adequate provision must be made both for national defence and for the administration of the British Empire. Further, statesmen and students now realise, much more than was formerly the case, that the greatest possible development in internationalism, and the greatest possible democratisation of the several parts of the British Empire, will involve, not less work for the Foreign Office and the Colonial Office than at present, but on the contrary, though work of a different kind, very much more than at present. The relations between governments, now marked by secrecy and mutual suspicion, will doubtless become ever more varied and voluminous as international intercourse expands. The mutual arrangements to be made, the points to be adjusted, the topics to be dealt with, instead of becoming fewer will become (as they have during the past half-century been becoming) each year more numerous, more varied and more complicated, as, with ever-increasing personal intercourse, the whole people of each nation, and not merely the aristocratic or the capitalist class, come into touch with one another, in the entire range of all their innumerable interests and tastes. What is vital to Democracy is that the management of these international relations should not be abandoned to the secretive manipulations of the bureaucracies concerned ; and that they should not only be conducted as far as possible with publicity, but also placed effectively under the supervision and control of the elected representatives of the people as a whole. Much the same may be said of the future of the Colonial and India Offices as of the Foreign Office. Even when full self-determination and adequate democratisation may have been achieved by every part of the British Empire, the relations between the several parts, including the relations between Great Britain and these parts, will not be less complicated than at present, but more complicated and varied. Not merely the process of democratisation, but also the conduct of relations with the fully self-governing States of the Commonwealth, calls for supervision and control by the elected representatives.

But apart from international relations, and the relations between the various nations of the British Commonwealth, the Political Democracy has plainly a great and even a growing sphere in the Ministry of Justice. The maintenance of civil order, in its crude form of repressing riots and tumults, will doubtless fill a smaller space in the state of the future than ever it has done in the states of the past. There may even be such a diminution of crimes of malice or violence, and such an advance in our knowledge of how to deal with them, that the prisons will be superseded by the hospitals and sanatoria in which the Health Authorities will seek to cure the physically or mentally defective. But the relations of one citizen to another, and of all citizens to the various organs of the community, will need regulating, and their mutual differences will need to be authoritatively adjusted, not less in the future than in the past ; but, on the contrary, with the growing interdependence of the population, very much more than in a simpler community. The growth of the work of the Courts of Justice, in the domain of civil proceedings, will, we imagine, more than keep pace with the decline in their criminal work. The Ministry of Justice will, moreover, be responsible for the codification and progressive amendment of the law, so that it may not lag behind the development of the community. In this connection there will have to be from time to time determined what kind of conduct, what forms of social behaviour, shall be proscribed or required with a view to maximising individual freedom. In all this vast range of work we can escape the unobtrusive rule of the bureaucracy only by providing for its effective supervision and control by the elected representatives of the community.

In deciding these large issues of national policy there is needed, it is clear, a national assembly, representing the common will of the whole body of citizens, and of the citizens as citizens, not as producers of particular commodities, or as consumers of commodities. The Political Parliament must therefore be popularly elected, and experience seems to us conclusive that, if we are to secure any continuous control by the people themselves, it must be elected proportionately to population, directly by the people and not through any intermediate body. We see every disadvantage, for an assembly in which issues of policy are to be determined, in any form of indirect election.[1] Whether election by single-member constituencies, or election by larger constituencies, returning five or more members, according

---

[1] See note to Chapter IV. " The Reorganisation of Local Government."

to some such system as that of the Single Transferable Vote, affords in practice the better guarantee that the elected persons will, in the aggregate, represent in the government the Common Will of the electorate as a whole, and likewise—a point often ignored— keep the elected persons themselves, and the Ministers, most effectually under the control of the whole electorate, is, we think, not yet decisively established. But what is clear is that the election itself must be on a register of all adults, based, as the sole qualification, on local inhabitancy.   Such a register has the unique advantage that it includes all the adult citizens, old as well as young, the infirm as well as the healthy, the home-keeping wives and mothers as well as those engaged in special vocations.   No other electoral basis includes all these citizens.   It affords these electors the opportunity of discussing as neighbours the relative merits of the policies submitted for their decision, and of seeing and hearing the candidates for election.   Moreover, all the subjects within the sphere of the Political Democracy concern the citizens, not in their characters of consumers of services or com- modities, nor yet in respect of their interests as pro- ducers of one among these, but by virtue of their ideals and prepossessions as citizens of a self-governing community.   It is upon their cleavage of opinion on these latter that it is essential that they should divide.

The Political Democracy must therefore have its own Parliament, directly chosen by an electorate based on inhabitancy ; and, as the action of each of the ministerial departments that we have named will be closely dependent on one or other policy being adopted as a whole, the Cabinet (reduced in numbers by the exclusion of all the Ministers concerned with the subjects that will pass over to the Social Parlia- ment) should, as it seems to us, continue to be held jointly responsible for all decisions, and should stand or fall together on a vote of the Political Parliament.[1]

THE SOCIAL PARLIAMENT AND ITS EXECUTIVE

The concentration and isolation of the essentially political functions of the Government in the Political Parliament and its Executive will permit of the development, for all the other functions of the House of Commons, of a distinct national assembly, with separate executive organs specially fitted for this part of the work.

There are, it is plain, two social purposes of the community as a whole for which this separate organ of representative government has to be provided : first, the determination of the mental and physical environment of the present generation—that is, the kind and temper of the civilisation which the citizens, as a community, desire and intend to enjoy ; and secondly, the provision for the community in the future. These two purposes will be, in the life of a vigorous democratic community, as they are in a devoted family, intertwined in every act and thought. It is important to emphasise the one which is usually too lightly regarded, namely the anticipation of the

---

[1] The retention of " Cabinet government," and full ministerial responsibility to the Political Parliament, does not exclude—it seems, indeed, to require—the appointment by the Parliament itself of a standing committee for each Ministry, charged with a continuous supervision of the work of the Department, in order to ensure that the policy from time to time prescribed by the Political Parliament, on the advice of the Cabinet, is in fact being carried out.

There is nothing in our proposals to call necessarily for any change in the constitutional law under which the Prime Minister for the time being may decide on a dissolution and a new General Election (in form, advise the King to dissolve Parliament). There is, however, much to be said for a restriction of this arbitrary power, which has gone far to place the House of Commons in subjection to the Cabinet instead of exercising control over it. It may be desirable, whilst retaining normally a five years' term, to make any dissolution of the Political Parliament within the first three years after a General Election, except on the occasions specially provided for, dependent on the concurrence of at least five-twelfths of the members voting in the division.

future.   But just as in a commercial enterprise the provision for depreciation, the creation of a reserve and the arrangements for expansion cannot well be made by any other authority than that charged with the supreme direction of the current administration, so we assume that both classes of functions can properly be entrusted to a single national assembly having its own executive.   This we propose to call the Social Parliament.

To the Social Parliament and its Executive will be assigned the function of exercising whatever national control may from time to time be required over the nation's economic and social activities.   To this organ of government we should transfer all the powers now vested in the Crown, not only over property as such, but also by way of taxation, including therefore the Right of Eminent Domain, so far as regards the absolute ownership of all land, minerals, tidal waterways and foreshores, together with the duty of deciding when it becomes necessary to expropriate private owners, whether of estates in these properties, or of other instruments of production, with whatever compensation and under whatever conditions may be deemed right.   The Social Parliament would also direct and control the administration of existing public services, and start any new ones that were considered desirable. This does not mean that the Social Parliament and its Executive would proceed at once to organise all the national resources and administer all the services and industries of the community, still less that it should do so without considering the established expectations of the present owners, organisers and workers in each case.   All that it means is that this supreme power of commanding that the instruments of production shall be owned, controlled and directed in any way that the community thinks fit, together with the power to tax, shall be vested, not as at present in the Crown and Parliament, as we know it, but shall be the concern of a separate and distinct national assembly, unconnected with the distinctive functions of the Political Parliament just described. Thus there would fall to the Social Parliament and its executive organs, in addition to the supreme control of the nation's economic resources, and of the industries by which these are made of use, such essential public services as the health and education of the community, including all public provision for the non-effectives (such as the children, the physically or mentally infirm or invalidated, and the aged) ; transport and communications ; the organisation of scientific research, and any provision for the encouragement of art and literature, music and the drama, recreation and religion that may be desired. Finally, there would be the necessary financial co-ordination and direction of the nation's ways and means, including such arrangements as the currency, prices and charges, the provision required for the future, the allocation of particular resources to particular needs, the equitable distribution of the national rent or surplus value, and, where necessary, the levying of taxation for the making up of deficits. The Department of Finance must in fact be one of the most important parts of the national administration.

It is not suggested that the Social Parliament should create or maintain a Cabinet of Ministers having collective responsibility, such as is proposed for the Political Parliament. The work of the Social Parliament would apparently be best done, on the model of the London County Council and our great Municipalities, by standing committees of the Social Parliament itself, each main department of work being thus supervised by its own standing committee electing its own chairman ; without the various chairmen necessarily agreeing with each other in

policy, or accepting, as such, any responsibility for
the work of other committees than their own. There
would clearly be, from the outset, separate Committees
and Chairmen of Finance, Health, Education, Transport and Communications, Mining, each other great
industry as it is taken into public hands, and it is
to be hoped also, on Economic and Social Research,
together with a general committee on all the branches
of industry and commerce not allocated to separate
committees, and presumably a General Purposes
Committee.[1] We shall deal in a subsequent chapter
with the organisation of the actual administration of
each of these industries and services, over which the
Social Parliament and its committees should have
only a general supervision and control, and the decision
of its annual budget, in order to secure the interests
of the community as a whole. As it is the interests
of the community as a whole that the Social Parliament
is to safeguard, and not those of particular vocations
or particular sets of consumers—and what has to be
weighed in each case are the claims of the future
against the insistent demands of the present—this
assembly, like the Political Parliament, must be
elected by the citizens as such, whether old or young,
well or ill, active or superannuated, home-keeping
wives or vocational workers. Moreover, any differences of policy or interest that will arise will turn to
some extent on geographical divergencies. For all
these reasons election for the Social Parliament should
be on the basis of inhabitancy by local constituencies
approximately equal in population. Whether proportional representation and a continuous control by

---

[1] Much valuable information as to the present functions of the British
Government, their distribution among the various departments, and the
manner in which they should be redistributed among Ministers will be found
in the *Report of the Machinery of Government Committee to the Minister of
Reconstruction,* Cmd. 9230, 1918. We have found our proposals in this
book fit in with the distinctions made, and with the principles of reorganisation enunciated in that Report.

the electorate can be ensured in practice best by relatively small Single-Member Constituencies or by larger constituencies, each returning five or seven members by the Single Transferable Vote, is an open question. But we hazard the opinion that the latter device is less appropriate for the election of the Social Parliament, which will need to express the public opinion of localities, than it might be for election to the Political Parliament, in which the issues may be expected to be more in the nature of the divergent opinions of persons than of differences among the interests of localities. The Social Parliament should be elected for a fixed term of years, and should not be liable to dissolution except on the occasions specially provided for, or at the request of a bare majority of its members for the time being.

THE RELATION BETWEEN THE POLITICAL AND THE SOCIAL PARLIAMENTS

We regard the separation of the two national assemblies as fundamental. They both have the function of expressing the desires and formulating the will of the community as a whole. But they will have distinct spheres, which will wax or wane in magnitude and importance at different rates. The issues of national policy on which they will be elected will, from the outset, be markedly different ; and they can, from the nature of the case, never be identical. Although both assemblies will properly demand the whole time and attention of their members, who must, accordingly, have an adequate livelihood provided for them, the persons presenting themselves as candidates for election, and those who ought to be chosen for such different duties, will be of different qualifications and tastes. Their executives will necessarily be differently composed, and must, as will subsequently appear, stand in different relations to other organs of public administration. The daily work of two such different national assemblies will itself be different, and its efficient performance will necessitate an organisation of each assembly appropriate to its own peculiar duties.

It has been explained why, seeing that both national assemblies have to express the desires and to formulate the will of the community as a whole, they should both be chosen by the same electorate, consisting of the whole body of adult citizens, and therefore (as the only way of including all such citizens) on the basis of inhabitancy in geographical constituencies. But although it is desirable that the two bodies should have the same number of members, it does not follow that both need have the same geographical constituencies, or that they should both be elected on the same day, or for the same term, or by the same method of voting. In our view, not the creation by devolution of new regional or provincial Parliaments,[1] but such a splitting up of the work of the House of Commons, and such a division of the present Cabinet, into two co-ordinate national governments, have already become necessary in our country to-day. In any populous community applying the principle of socialisation, such a division seems to us absolutely essential.

It may be suggested that the two national assemblies —the Political Parliament and the Social Parliament— together with the national executives which they will create and maintain, should be equal and co-ordinate. Each should be, within its own sphere, supreme ; but, as will be indicated, provision must be made for those cases in which, by the nature of things, they will

---

[1] It should be emphasised that, in so homogeneous and closely knit a community as that of Great Britain, any division of the administration of services extending throughout the whole island both impairs efficiency and increases cost. On the other hand, national feeling may be so intense as to require the sacrifice of a division of administration as well as of legislation.

necessarily impinge on each other's sphere. Laws or commands, whether by the one or the other, will be legally valid only in so far as they are warranted by the powers conferred by the statute, which will have to be interpreted, in case of dispute, on particular issues brought before the law courts as in the United States.[1]

Although the two national assemblies will be independent of each other, they will necessarily in many matters have to work in consultation with each other, probably by the machinery of joint committees or conferences. Thus, the laws passed by the Political Parliament with regard to national defence and the maintenance of armed forces, or the negotiations with foreign nations on such subjects as commerce and shipping, migration and naturalisation, cannot fail to affect the administration of industries and services within the sphere of the Social Parliament and of the various administrative bodies within its jurisdiction. Conversely, some of the decisions of these administrative bodies, and of the Social Parliament, will touch on the sphere of the Political Parliament and its Executive. This is not to suggest that the concurrence of the Political Parliament would be required before the Social Parliament could organise

---

[1] It is not suggested that there need be any formally enacted or " written " constitution, otherwise than at present ; but the establishment of the Social Parliament (and, indeed, any relief of the congestion of the House of Commons by " devolution ") necessitates a statute defining the powers and functions of the new body ; and this statute will, anyhow, be construed by the Courts of Justice like any other. No " Conseil d'État," or other system of special tribunals applying " administrative law," is involved. Cases would come before the ordinary Courts in the accustomed way, and be finally disposed of by whatever was the Supreme Court of Appeal.

The objections taken in the United States to the action of the Federal Courts in declaring statutes to be incompatible with the Constitution, and therefore void, really turn on the difficulty which the United States Constitution places in the way of its prompt alteration. If any judgment of the Supreme Court that was contrary to the desire and purpose of the community could be, as regards future cases, overruled by the national legislature without undue difficulty or delay, all substantial grievance would be removed. Under the scheme here proposed, nothing more dilatory or onerous than a Joint Session of both Parliaments, equally responsible to the same electorate, would be required.

any industry or service, set up any institution, or even take over any privately owned property. But if any alteration of the criminal law was desired, which affected the personal liberty of the citizens, this encroachment on individual freedom should need the concurrence of the Political Parliament upon the motion of the Minister of Justice.[1] Examples are the bye-laws or regulations creating new offences which are required in the ordinary administration of public services or industries, whether connected with institutional care of children, the sick or the insane ; with the maintenance of order by municipalities or other local authorities ; with the regulation of new buildings or road traffic ; or with the striking off the professional register of practitioners guilty of improper conduct. All these regulations creating new offences should come before the Minister of Justice, part of whose function should be the safeguarding of personal liberty. But the Minister of Justice is responsible to the Political Parliament ; and in fact, all such bye-laws and regulations creating new offences, that may be required by any Department responsible to the Social Parliament, and approved by it, should require the authority (either under some general statute or by specific resolution of approval) of the Political Parliament, which should have, as one of its functions, the protection of the liberty of the individual citizen against undue encroachments by any legislative or administrative authority, whether communal or vocational.

---

[1] The connection of the Home Office or of any Ministry of Justice with prisons is, of course, merely accidental, and we may hope, only temporary. With the substitution of the idea of curative treatment for punishment, and of that of preventive seclusion for imprisonment, we may expect to see our prisons, like our lunatic asylums, superseded by mental hospitals and convalescent settlements which would naturally be placed under the supervision and control of the Standing Committee on Health of the Social Parliament. The bias of the Ministry of Justice should be to get people out, not to put them in ! It would be the duty of the Ministry of Justice to take care that no person was secluded without adequate cause, or treated otherwise than with a view to cure or prevention.

One of the most important of the questions for both the Political and the Social Parliament will be that of finance. The assessment and collection of all national taxation should be entrusted to the Social Parliament, which will necessarily have to adjust the national balance-sheet, in conjunction with the receipts derived from the national resources in public owner- ship and with the balance - sheets of the various industries and services in public administration. The Political Parliament will accordingly decide what total expenditure it thinks necessary for the ensuing year in respect of the services under its supervision and control, and then present this to the Social Parlia- ment. This body may accept the total, and in that case would include the amount in the budget, and make provision for raising the necessary revenue. There seems to be no necessity for the Social Parlia- ment to be authorised to amend in detail the ex- pénditure so proposed ; but it seems necessary to permit the Social Parliament, if it thinks fit, to make objection to the aggregate amount of the demand ; and, of course, in objecting to the total, discussion of details could not be avoided. The Social Parliament must be permitted to urge that the requirements of the Political Parliament would make a draft upon the resources of the nation that would be excessive and injurious, either to contemporary interests or to those of future generations. If after conference between the two assemblies, a total could not be agreed upon, the difference might be settled by the aggregate vote of the members of the two Parliaments in joint session assembled.

Similar machinery might be used for obtaining that concurrence of the two Parliaments which should certainly be required for any change in the constitution itself. There might also be available for the decisions of deadlocks the device of an appeal to the electorate whether by referendum vote, or by a double dissolution resulting in the election of new Parliaments.

We do not ignore the difficulty inherent in any division of legislative authority between two co-ordinate assemblies, especially in the realm of finance. It may be said, on the one hand, that two national assemblies would lead to constant deadlocks ; and, on the other, that supremacy will inevitably accompany the " power of the purse." The difficulty is inherent in any form of bi-cameral legislature ; and it cannot logically be made a ground of objection to our proposals by those who cling to a Second Chamber of any kind, or by those who propose, as an alternative, the creation of provincial Parliaments. There is only one way completely to escape this difficulty, and that is to vest all authority in a single national assembly, controlling a single national executive. Such an alternative we reject, not only because of the danger to liberty which it may involve, and not merely because of the excessive burden of business by which Members and Ministers would be overwhelmed ; but because, as we have endeavoured to show, no one elected assembly can possibly express the General Will of the inhabitants on all subjects whatsoever. If, as we think, it is essential, if Democracy is not to result in paralysis, to provide, not one but several channels for the expression of the nation's Common Will, the chance of deadlocks will be minimised by arranging for each organ to deal with its own appropriate subjects, and to deal with them, as far as possible, completely. Thus, it is better to have, in addition to the most extensive system of Local Government, supplemented by voluntary Democracies of Consumers and Pro-ducers respectively, two national Parliaments with distinct spheres, than two legislative chambers dealing with the same subjects. The corresponding divisions of the executive, to which Anglo-Indians have lately applied the word " dyarchy," are required on the same grounds as the division of the legislature. It may well be that our proposals do not adequately provide for the difficult problem of the " power of the purse." The joint session of the two Parliaments may become, not an exceptional expedient but the regular way in which the year's estimates are voted. It may be found necessary to make the Standing Committee on Finance, which will have at its disposal the department growing out of the present inadequately equipped Treasury, a standing joint committee of the two Parliaments ; and to entrust the preparation of the estimates for all the departments, those under the Political as well as those under the Social Parliament, to this standing joint committee. What cannot be avoided is the necessity of coming to a decision as to the way in which the nation's resources shall be allocated as between one form of public service and another ; and that decision democrats will not be prepared to entrust to any other authority than the elected representatives of the nation in joint session assembled.[1]

It will be clear that the relation of the Political Parliament to the Social Parliament will not be that of a Second Chamber in the ordinary sense ; any more than the Social Parliament will occupy that position to the Political Parliament. We see no need for any " Second Chamber " to either of the Parliaments within their respective spheres. A " Second Chamber,"

---

[1] We need not elaborate the various constitutional devices that might be adopted in order to facilitate the adequate consideration of conflicting claims to expenditure, and to prevent deadlocks. The effective discussion would naturally take place (as ought to be the case at present in the dealing with the departmental estimates by the Treasury, and actually takes place in the work of the London County Council) in the course of the examination of the departmental estimates by the Finance Department, and in the Standing Committee on Finance, which would naturally be in full and frank consultation with the Ministers, Chairmen of Committees and chief administrative officers of all the departments. It could easily be provided that (subject to a maximum number) the Ministers of the Political Parliament and the Chairmen of Committees of the Social Parliament should be free to take part in the proceedings of the other assembly.

even if restricted to its appropriate function of revision in the case of errors or omissions, and suspension in the case of undue haste or doubt as to popular mandate, has—possibly owing to the historical confusion with the former separate Estates of the Realm—almost invariably (but as democrats would now say illegitimately) presumed to have an opinion of its own on the substance and on the merits of the decisions of the popular assembly, an opinion which has naturally sometimes been divergent, and has thus produced obstruction, ill-feeling and delay.[1]

In addition to the contingency of changes being desired in the constitution itself, there are, however, two classes of subjects on which it may be desirable to provide for safeguards to the individual citizen on the one hand, and to the widest and most durable interests of the community on the other, against the possible zeal and eagerness of either of the two Parliaments.   In the first place there is the personal liberty of the individual citizen, which, from the very nature of things, is, in the densely peopled, highly organised modern community, always in danger.   In the long run it will be advantageous to all concerned, that no proposal to lessen the existing freedom of the indi-

---

[1] It follows that each of the Parliaments should have its own internal organisation for securing all the necessary protection against error and haste that any Second Chamber can afford. We suggest that the best hint is offered by Norway. Each national assembly might elect, at its first meeting, a Committee of Revision of eminent legal, administrative and other experts, statutorily entitled to sit for the whole term of the assembly, and to have submitted to it for revision every legislative Act. It should be required to submit any amendments which it thinks necessary in order to carry into effect the decisions of the assembly (including therefore the correction of mistakes and the avoidance of inconsistency with existing legislation) to the assembly itself, in a statement published to the world, in which the reasons for the proposed alterations would be adduced. The assembly should thereupon be required to reconsider its measure, taking a vote on each of the amendments suggested.

Any power of suspension that may be thought desirable (whether for a single session only, or until the next assembly) on the ground that the proposed legislation had been undertaken with undue haste, or that public opinion had not yet accorded its approval to it, might be entrusted to the same Committee of Revision.

vidual by the creation of new statutory offences should lightly become law. Socialists are at least as anxious as Liberals or Conservatives to protect individual liberty against the enthusiasm of a Social Parliament, which might be carried away by its absorption in improving the mental and material environment of the present generation, or in making provision for coming generations ; and likewise against the zeal of administrative bodies, eager to surmount difficulties, or tempted to " make people better by Act of Parliament." Thus, whilst it would be open to the Social Parliament to organise the public services in whatever way was thought fit, and to provide any kind or quality of commodity or service that was desired, it would not be within the power of the Social Parliament, without obtaining the concurrence of the Political Parliament, advised by the Minister of Justice, either to make the use of any public service legally compulsory under penalty, or to make it an offence for the service to be supplied in any other way.

In the second place, there is the danger that the Political Parliament, absorbed in its task of maintaining the national interests throughout the world, might be led to the expenditure upon the army and navy, or upon an aggressive policy towards other countries, of a larger proportion of the nation's resources than would be, on reflection, desired by the community. As the Social Parliament, from the very nature of things, must have the administration of the nation's resources, it is this Parliament that must necessarily have the power of deciding what taxation upon individuals is required. It is in order that the claims of all the varied interests and desires of the community may be properly compared and weighed, one against another, that it is proposed that the Political Parliament should be required to submit its estimates of expenditure to the Social Parliament for sanction, and for provision of the necessary funds. In both cases a reference, not to any outside authority or privileged section, but to the elected representatives of the community itself organised in a different way, affords the best possible safeguard against the outcome, either in the Social Parliament or in the Political Parliament, of an undue zeal or an excessive absorption of national resources on either side.

The argument may be summed up as follows : It is desirable to separate and isolate the governmental power over persons, exercised through the criminal law, from the governmental power over things, exercised through their administration. The organ of the community in which the execution of the criminal law is vested should have no power over things except such things as (by vote of money) have been entrusted to it by the organ of the community charged with economic and social administration. On the other hand, the organ of the community charged with the administration of things should have no power to use the law for the coercion of persons, except by resort to the Law Courts under a Minister responsible to the other great organ of the community, and under a criminal law assented to by that body.

There seems to be no reason for giving either of the two national assemblies a general supremacy over the other. In particular, it is entirely pernicious that the prestige of the Crown should be associated more closely with the army and navy than with the public health or education service, or with the administration of industry. The idea that what have been called the primary functions of the State— defence and foreign relations, police and justice—are of greater importance than the economic and social functions which have grown up almost entirely within the last century, appears to be merely a traditional error. In peril of invasion, it is true, the Executive of the Political Parliament would doubtless have to be granted exceptional powers (as was, in fact, done by the Defence of the Realm Act) ; and the Executive of the Social Parliament would, for the time being, take a subordinate place. On the other hand, in times of peace the work of the Political Parliament and its Executive would perhaps not loom so large in the public mind as that of the Social Parliament and its Executive ; and it would be the proposals of the latter that would evoke public discussion in and out of Parliament. The relations of the two Parliaments, and of their several Executives, with the Crown, and with all the ceremonial functions of the Monarch, should be precisely equal.

DEVOLUTION AS AN ALTERNATIVE SCHEME OF REFORM

So far for the scheme that we propose. We do not disguise from ourselves that a proposal so contrary to the existing categories of political thought as the division into two of the supreme national assembly —not, as at present, into two Chambers with concurrent powers on the same subjects, but into two groups of subjects each allocated to its own Parliament —is, at first sight, unacceptable. Nothing is so painful as to be hustled out of deep-cut ruts of thought ! But there are two questions which the critics of the scheme will have to answer. Is there not an unbearable evil to be remedied ? If so, what alternative proposal of reform can be made ?

We must recall to the reader our previous analysis of the failure of Parliament to cope with the collective business of the community, and the dangerous disillusionment with parliamentary institutions, and even with Democracy itself, which this failure has caused. There is, first, the admitted congestion of business in the House of Commons and the Cabinet, which is making parliamentary government a byword. Every one agrees that some remedy for this congestion must be promptly found ; and the suggestions [1] for the purpose range from a mere revision of the procedure of the House of Commons to the establishment by " devolution " of a litter of subordinate legislative assemblies for particular parts of Great Britain, whether " nations," " regions " or " provinces." It is, however, difficult to see how a mere devolution of legislation to subordinate Parliaments—a project which is found to bristle with difficulties of its own—will amount to much, unless each of the new Parliaments is allowed to control the administration of the " nation," " region," or province committed to its care ; and the splitting up of the administration of a country so nearly homogeneous and so closely integrated as Great Britain has become appears to be open to grave objections.   It seems plain that national de-fence, Customs, the Post Office, the administration of the Income Tax and Super Tax, the Supreme Court of Appeal, and many other important departments— not to mention such nationalised industries as the railways and mines—could not be divided without the most serious practical inconvenience and loss of efficiency ; whilst any divergence among different parts of Great Britain in such matters as Factory Legislation, the Mines Regulation, Merchant Shipping and Trade Boards Acts, Unemployment Insur-ance, and the Employment Exchange, whether in law or in administration, would lead to disabling inconvenience. How far it is desirable to permit of variations between one part of Great Britain and

---

[1] The present chapter deals only with the problem of how to make effective a representative assembly, *however elected*. Those who desire a change in the method of election, especially those who advocate election on a vocational basis (the " Soviet ") will find that issue discussed in Chapter VI. " The Reorganisation of the Vocational World."

another in the minimum standards enforced in any
application of the Policy of the National Minimum
raises difficult economic and industrial problems.
With regard to health and education, for instance,
where the central administration confines itself almost
entirely to prescribing the National Minimum, supervising the Local Authorities and subsidising such of
their activities as it approves, practically the whole
field of variation to suit local conditions is already
open to the responsible elected assembly for each
locality (the County, Borough or District Council).
In fact, it is very forcibly argued by those who oppose
" devolution " that the case for what is called
" regional " or " provincial " Parliaments is, in effect,
no more than an argument for the concession of a
greater measure of independence in self-determination
to the existing Local Authorities, possibly with suitable enlargement of their areas, without any alteration
in the constitution either of the legislative body or of
the central administrative departments. It comes to
no more than an alteration in the powers and areas
of Local Government, a matter dealt with in a subsequent chapter.

But even assuming for the moment that the House
of Commons and the Cabinet could, by the expedient
of creating several new Parliaments for particular
localities, rid themselves of any important part of
the business by which they are now overwhelmed—
an assumption which few experienced officials would
allow—no such multiplication of Parliaments, each of
them dealing with all the business of its geographical
province, would remove the second cause that we have
assigned for the creeping paralysis that has come over
parliamentary government and the Cabinet System.
What to-day renders impotent both the House of
Commons and the Cabinet is not wholly, or even
mainly, the mere volume of the business with which

they have severally to deal. The main cause of their
failure is the heterogeneity of the issues on which
they are supposed to express and to carry out the
Common Will of the community. Upon such a
heterogeneous mass of issues, simultaneously presented
to it, the community has not, and never can have,
any Common Will. The community as a whole, like
the individual elector, has simultaneously several
different wills ; and the attempt to merge them at
one and the same General Election results, for the
most part, not in any " Greatest Common Measure "—
for it is not a sum in arithmetic—but in uncertainty
and paralysis. Only when one question is made
temporarily to predominate can any clear decision
be obtained ; and this is then obtained at the cost of
paralysis of the national will as regards all the thousand
and one other subjects needing to be attended to.

The Argument summarised

We now resume the argument in favour of the
scheme already outlined. It will be plain that it is
impracticable to set up a separate national assembly,
or even to have a separate General Election, for each
of the various subjects on which the Common Will
.has to be ascertained and formulated. Even the use
of the Referendum, itself open to many objections,
does not provide for what is, after all, the most continuous, and it may well be the most important, function
of democratic institutions, namely, the control over
administration. What can be done is to divide the
business, according to its nature, first apportioning
to Local Authorities, and to the new factors in the
Socialist Commonwealth, what can most appropriately
be dealt with by these bodies ; and then dividing
what must necessarily remain as the burden of the
central democratic organs of the community in such

a way as to enable the Common Will for each portion to be ascertained, and the difficulties in the execution of that will to be grappled with. The analysis reveals two main complexes [1] of public business, each of them forming a coherent and interdependent whole on which the community may, by appropriate channels of expression,[2] be enabled to formulate a Common Will ; to be embodied in legislation of a particular type. The administration of the resulting services does, in fact, so far hang together as to make it possible, and indeed easy, for them to be controlled by the executive organs of a single national assembly. At the same time these two complexes are sufficiently distinct in character to enable them to be dealt with apart (although, of course, not without periodical

---

[1] To avoid misunderstanding, it may be well to explain that we use the word "complex" in its old-established meaning of a system of inter-related parts ; and without any reference to the peculiar meaning lately given to it by the psycho-analysts.

[2] Mr. Graham Wallas, in *Human Nature in Politics*, has brought out the subtle reaction of well-devised and safeguarded channels of expression on right methods of thought: "Trial by jury was, in its origin, simply a method of ascertaining, from ordinary men whose veracity was secured by religious sanctions, their real opinions on each case. . . . The process . . . by which that opinion is produced has been more and more completely controlled and developed, until it, and not the mere registration of the verdict, has become the essential feature of the trial.

"The jury are now separated from their fellow-men during the whole case. They are introduced into a world of new emotional values. The ritual of the court, the voices and dress of judge and counsel, all suggest the environment in which the petty interests and impulses of ordinary life are un-important when compared with the supreme worth of truth and justice. They are warned to empty their minds of all preconceived inferences and affections. The examination and cross-examination of the witnesses are carried on under rules of evidence which are the result of centuries of experience, and which give many a man as he sits on a jury his first lesson in the fallibility of the unobserved and uncontrolled inferences of the human brain. The ' said I's,' and ' thought I's,' and ' said he's,' which are the material of his ordinary reasoning, are here banished on the ground that they are ' not evidence ' ; and witnesses are compelled to give a simple account of their remembered sensations of sight and hearing " (pp. 207-9). He adds in another place : " If at the assizes all the jurors summoned were collected into one large jury, and if they all voted Guilty or Not Guilty on all the cases, after a trial in which all the counsel were heard, and all the witnesses were examined simultaneously, verdicts would indeed no longer depend on the accidental composition of the separate juries ; but the process of forming verdicts would be made, to a serious degree, less effective " (*ibid.* pp. 218-19). See also *Public Opinion and Popular Government*, by A. Lawrence Lowell.

conferences and consultations), alike as regards legislation and the control of administration.

THE POLITICAL COMPLEX

These two complexes are, as has been explained,
first the essentially " political," comprising the relations of the community as a whole with other communities which, it may be hoped, will be increasingly
a matter of international law ; and the maintenance
of order and individual freedom within the community,
which may be assumed to be already a matter of
national law. As things are, the business of the
Foreign Office has, for the sake of national defence,
to be very intimately connected with the War Office
and the Admiralty, and that of the Colonial Office
and India Office with all three. It is not too much
to say that upon the complex of policy embraced
within these five departments there is ascertainable
from the community as a whole something that may
fairly be described as a Common Will, unparalysed by
the intervention of desires and purposes with regard
to other issues. There is, in fact, a policy on which
the electorate can decide. In this complex we place
also the Ministry of Justice, with its functions of
maintaining internal order, preventing crime, and
administering justice, including the development of
law and the protection of personal liberty, partly
because these all form part of national defence in the
fullest sense, just as law is or should be the basis of
international as well as of internal relations. The
naturalness and, so to speak, the practicability of this
complex, in exactly the form in which it is here proposed, is borne out by the fact that it represented
right down to the middle of the nineteenth century
practically the whole business of national government,
which Treitschke could describe as confined to the

levying of war and the execution of justice. This complex was, as their letters and biographies reveal, substantially all that " politics " really meant to the majority of Victorian statesmen and politicians. Nor can we look forward to any lessening of its essential consequence. Whilst aggression and violence may gradually disappear, the relations of one community with another, like those of individuals within a community, must inevitably become ever more extensive and complicated, leading on the one hand to a development of law and of international law, and on the other to an enlargement of personality and experience of which it is difficult to exaggerate the importance. If we come to think about it, all the functions assigned to the Political Parliament and its executive, whilst becoming ever more complicated and, as we should say, more scientific, are likely, if civilisation is to endure, to become increasingly matters for international arrangement.

THE SOCIAL COMPLEX

The other complex is that of the business which is as essentially " economic " in character, in the oldest sense of this word, or, as we now say, " social," as the other was " political." Comprised within it is everything connected with conservation of the resources of the community ; the administration of its industries and services ; the maintenance in health of its population ; its education ; the development of literature, science and art ; and generally the determination, for the present generation and for the future, of the kind of civilisation that the community desires to maintain. On this complex of business there is, it may be suggested, the possibility of eliciting from the community a fairly distinct and definite Common Will, untrammelled by contradictory desires and purposes with regard to the " political " complex ; and of formulating and carrying out a coherent policy of some efficiency. The work of the central democratic organs in this field is of comparatively recent growth ; but included in the complex would be the present Departments of Health, Education and Employment, together with the Board of Trade and the Board of Agriculture and Fisheries. This group of social and economic activities, including all the industries and communal services, is the very stuff out of which the material and mental environment that the members of each community desire and intend has to be constructed. And although each service has its own technique, and must be undertaken by a distinct administration,[1] the daily work of these administrations have to be continuously co-ordinated one with another—the service of education with that of health ; the organisation of employment with technical education on the one hand, and with the management of all the various industries on the other ; housing with both health and transport ; afforestation and agriculture with water supply and open spaces, with health resorts and the enjoyment of lake and mountain. In view of the necessity of weighing always the demands of the present against the needs of the future, and of the importance of the control over the administration of industries and services, the nation's financial business, including taxation, naturally falls into the same complex. As all these public activities must coincide, if any one of them is to attain a high degree of efficiency, and must all march together if the common standard of life is to be raised, their administration rests essentially on a common policy, which can be put before the electorate

---

[1] The appropriate division of work among public departments has been authoritatively determined for Great Britain in the *Report of the Machinery of Government Committee*, Cd. 9230, 1918.

as a whole, and independent of the issues of policy raised by the other complex of subjects that we have styled political ; and the two together seem fairly to exhaust the business under which Parliament and the Cabinet are at present crushed. It is only by cutting the business into two halves, according to its nature, and entrusting each to its own national assembly, with its own executive, that the load upon legislators and statesmen can be brought within a manageable compass. No other method of division seems calculated to remove the real cause of the present breakdown, which is not merely magnitude of business, but paralysis of will. Only by making it possible for the electorate to separate its present conflicting wills, so that it can give one mandate on policy for all the national business of one kind, and another mandate on policy for all the national business of another kind, does it seem possible to avoid the paralysis. Only by some such differentiation of business can the Members of Parliament concentrate their thoughts and attention on something like a homogeneous range of subjects. Only by the establishment of separate executives, each concentrating its attention on its own complex—thus rescuing the Cabinet from a wilderness of entirely disparate affairs : first, say, our relations with China or Peru, then the price of coal ; now the prevention of war with an unfriendly neighbour, and the next moment the prevention of tuberculosis —does it seem that the nation's common business can be done.

THE PROTECTION OF THE INDIVIDUAL AGAINST THE GOVERNMENT

It is an incidental advantage of the proposed division of the overwhelming power of Parliament between two separate national assemblies, each with

its own executive organs, that it creates a new safeguard for personal freedom. One of the natural
apprehensions about any considerable increase in the
functions of government—or even in municipal enterprise and vocational organisation on any large scale—
is that its authoritative influence over the life of the
individual might thereby become tyrannical and all-
pervading. In the scheme set forth in this book no
addition is proposed to the existing constitutional
authority of government in Great Britain. Yet if the
present powers of the Crown, the Cabinet, the House of
Commons and the Civil Service were to be applied to
the ownership and administration of industrial capital,
the individual might easily find himself practically
helpless. This is, in fact, the tendency of nearly all
the legislation of to-day ; and, irrespective of Socialist
projects, the danger is one to be guarded against. The
constitution now proposed would provide a not inconsiderable safeguard for individual liberty.

In the first place, the very establishment of two
national assemblies by statute would, in itself, supply a
much-needed corrective to the omnipotence of Parliament. At present, in Great Britain, the power of
Parliament is without any legal limitation—a fact
which the predominance of the House of Commons over
the Crown, on the one hand, and over the House of
Lords on the other, together with the practical control
of the elected assembly by the Cabinet, renders all the
more alarming. The transformation of Parliament into
two distinct national assemblies, each of them defined
by statute, would, in itself, bring their legislative
enactments within the purview of the Law Courts,
which would necessarily have to construe each measure
on any case that arose under it, not merely as at present,
in order to discover its meaning, but also to see whether
it fell within the powers conferred upon the assembly
by which it was enacted. As in the United States

to-day, any enactment by either the Political Parliament or the Social Parliament which went beyond the powers entrusted to that assembly would, in effect, be declared unconstitutional. At the same time, it would be neither unduly difficult nor productive of dangerous delay to cure any such defect, if it were really the popular will that it should be cured, by making the necessary alteration in the constitution by a Joint Session of the two assemblies.

But the proposed division of powers and functions between two co-ordinate Parliaments, controlling two distinct national executives, with two separate complexes of administration, affords an even more important safeguard for individual liberty. One of the objections made to the assumption by government of even the most indisputably public services, involving the direct employment of large bodies of men and women, is that the government loses its position of impartiality in the maintenance of order. If the three hundred thousand employees of the Postmaster-General were to strike, the Cabinet, which would certainly make every effort to maintain the postal service, would be hampered in the maintenance of order by the fact that it would probably be using the army, navy and air force, not merely to "keep the ring," but actually also to convey the mails. If the present Cabinet, responsible to the House of Commons as we know it, were to become the direct employer, not only of the 300,000 postal employees, but also of the 600,000 railway workers, and the 1,100,000 coal-miners, not to mention other industries, the danger of a grave national conflict would be greatly increased. When a government controlling a standing army sets to work, in its capacity of employer, to "break" a national strike among its own employees, the process is perilously apt to take on the character of the suppression of a rebellion. On the other hand, the community, which needs to be protected against aggression by the members of any one vocation, has an even greater interest in the maintenance of law and order ; and it could not afford to allow its government to be defeated. For this reason among others, it is essential that the executive government and the national assembly which are responsible for the maintenance of law and order, and have the control of the nation's armed forces, should not themselves be responsible also for the conduct of the nation's industries and public services. It should remain unimplicated in the disputes between the postal workers and their employer; between the railwaymen and those responsible for the administration of this vital public service ; between any section of the coal-miners and those whose task it is to see that the community regularly gets the coal that it requires, and generally between any one portion of the population and the remainder. Under the constitution now proposed, the Minister of Justice and the Minister of Defence would have no more connection with the policy of those responsible for the administration or the control of the nation's industries and services than the Home Secretary or the Secretary of State for War has at present for the policy adopted by the Town Council of Manchester or the Co-operative Wholesale Society. Any strike of persons in national employment would not be a strike against the government responsible for the maintenance of law and order, and wielding the instrument of the standing army ; or against the national assembly by which that government would be controlled ; but primarily against the National Board for the industry or service ; and secondarily against the entirely distinct Social Parliament and its particular Standing Committee, which would have no more, and also no less, right to call in the police and the troops for the protection of their premises and plant than a Local Authority or a Co-operative Society.

But even within its own legitimate sphere each of the two national assemblies and national executives must necessarily exercise, in a great and densely peopled community, very extensive powers. Merely to halve by division the whole power and authority of the present government departments, Cabinet and Legislature, would not, in itself, afford much new protection to individual liberty. For this reason it is suggested that neither of the two governments and legislatures should be entirely unlimited in its autocracy. The Social Parliament may enable anything whatever to be provided for, or supplied to the citizens, whether by National Boards or Local Authorities ; but it cannot, of its own authority, compel the citizens to take advantage of its enterprise, or forbid any one among them to carry on the business for himself. But if in its zeal for the well-being of the citizens, it wishes to compel the individual citizen to do anything, or to forbid him to do anything under pain of fine or imprisonment, it must seek the concurrence of the Political Parliament, advised by the Minister of Justice, whose duty it will be not lightly to consent to any curtailment of individual liberty. Conversely, whilst the Political Parliament and its responsible Cabinet of Ministers will be free to conduct the nation's international relations and to direct its armed forces for the maintenance of law and order, they will have no power to deprive any citizen of his property, or to levy any tax, and they must come to the Social Parliament for whatever funds they deem it necessary to expend for the duties entrusted to them. Through the Political Parliament the community will wield the coercive instrument of the criminal law, and the power of the nation in the counsels of the world ; but the Political Parliament will need to ask the Social

Parliament for all the funds it requires for action either at home or abroad. Through the Social Parliament the community will control the nation's economic resources and wield the power of taxation ; but whenever the Social Parliament desires to prohibit private enterprise or penalise individual action, it must seek the concurrence of the other body. In short, in both classes of encroachment on the sphere of the individual, personal freedom will have the new safeguard of the requirement of concurrence by two separately elected national assemblies, examining the proposition from two distinct standpoints. This feature of the scheme runs, like a red thread, through the detailed proposals of the following chapters.[1]

---

[1] What effect will this proposed reconstruction of our National Government have on the organisation of Political Parties ? Will it make for the continuance of the Party System ? Will it mean two parties or many groups ? Or will the Party System be superseded altogether ? These questions are outside the realm of constitutional reconstruction. Political organisations are and must always remain voluntary ; and they will grow or decay, diminish or multiply, remain fixed in their principles or change from one basis to another, according to the promptings of the time-spirit. We can only hazard a prophecy. The division of the work of the national government, and its relegation to two Parliaments and two Executives, concentrating their attention respectively on political and social issues, will tend to weaken but not to destroy the organisation of the electorate into two or more political parties. At present our civilisation is predominantly capitalist in its basis, and during the past few decades—unlike the preceding half-century—our capitalists have become predominantly imperialist in policy. So long as this is the case, the dominant tendency will be for the cleavage of parties, apart from individual adherents on one side or the other, to be between those who are essentially property-owners, whether or not they are actively pursuing a vocation, and those who are essentially dependent on wages or salaries, irrespective of any exiguous possessions that they may call their own. As it is impossible to expect any sudden or simultaneous supersession of the capitalist basis of society, or even the reversion of the capitalists to the pacific non-interventionism of their Victorian predecessors, we have to contemplate the starting of the new constitution amid much the same cleavage of opinion as exists to-day. In that case it may be inferred that the political parties would seek to influence equally the Political and the Social Parliaments, and even the Local Authorities. But, as we see to-day in the case of the municipalities, the difference in subjects and issues between the two Parliaments would tend to weaken the party influence in the elections to one or the other of them, and conceivably in both.

When, however, with the change in heart and the progress of socialisation, our civilisation has ceased to be predominantly capitalist in its basis, and when those who " live by owning " have sunk to a despised remnant, the cleavage of opinion will necessarily be different. What the issues at

It must, however, be made clear that there is
no idea of the Social Parliament with its standing

elections will be in a predominantly Socialist community it is, of course,
impossible to predict. We are inclined to think that the organised political
parties as they exist to-day will pass away ; and that their place will be taken
by more or less sporadic propagandist organisations, seeking to influence
the electorate and the national assemblies on particular subjects. The
political party organisations of the past half century are commonly said to
have arisen and grown with the creation of an extensive electorate. It
may equally be said that their origin and growth have coincided with the
development of a permanent cleavage of financial interests between the
" haves " and the " have nots." The recurrent disputes among different
vocations, or those arising between various sections of a community in which
there is no " living by owning," may quite possibly produce no lasting
division into political parties. The most influential agencies may be such
propagandist bodies as the Anti-Corn Law League, or the Woman Suffrage
societies in the past, or the Proportional Representation Society or the
League of Nations Union in the present. The more complete and intensive
becomes the education of the community, the more numerous and varied
may be these propagandist bodies ; and also the shorter the duration of
life of each of them, as one question after another gets decided. This
tendency to substitute transient propagandist bodies, inspired by enthusiasts,
for permanent political parties controlled by the wirepullers, will probably
be stimulated by the altered relations between the representatives and the
electorate. At present the Member of Parliament—with a so-called " Payment of Members " that hardly meets his bill for postage stamps—feels
that he is doing a favour to his constituency by " serving " it at Westminster ; and will do so only in the way that suits his own convenience,
his own amateurish prejudices, and his own pecuniary interests. The
" whole-time " member of the Social or the Political Parliament, provided,
like his colleague devoting himself to analogous duties in a reorganised
Local Government, with an income adequate for full maintenance, will
tend increasingly to regard himself, and to be regarded, as pursuing a
definite vocation—that of the Elected Representative—requiring no less
continuous a devotion to duty, and the mastery of no less technique (though
of a different kind), than the vocation of the professional expert or that
of the civil servant. Those who pursue this vocation in the highest spirit
will find themselves relatively impartial as between the ideals of different
reformers, in all of which they will discern much that is good, and will be
concerned rather to discover how the particular projects of the idealists and
the half-articulate desires of the electorate can be adjusted to the circumstances, in such a way as to be made, in a democratic community, to work
for the common benefit. The task of the propagandist organisations will
therefore lie much more in educating the electorate than in lobbying the
elected representatives. With the increase in an educated community both
of public spirit and of interest in public affairs, this diversion of voluntary
effort from political parties to propagandist bodies may be expected to be
progressive.

The business of " electioneering "—at present an arduous and costly
burden on the candidates or their party organisations—will be transformed
when all the necessary work and expenditure (including not merely the
registration of the electors and the conduct of the poll, but also the printing
and addressing as well as the postage of election literature and poll-cards,
the free provision of halls for meetings, and their adequate advertisement),
is devolved on public officers and paid for from public funds.

committees itself undertaking the complicated work of the administration of the socialised industries and services, any more than of its undertaking the duties of the Local Authorities. A second cardinal feature of the present proposals is the separation, throughout the whole range of the work of the Social Parliament, of Control from Administration. Here we come, at last, to what is perhaps of most interest to the Labour and Socialist Movement : namely, how should industry and services be organised ?

CHAPTER II

SOME LEADING CONSIDERATIONS IN THE SOCIALISATION
OF INDUSTRIES AND SERVICES

WE pass straight from the proposed constitution of
twin national assemblies, in which the supreme
control of the community should be vested, to the
other end of the problem of the constitution of the
Socialist Commonwealth : namely, the organisation of
industries and services ; leaving to future chapters
the relation of the national Parliaments to the various
administrative organs to be proposed. In so doing
we must again emphasise the fact that, with Socialists,
it is not a question of " socialising," at one blow or in
any one way, the whole of industry, and all services,
but of providing the most advantageous form of
administration for each industry or service, as, one
after another, in the course of industrial and social
evolution, each passes from capitalistic to public
ownership and control. Nor need it be imagined
that this progressive " socialisation," which has already
been going on for some time, will ever become so
universally complete, even in any one country, that
there will be no " unsocialised " enterprise. It may
even be predicted with confidence that there will
always be a toleration of unsocialised industries
and services—such as the whole realm of individual
production in horticulture, peasant agriculture and
the artistic handicrafts ; the purely personal vocations

of the poet and the artist ; the prosecution of many
minor industries and services that may be most conveniently conducted on an individual basis ; possibly
the experimental promotion of some new inventions
and devices ; not to mention the co-operative organisation of religious rites and observances. There may
also be a persistent though always varying residuum
of capitalist profit-making industries, such as the production of articles for export to barbarous races or
unsocialised States, for which no other provision
has been made, the going to and fro of privately
owned ships in the oceans of the world, and even, in
the most completely socialised communities, the carrying on, by way of experiment or for the sake of comparative costing, of parts or sections or varieties of
industries or services that are otherwise socialised.
And it must always be remembered that Socialists
accept, as one form of socialisation, not only Local
Government in all its manifestations, but also the
free and voluntary association of groups of consumers
for the production and distribution of those commodities and services for which they feel themselves
to have an exceptional need, or for which they prefer
this form. The scheme of organisation must therefore be so framed as to cover not merely the various
industries and services that may at any particular
moment have already passed out of capitalistic ownership, but also, in appropriate ways, whatever national
supervision and control is required in the public
interest over Local Government and the Co-operative
Movement, as well as over the residuum that will, for
the time, remain in individual or group ownership.

Starting from the present stage of development of
the various industries and services in Great Britain,
and the materials available for the rebuilding of our
constitution, there are three different forms of organisation of the industries and services, now in public

ownership or (as may be thought) ripe for socialisation. We shall set forth a form of national organisation which seems to us appropriate, with particular variations to suit each case, for those great industries and services, probably fewer than a dozen, which require to be dealt with primarily on a national basis. We shall deal separately with the much larger number of enterprises which will be more advantageously conducted by Municipalities and other forms of Local Government. The third class of enterprises, comprising the production and distribution of the great mass of commodities prepared directly for household consumption or use, we shall describe as falling most appropriately within the sphere of the consumers' Co-operative Movement, and of federal organisations of like character. A separate chapter on "The Transitional Control of Profit-making Enterprise" will deal with the supervision and control that the public interest may require to be exercised over industries and services still in individual ownership, including compensation and taxation. All this development demands, for the most efficient working, a much higher degree of organisation of the producers themselves than at present exists in this or any other country. Hence we shall describe the transition from the present Trade Union Movement in Great Britain, as now organised both industrially and politically, for its long-drawn-out secular warfare against the capitalist class, to a world of vocational organisation of brain workers and manual workers, each section of which will have for its purpose the elevation of its vocational status in the community, the elaboration of its professional technique, the development of its professional honour, and the perfecting of the science and art of the particular service that its members render to the community as a whole. But before elaborating our suggestions under these five heads, it will be convenient to recapitulate the teachings of experience as to what may be expected from each of the social materials out of which the new constitution has to be built.

Three separate Aspects of Economic Man

Our analysis of the existing structure of society has shown that, whenever the capitalist profit-maker is eliminated, the human beings concerned have three separate and distinct purposes, as to which, in constructing a democratic government of an industry or service, their Common Will needs to be represented. There is first the primeval cleavage of interest and purpose between the producer of a particular service or commodity and those who desire to use or consume it. In the whole range of animal life this cleavage of interest is manifested in the simple device of forceful seizure of the desired commodity by the would-be consumer, if he be the stronger party, without compensation : a device which may still be detected in practice in human society in undeveloped countries wherever one race holds another in subjection by force of arms. But over and above this cleavage there arises, in any self-governing civilised community, the consideration of the interests of the whole body of citizens, many of whom neither produce nor consume the particular product, including notably the interests of future generations. Thus, democratisers of industry have to consider, not only man as a producer and man as a consumer, but also man as a citizen desiring the permanent maintenance of the community of which he forms part, and the continuance of a particular type of civilisation. It would, however, be a mistake to assume either the practicability or the expediency of always differentiating, in the government of an industry or service, between these two aspects of consumption. In some industries (we may instance the supply of household requisites by the Co-operative Movement) the actual body of consumers—the members of a particular Co-operative Society—may not unfairly be taken to represent the interests of the whole community of citizens, whilst in other services, such as the main drainage system or the maintenance of public parks, the citizens on the electoral register form the only practicable constituency for representing the day-by-day users or consumers of these municipalised services. On the other hand, when what is in question is the organisation of the natural resources of a community, and their wise conservation over successive generations (as is the case with coal, oil, timber and species of animals in danger of extinction) ; or the inevitable conflict between the cheapest possible exploitation and the maintenance of such priceless amenities as pure air, unpolluted streams and unspoilt scenery, the divergence of interests between the present generation of consumers and the permanent interests of the community—which the economic apologists for Capitalism have hitherto almost ignored—compels a Socialist community to provide special machinery for the protection of the future.

The Relative Functions of Democracies of Consumers and Democracies of Producers

It will be helpful to a solution of the problem of the functions to be assigned to the several parties in the administration of industries and services to recall what has been the experience of Democracies of Consumers and Democracies of Citizens, as Co-operative Societies, Municipalities or national departments on the one hand, and on the other of the Democracies of Producers, whether in the form of Trade Unions of manual workers or in that of Professional Associations of brain workers.

DEMOCRACIES OF CITIZEN-CONSUMERS [1]

Democracies of Citizen-Consumers have been not-ably successful in the ownership and organisation of the instruments of production, alike in importation, in manufacture and in distribution—a success which has been shown, not merely by the fact that their enterprises have survived, and even grown, in com-petition with the Capitalist System, but in the more important result that this form of organisation of industries and services, in so far as it includes the corporate ownership of the land and other instruments of production, does what the Capitalist System has never done and can never do, namely, ensure the distribution of the inevitable surpluses that we know as rent and profit—that is to say, surplus value—equitably among all the consumers. And all experi-ence points, as the essential cause of their success, to their principle of setting themselves to satisfy the ascertained desires or demands of their members. The whole of the activities of the Co-operative Society start from the sales - counter of the store. In like manner, the members of a municipal council are bound to consider the desires and needs of their electors, as the users or consumers of the municipal services, otherwise the councillors may not secure re-election. These Democracies of Citizen-Consumers have shown themselves to have, by their inherent nature, the unique characteristic of remaining open democracies, free from any tendency or desire to close their ranks against newcomers. Their repre-sentatives and officials, compared with the representa-

---

[1] In our preceding analysis we distinguished between those Democracies of Consumers in which membership was voluntary (such as the consumers' Co-operative Movement) and those in which membership was obligatory (such as the Municipality). For the purpose of this section the distinction is immaterial, as we are here concerned only with their relation to Demo-cracies of Producers. We shall therefore use the term " Democracies of Citizen-Consumers " to include both.

tives of such Democracies of Producers as exist, or
as have ever existed, are inclined actually to favour
new processes, new materials, new products, and, be
it added, to give opportunity to new types of skill,
whether of hand or of brain. The consumers'
representative has, in fact, as such, a continuous bias
towards two types of personal freedom : the freedom
of the individual producer to take up any work that
suits him, and the freedom of the individual consumer
to use or consume any product or service which he
happens to desire.

On the other hand, Democracies of Citizen-
Consumers tend to be, by their very nature, soulless
and callous constituencies, testing all things by the
satisfaction of the desire of the members in their
consumption of particular commodities or services in
the production of each of which the majority of the
members (even if they all work) take no part. When
permitted to exercise undisputed authority over their
employees, they have tended, often out of mere
thoughtlessness, to refrain from improving, and even
to worsen the conditions of employment ; and, more
especially, to ignore any desire of the workers concerned, when once they find themselves under contract
of service, for any personal freedom beyond what has
become customary in capitalist employment. They
have done practically nothing, any more than does
the Capitalist System, to secure the willing co-operation
of each section of workers in the running of the service.
They have too often developed the evils of bureaucracy which characterise every form of uncontrolled
" government from above " : red tape, secrecy, arbitrariness and, in some cases, favouritism in the selection,
promotion and dismissal of employees. For all these
reasons, experience demonstrates that Democracies
of Citizen - Consumers cannot implicitly be trusted,
any more than even benevolent capitalists can be

trusted, with complete authority in industry. They need to be complemented by Democracies of workers by hand and by brain.

DEMOCRACIES OF PRODUCERS

Democracies based on vocation or, as we say, on production, whether Trade Unions of manual workers or Professional Associations of brain workers, have proved equally successful, but in another sphere. They have achieved far-reaching results, not only in maintaining and improving the conditions of employment, but also in protecting the personal freedom of the worker in and outside the working hours. They stand for full livelihood, personal dignity and individual initiative in the exercise of a vocation. The liberty they assure and develop is an intensive liberty, applying to the more continuous and more specialised factors in each member's life, as against the extensive and diffused liberty typical of the Democracy of Consumers, applying to fragmentary and changing parts of the life common to all men. Further, this form of Democracy does what the Capitalist System and Democracies of Citizen-Consumers fail to do: namely, supply machinery by which the consciousness of consent and active co-operation in the productive process may be evoked among the workers. In the case of " Subject Associations," or scientific societies — hitherto confined to Professional Associations of brain workers, but equally open, with increasing general education, to Trade Unions of manual workers — these Democracies of Producers have, even under the Capitalist System, enormously assisted in the continued improvement of technique and the progressive advancement of knowledge required by the existing members of the vocation. No less important has been, in some vocations, the development of professional honour and the imposition of a code of professional morals, by which the standard of conduct has been raised. There can, we think, be no doubt that vocational organisation, in all these ways, promotes not only the development of personal character, but also the efficiency of production, alike of commodities and of services.

But Democracies of Producers, as all experience shows, have their peculiar weaknesses and drawbacks. These vocational Democracies have hitherto failed, with almost complete uniformity, whenever they have themselves sought to own and organise the instruments of production. In the relatively few instances in which such enterprises have not succumbed as business concerns, they have ceased to be Democracies of Producers managing their own work, and have become, in effect, associations of capitalists, though often capitalists on a small scale, making profit for themselves by the employment at wages of workers outside their association.   And this practically invariable failure of Democracies of Producers in the actual ownership and organisation of the instruments of production is, as all history indicates, not a matter of social class. It is, for instance, demonstrably not due merely to those concerned being manual workers, or to their lack of mental ability or training, or to any difficulty in their obtaining sufficient capital. The twenty-eight flannel weavers of Rochdale who in 1844 started the Co-operative Store of the Rochdale Pioneers, and their countless imitators in other industrial centres, and in many different countries, who have built up, by the device of Dividend on Purchase, the gigantic business of the consumers' Co-operative Movement, had no more brains and commanded originally even less capital than the self-governing workshops started by groups of enthusiastic co-operators or by the Trade

Unions. The plain truth is that Democracies of Producers cannot be trusted with the ownership of the instruments of production in their own vocations. Each vocation, however large and important it may be, is but a fragment of the community. The commodities and services that it turns out are, almost entirely, not for consumption or use by its own members, but for consumption or use by the rest of the community. Hence the self-governing workshop, or the self-governing industry, necessarily producing for exchange, is perpetually tempted to make a profit on cost : that is to say, to retain for its own members whatever surplus value is embodied in the price for which it can dispose of its product ; or, to put it in another way, to retain the equivalent of the advantage of all differential factors in production (such as superiority of soil or site, of machinery or administrative skill) that it controls—this equivalent being exactly what, in the Capitalist System, appears as rent and profit. Further, in the practical administration of its own industry, a Democracy of Producers, whether it be of manual workers or of brain workers, is, by the very nature of its membership, perpetually tempted to seek to maintain existing processes unchanged, to discourage innovations that would introduce new kinds of labour, and to develop vested interests against other sections of the community of workers. The very concentration of the members' attention, not on the market-place, where the demands of the consumers are paramount, but on their own particular workshop, and on their speciality in productive capacity, is inimical to success. Throughout all history, disputes among different vocations and sections of vocations, whether they were brain workers or manual workers, as to which of them were " entitled " to particular jobs, have been specially characteristic of every form of associations of producers. This tendency to exclusiveness is inherent in any association based on vocation in production and is absent from every association based on community in consumption, for the simple reason that exclusiveness is normally of material advantage to the members of the one, and of no such advantage to the members of the other. The members of any association formed among the producers of a given commodity or service, just because they are necessarily producing almost entirely not for their own use but for exchange, can normally increase their own incomes, apart from any increased efficiency in production, by restricting their membership and limiting their output in relation to the demand in such a way as to enable them to raise the aggregate exchange-value of their product. On the other hand, any Democracy of Consumers, based on community in the consumption of commodities or services, can hardly fail to become aware, just because it is producing not for exchange, but for its members' own use, that the greater the number of consumers supplied the larger the amount produced ; and that the more open the industry or service is to new kinds of producers, the greater will be the economic efficiency, the better the quality and the lower the cost.

There is, finally, the hotly-disputed issue raised by the controversy as to the relative functions of Democracies of Citizen-Consumers and Democracies of Producers : the group of questions included under the invidious term " discipline." Who is to appoint the hierarchy of managers, from the foreman up to the principal executive officer, a hierarchy which must exist in some form in any extensive enterprise, whether national, municipal or co-operative ? To whom is this hierarchy to be responsible ? In whom is to be vested the power of reprimand and dismissal of these managers, a power which necessarily influences them in the exercise of their vocation of management ?

Let us first approach this question from the standpoint of democratic theory. Those who advocate vesting the power of appointment and dismissal of the managerial staff in the hands of the particular groups of employees who have to carry out the directions of this staff do so on the ground that this course is essentially the democratic one : that is to say, the one which conforms to the maxim that " governments derive their only just power from the consent of the governed." The implication is that those whose function it is to give orders should be appointed by, and be dismissed by, the particular groups of persons whose function involves obedience to these orders.[1] But is this not a primitive, and indeed obsolete conception of Democracy, dating back to the time when Democracy was conceived of as an " organ of revolt " ; and had not yet acquired its meaning as an " organ of government " ? In the completely democratised community those whom the people elect are not their governors, but their agents or servants, chosen for the purpose of carrying out the people's will. Democracy nowadays means, not a curb upon an alien or an irresponsible government, but government by the electors themselves, exercised through those whom they designate for the purpose. To give a concrete example : when the members of a national Trade Union wish to provide for their organisation a completely democratic government, the members as a whole elect an executive council, which is instructed to carry out the decisions as to policy formulated by the membership as a whole, or by its delegate meeting.

---

[1] It may be noted that some of the applications of this conception of election by those who are to obey the orders of the elected person run counter to the conceptions of (a) election by the " producers " or (b) the self-government of each vocation. Thus, in the experiments alleged to have been made in Russia in the election of school teachers by the scholars, we have a case of " government by the consumers." Similarly, when (as in the United States) experiments have been made in " self-governing prisons," it is not the warders but the prisoners who have been entrusted with the election of the governor of the gaol.

This involves a considerable staff of clerks and account-ants, office-boys and charwomen, who spend their working lives in carrying out the orders of the execu-tive council. Is it suggested that democratic theory requires that the clerks, accountants, office-boys and charwomen should elect the members of the executive council, the General Secretary and the Assistant Secretaries, whose orders the office staff has to obey; instead of the right of election being vested in the whole membership of the Trade Union? Or, to pass to another form of enterprise, every Local Educa-tion Authority, responsible to the citizens for providing a sufficient supply of schools for their children, has in its service a heterogeneous staff of teachers and in-spectors, school keepers and attendance officers, doctors and nurses, besides a secretariat of all grades. Does democratic theory require that these employees of the Local Education Authority, whose daily life is spent in obeying its orders, should elect that Authority, instead of the whole body of citizens whose policy it has to carry out? Or is it suggested that the Post-master-General, whose duty it is to provide the whole nation of citizens with the postal service that it desires and needs, should be made responsible, not to the elected representatives of the citizens, whose decisions as to policy he has to carry out, but to the varied mass of postal employees, whose function involves their obedience to the directions that are given by the head of the hierarchy? Or, to take an extreme case, the workers under the orders of the Secretary of State for Foreign Affairs are the clerks and messengers of the Foreign Office, and the members of the Diplo-matic and Consular Services in foreign parts. Does the principle of Democracy require that these persons should elect the Foreign Minister, and control the policy that he pursues, in place of the whole com-munity of citizens whose concern it is?

We think that the proposal that the employees should elect their managers, however consonant it may have been with some of the definitions of Democracy when the people were "subjects" and not themselves the sovereign power, springs from confusion of thought as to the meaning of Democracy when it is an "organ of government." Pushed to its logical extreme, the election and dismissal of the executive officers of government by the persons immediately concerned in carrying out their directions would lead to each specialised part of the mental and physical environment of the community being determined by the desires and wills of relatively small fractions of the community, instead of by the community itself. It would not be "government of the people by the people," but government of the people, in each separate aspect of its life, by a specialised and peculiarly "interested" oligarchy. To us it seems that this would not be Democracy, but the negation of Democracy.

This is not to say that the persons employed in each democratic service—whether they be managers or mechanics, labourers or lift attendants, clerks or chemists—have not a right to "control their own working lives," just as valid as the right of the people, as such, to its own "self-determination." To the consistent democrat this is not a "right" of each individual employee, but a "right of self-determination" of the vocation as a whole.[1] It must be observed that the "right of self-determination" for any vocation does not include the right to determine the conditions under which any other vocation—such as that of the directors or those of the several kinds of technicians—shall carry out its own social function.

_____
[1] This aspect of Democracy will be specially dealt with in the subsequent chapter on "The Reorganisation of the Vocational World."

But, however furiously rival theorists may dispute as to what Democracy involves, the issue will plainly be determined by results. Upon the essential point of whether the power of appointing and dismissing managers should be placed in the hands of the particular groups of employees whose function involves obedience to the directions given by such managers, or in the hands of those for whom the function is exercised, the teaching of experience seems clear. No Trade Union or Professional Association, no Co-operative Society or Local Authority, and no office or industrial enterprise belonging to any of these, however democratic its sympathies have been, has yet made its administration successful on the lines of letting the employees elect or dismiss the executive officers whose directions these particular groups of employees have to obey. This is not for want of trying. There have in fact been innumerable experiments in almost all industries and services, in all civilised countries, during the past hundred years, in every form of the " self-governing workshop " ; and it will not be disputed that their experience has pointed uniformly in the same direction.[1] It is, in fact, a matter of psychology. The relationship set up between a manager who has to give orders all day to his staff, and the members of that staff who, sitting as a committee of management, criticise his action in the evening, with the power of dismissing him if he fails to conform to their wishes, has been found by experience to be an impossible one. A Democracy of Citizen-Consumers may err on the side of arbitrariness, or in its preference for merely mechanical tests of efficiency, but what it is always seeking is the greatest extension

---

[1] *The Co-operative Movement in Great Britain*, by Beatrice Potter ; *Co-operative Production*, by Benjamin Jones ; *Co-operative Production and Profit Sharing*, by S. and B. Webb (*New Statesman* Supplement of Feb. 14, 1914 ; the articles by Joseph Cernesson in *L'Association ouvrière*, March 15 and 25, and April 15, 1913.

of the service for the largest number of consumers. On the other hand, a Democracy of Producers tends to select its own managers, not because of their ability to organise most efficiently the industry or service, but because they will organise it in a way that suits the convenience of the fraction of the community who earn their livelihood by it. Hence the Democracy of Producers develops a bias which, though of great advantage as a counter-balance to the bias of the dominant Democracy of Citizen-Consumers, just as it is as a defence against the Dictatorship of the Capitalist, becomes, when unchecked, a means of restricting production and securing a position of relative plenty and ease for the existing workers in one particular industry, as against other sections of producers and the whole community of consumers.

Our conclusion is that the selection of persons to exercise the extremely important functions of management and direction in any grade whatever—functions which must inevitably become of ever greater importance as enterprises become more extensive and more complicated—should not be looked upon as a question of appointment either " from above " or " from below." What is required, and what ought to be the sole consideration, is to obtain the services of the person best qualified for the particular post to be filled. What has to be contrived is social machinery that will, as far as may be practicable, ensure not only that the selection will be rightly made, but also that all those concerned will have confidence that it is rightly made. This excludes, in the Socialist Commonwealth, any exclusive reliance on the sagacity of the autocrat who prides himself, often very erroneously, on his instinctive capacity for picking out the right man. The community, no less than the candidates, needs to be protected against individual bias or " faddiness," not to say also against favouritism on the one hand and intolerance on the other. Experience indicates that managerial appointments, like all promotions, should be made on the well-considered and authoritative recommendations of a Selection Committee or Appointments Board. Where possible this should be a standing committee, whose members would acquire special competence in the art of selection ; but there should be added to it, for particular appointments, representatives of those from whom the person to be appointed will receive orders, of those to whom he will give orders, and sometimes also outside experts, such as members of the Professional Association concerned with his work. This, at any rate, is the method of selection to which, on the whole, experience points. Yet the door need not be closed on further experiments ; and in our chapter on " The Reorganisation of the Vocational World " we shall examine the conditions under which, in a Socialist Commonwealth, such experiments might be tried by any group of producers claiming to have found a more excellent way of carrying out their social service.

OWNERSHIP AND DIRECTION

Two fundamental conclusions stand out. The minimum participation of Democracies of Citizen-Consumers must be the ownership of the instruments of production. The minimum participation of Democracies of Producers is control over the conditions under which the producers by hand or by brain fulfil their vocation. But both these highly generalised phrases demand specific interpretation.

It is plainly necessary to include with the ownership of the instruments of production what has usually gone with property rights, namely, the power to decide, subject to the limits prescribed by the law of the land, what disposition shall be made of these instruments, what commodities or services shall be produced, and in what quantities and qualities, and how the product shall be disposed of. It is thus not a bare legal ownership of land and raw materials, or of buildings and plant, that is here in question, but the actual power of deciding to what use the instruments of production shall be put, and to what end each productive process shall be directed. On the other hand, what is referred to as instruments of production is not, pedantically, every tool or accessory by which production is assisted —there is no suggestion that a carpenter should not individually own his kit of tools, the seamstress her needle, or the clerk his fountain-pen—but merely what is commonly included by the business man as capital, such as is provided by a joint-stock company engaged in manufacture or commerce.

The Participation in Management by the Producers

Similarly, there must be included in the conditions under which the producers by hand or by brain fulfil their vocation, and over which they must exercise control (though not necessarily dictatorship or exclusive control) not merely their pay, their working hours, and the sanitation, safety and amenity of their places of employment, but also the character of the operations that they are called on to perform, and the persons with whom they are required to associate in work, their intellectual liberty both inside and outside of their employment, and—what is often forgotten—their practical freedom or opportunity to exercise their vocation in an efficient way.

It is exactly at this point that the great mass of productive workers, probably nine-tenths of the whole, are under the Capitalist System most restricted, and it is here that the Socialist Commonwealth will seek to provide for the greatest development. Exactly as a nation feeling itself to have a common heritage in a distinct culture is morally entitled to self-determination in matters of government (and cannot with advantage be denied it), so each vocation that is conscious of itself as a distinct vocation, with its own training, its own standard of qualification, its own technique, its own code of honour among fellow-members and towards the community, and an interest in the development of its own science and the promotion of its own art or craftsmanship, is equally entitled to its own measure of self-determination in the specialised service that it renders to the community. The most disastrous of all the effects of the Capitalist System has been the destruction of this " instinct of workmanship " among nine - tenths of the people. With relentless pressure the Capitalist System is always seeking, whilst magnifying the sphere of the brain-working specialist, to " unspecialise " the wage-earner, or, what amounts to much the same thing in terms of individual development, to reduce the workman's function to one endless repetition of a purely mechanical task, under the direction, not of his own but of another's brain and will. It will be one of the functions of vocational organisation in the Socialist Commonwealth — to be described in a subsequent chapter—to restore to the manual worker his " instinct of workmanship."

Now it is obvious that these various minimum requirements of the different sections of producers, of the consumers of different commodities and of the citizens as a whole, not only impinge on one another theoretically, but must, in practice, often lead to a clashing of decisions. It follows, therefore, that every constitution for a socialised industry or service must include, as an indispensable feature, not only a well-balanced constitution for carrying on the day-by-day administration, but also well-devised machinery for consultation, for accommodation and, in fact, for bargaining, between the representatives of the Citizen-Consumers and those of the various grades or sections of the producers in the particular industry or service. And no one party can be treated as homogeneous, or even necessarily as united. Control merely over an aggregate of commodities and services is illusory and valueless, unless it includes the right to decide about each of them ; and the self-determination of a whole crowd of heterogeneous producers is equally illusory and valueless unless it includes self-determination for each group feeling itself to constitute a distinct vocation. There will be divergencies among different sections of Citizen-Consumers as to how much of the national production shall be directed to this or that commodity or service, and between the Democracies of Consumers as such and the Social Parliament as to the relative claims of what we may call " consumption goods " as against what is required for the general interests of the community—to say nothing of the perpetual conflict between enjoyment in the present and provision for the future. And on the other side, each grade and section of the producers will have its own claim, not necessarily to exceptional remuneration, but often to specialised conditions of work, and sometimes to exceptional allowances for functional expenses ; and every group that is in a minority, including therefore the various kinds of brain workers, will need to make good its own right, not merely to equality in the common liberties enjoyed by producers as such, but to its own freedom, including practical opportunity to each kind or grade of producers to fulfil efficiently its own particular vocational function —the labourer to dig, the mason to build, the engineer to construct machines, and the violinist to play the fiddle—but equally, the inventor to invent, the auditor

to audit, the architect to design, the orchestral conductor to give the time, and the director to direct.
The freedom that the Socialist Commonwealth will
seek to maximise can be no other than an individual
freedom, an individual freedom for each vocational
organisation to protect and develop so long as this
freedom does not conflict with a like freedom of other
vocations or with the welfare of the community as a
whole. In considering any scheme for the socialisation of particular industries or services, or for any
reconstitution of vocational organisation, it is accordingly imperative to bear in mind and arrange for a
due consideration and representation of the interests
of the community as a whole, not merely in the
present generation but also in the future.

CHAPTER III

In view of the enlarged spheres of Local Government and of the consumers' Co-operative Movement in the Socialist Commonwealth, it is possible that, out of all the many hundreds of industries and services that go to make up the economic and social life of the nation, only half a dozen or so will need to be organised and directed nationally. At present, in Great Britain, only the Post Office is so administered. The nation ought clearly to contemplate an immediate nationalisation of the railways and canals, on the one hand, and of the mining industry (including oil) on the other. Afforestation for the sake of the timber supply is equally pressing. It may be suggested that insurance is no less ripe for nationalisation, and also the service of keeping current and deposit accounts, which is the basis of British banking. What other industries may, in the near future, be promoted from profit-making enterprises to public services (such, for instance, as the smelting of metals from the ore, and the conduct of the main lines of passenger steamers) may be left to experience to decide.

Each of these national services will require substantially the same constitutional framework of administration and control, subject to the particular variations that its circumstances may demand. It may be taken for granted that the object to be aimed at is, not only the utmost practicable efficiency and continued improvement of the service, but also the fullest practicable participation in the management by the workers concerned, and at the same time the most effective safeguarding of the interests of the consumers and of the permanent welfare of the community as a whole. The essential feature of our proposal is the separation of current administration on the one hand from the decision of policy on the other. In the whole sphere of policy — such as the quality and quantity of the service to be rendered, and how, when and where the commodity or service is to be made available for the needs of the community—the Social Parliament will be, through its standing committee, the supreme authority. But with the day-by-day administration in the widest sense, including appointments and promotions, purchases and sales, and the choice between this or that method or technical device of the service, the principle should be that there should be no more Parliamentary interference, in the case of the nationalised services (such as the Post Office, the railways and canals, or the mining industry) than in those, like education and health, that are entrusted to the Local Authorities ; substantially, indeed, no more than in that of the supply of household requisites that will remain in the hands of the consumers' Co-operative Movement.

THE ABANDONMENT OF MINISTERIAL RESPONSIBILITY

It will accordingly be seen that, as already indicated, it is proposed to depart altogether, in the relation of the nationalised industries and services to the Social Parliament, from the existing British plan of placing each department under the autocratic government of a political Minister, who is supposed to be responsible to Parliament for every act and decision of the hundreds

of thousands of officials who are nominally his personal
servants, and who yet stands or falls with the Cabinet
as a whole. This plan purports to enable the whole
body of citizens, through their elected representatives,
to control both the policy and the administration of the
several government departments. This professedly
democratic control is assumed to be exercised, by
requiring each department to be represented in each
of the two Houses of Parliament by a Minister, who
has to stand the fire of " questions " as to the failures
and mishaps of his department, who has once or twice
a year to justify the estimates and supplementary
estimates of its expenditure, and against whom an
adverse vote may any day be carried.

Now, however useful may have been this conception
of " ministerial responsibility " in the early stages of
the assertion of popular control over an autocratic
government—whatever advantages it may have offered
in the days when the sphere of government was
restricted practically to defence and foreign relations,
the maintenance of order and the administration of
justice, it has become, in the Great Britain of to-day,
illusory as an instrument of democratic control over
a great and complicated administration. Even in
such a comparatively simple service as that of the Post
Office it fails altogether, either in enabling Parliament
to ascertain with what efficiency, or even with what
comparative results, the service is being conducted,
or in putting the House of Commons in a position
to come to an independent and properly informed
decision upon even the greatest issues of policy. When
Parliament has given a decision (as, for instance, a
generation ago, that life assurance should be conducted
by the Post Office ; or, in 1917–18, that immediate
arrangements should be made by the Local Government
Board to enable the shortage of houses to be made
good from the very day that hostilities ceased) there

are no means (as experience has shown) by which
the House of Commons can ensure its being carried
out, or by which it can even ascertain what is obstructing its execution. The " questions " which Members
can put to the Ministers are habitually answered in
such a way as to reveal as little as possible of what is
going on ; and especially with the object of concealing
anything to which it is imagined that objection may
be taken. The estimates and supplementary estimates are prepared in such a way as to present as
little opportunity as possible for effective discussion
of the details of the administration ; and, above all,
so as not to let it be inferred that any other course
is practicable than that which the department has
followed. Even when zealous Members have labori-
ously got up the subject, and are seeking to criticise
the department for independent information, there is
habitually no time for adequate discussion of more
than one or two points. When an issue of policy
presents itself, on which the decision of Parliament
has necessarily to be taken, the Minister himself,
primed by his officials, is the only source from which
Members can get information ; and what the Minister
says almost invariably controls the vote. Finally, the
fact that any adverse vote, however small may be the
detail, involves a " defeat of the Government " compels the Government to " put on the Whips," who
almost invariably manage to secure the support of a
docile majority uninterested in the matter under discussion, and naturally concerned to maintain the
Cabinet with whom, in the main, they feel themselves
in sympathy. The very conception of the joint and
several responsibility of the Cabinet for everything
done or said by any of its members — useful as
this may be in enabling the electorate to choose
between one or other main lines of national policy,
as presented at a General Election—actually prevents

the House of Commons, as regards the hundred and one departmental issues that arise, from expressing its disapproval of the policy of any particular Ministry. There remains only the instrument of what is called the general sense of the House ; and this has for many years been impotent to cause the dismissal of even the most unpopular Minister, or (where fresh legislation is not required) hardly ever to require a change in the administrative policy that has, in any one department, been definitely adopted.

What has happened, in fact, during the past half century, with the continuous increase of the functions of government, has been the gradual establishment of a largely unselfconscious bureaucratic conspiracy against Parliamentary interference or control. The Minister, overwhelmed with the immensity of the administration for which he is nominally responsible, welcomes the assistance of his able and well-trained officials in keeping at arm's length, not only the newspapers and the public, but also the inquisitive M.P. Official secrecy becomes a disease. The evasion of questions in the House is reduced to a fine art. Comparative statistics as to output or result, all the discoveries of costing, and all means of comparison with the corresponding services of other countries are withheld from publication. Discussions on the estimates are as far as possible curtailed. The happiest Ministers, and the most complacent departments, are those to which the House of Commons can be hypnotised into giving the least attention. Parliamentary control, even over policy, has become an illusion and a sham. Ministers and officials have the excuse that, as things are at present arranged, the pertinacity of Members of Parliament is almost always badly informed, the criticisms are ill-instructed, the discussions in Parliament usually extraordinarily futile ; and " Parliamentary control " seems to them to mean merely an increase of official work and anxiety, without the counterbalancing advantage of useful criticism or constructive suggestions.

The Differentiation of Control from Administration

It would, however, be a mistake to ascribe the failure of the existing Parliamentary system to provide any genuine or effective democratic control over any public department, either wholly or mainly to the Cabinet system, or to that of ministerial responsibility to Parliament. Even if these were superseded by a more efficient organisation of Parliament itself, such as is now proposed, it would still remain impossible for the conduct of the nationalised industries to be properly managed upon the lines on which the Post Office, for instance, is now administered. For such colossal services as those of the railways and the mining industry — we should say throughout the whole sphere of the Social Parliament — what seems essential is that the function of the national assembly should be sharply differentiated from the day-by-day administration.

This separation of current administration from the decision of great issues of policy, to which we attach the greatest importance, involves, it will be seen, for each of the nationalised industries or services, not one central organ only, but two. To secure to the Social Parliament, representing the community as a whole, and concerned no less for the future than for the present, an effective control over the national services, it is proposed that there should be, for each great service, a separate standing committee, charged with the continuous oversight of its own service, and responsible for advising the Social Parliament upon any issue that arises connected with that service. But merely to appoint a standing committee is not enough. The Social Parliament — even a standing committee of the Social Parliament—can never know enough, and can, merely by the eyes and ears of its own members, never know anything accurately enough, even to come wisely to an independent decision upon issues of policy, let alone ensure that its decisions as to policy are thoroughly carried out. The community needs a much more effective democratic control over its affairs, and more adequate safeguards for both efficiency and improvement—not to say more protection against the evils of uncontrolled bureaucracy—than can be given by the amateur supervision of busy Members of Parliament, advised only by heads of departments who are themselves part of the very administration to be directed and controlled. For each nationalised industry or service it is therefore necessary to provide an organisation apart from that of the administration, not merely for the registration and authoritative communication to the administration of the decisions as to policy to which the Social Parliament may come from time to time, but also for authoritatively ascertaining and informing the Social Parliament and public opinion how the service is in fact being conducted. The germ of such an organisation (but only the germ) is to be found, for the railways and canal service, in the present Board of Trade, and for the mining industry in the Home Office. The greater part, however, of the work required in order to make really effective the control of Parliament and of public opinion has been so far, in the British Government service, hardly yet begun. What is needed is the systematic organisation, with regard to each nationalised industry, of comparative statistics of output or results in the various parts of the service, of detailed costing, of continuous test audits and of sample inspections ; and with all this there should be associated not only the organised study of other analogous administrations, but also original research into the subject - matter with a view to new discoveries. Let us take the existing Post Office as an example. The present headquarters staff would be separated out into two distinct departments, one concerned primarily with the current administration, under its independent departmental hierarchy of Boards, Councils and Committees, and the other (somewhat analogous to the Mines Department of the Home Office in respect of mining, or to the Railways Department of the Board of Trade in respect of railways) responsible for keeping the Social Parliament and the nation fully and frankly informed how the service is being conducted, at what cost and with what results. The function of the administration will be to do ; that of the control department will be to know what is being done, in order that the Social Parliament and public opinion may be able to discover with what fidelity and success the policy from time to time laid down by the Social Parliament is being carried out.

The development of the various departments of " control " will introduce to the Civil Service work of a type which it has so far been allowed to undertake only in an imperfect and, so to speak, a half-hearted way. The government departments have not, as a rule, been told that original investigation and research was within their function ; their conceptions of accountancy and audit, costing and comparative statistics have been, until lately, quite rudimentary; and their function has been regarded as inhibitive of what was bad rather than as stimulative of what was good.[1] It will clearly be necessary to train, for the

---

[1] See, for instance, the suggestive remarks of an experienced Treasury official, in *National Economy*, by Henry Higgs, C.B., 1917 ; and his *Financial System of the United Kingdom*, 1914. Compare the remarkable reports of the President's Commission on Economy and Efficiency, insti-

control departments, a Civil Service of a new kind ; to set these officers to develop a new administrative technique ; and to enable them to study, on the spot, the various devices by which other nations, and other forms of organisation in our own country, are coping with analogous problems. But any permanent cleavage of the Civil Service would be injurious. It would be desirable that officials should, as a matter of course, pass from one department to another, bringing to each successive sphere of work an invaluable " inside " knowledge of other departments. Departmental interchange should become the rule instead of the exception.

THE ADMINISTRATIVE MACHINE

For the current administration of each nationalised industry or service there should be a National Board with full power over administration in its widest sense, and subject only to such specific directions as to policy as it may from time to time receive from the Social Parliament itself. Each National Board should be appointed by the Social Parliament, on the advice of the standing committee concerned, for a specified term of years (in form, this would be appointment by the Crown on the petition of the Social Parliament). The exact composition of each National Board may be left to be decided from time to time according to the nature of the service or the conditions of organisation of the industry ; but it may be suggested, as a type, that the Boards might each consist of sixteen members, five of whom might be taken from among the heads of the principal branches of the administration, five should be representatives of the various

tuted by President Taft in 1910, which seem to have worked almost a revolution in the administrative methods of some of the Washington departments.

vocations (manual working and clerical) employed, five should be appointed to represent the interests of the consumers and of the community as a whole, whilst the principal executive officer should preside. This is, as will be seen, quite frankly to entrust the administration in each case to a body the large majority of which would be either engaged as principal officers in the service or would be representative of the vocations to which the bulk of the employees belonged ; with a minority representing the interests of the remainder of the public. We make this proposal deliberately in the conviction that, in this way and in this way only, will the community be able to secure that highest efficiency which is dependent on the full and cordial co-operation of all the producers. The presence, as full members of the National Board, of representatives of the various vocations engaged in the industry will conduce, in more ways than one, to a progressive improvement in the service. The association of these representatives with the principal directors of the service, including financial, technological and managerial technicians, cannot but afford the best guarantee for the adoption of the most efficient technique. It will be the duty of the representatives of the consumers and citizens to ensure that all legitimate interests are taken into account. But more is involved than cost and price. There are always arising new needs which the producers themselves may easily overlook, and inventions and new processes against which they may be biassed because they involve a certain measure of supersession of that to which the producers have been accustomed. Moreover, other industries and services are often vitally concerned in that which is being administered, and some authoritative exposition of their requirements seems essential. The National Board should, accordingly, be a tripartite body.

How the members should be in each case selected must necessarily differ from service to service. It is of course plain that the vocational representatives must be the nominees of the vocational organisations, whatever these may be. Whether they can be simply elected by one Union or Federation of Unions depends on the state of organisation in each industry—a point to which we shall recur in the subsequent chapter on " The Reorganisation of the Vocational World." Here it suffices to say that where the organisation is imperfect, it will probably be necessary to allocate the five members among the various Unions concerned in such a way as to secure the widest possible proportional representation of the various grades and sections. In like manner, the five members representing the direction and management should usually be chosen from among the heads of the principal branches of the work; whilst the representatives of the consumers and citizens should include one, at least, nominated by the consumers' Co-operative Movement, and one or more able to speak for other industries or services. The final choice can hardly be entrusted to any other hands than those of the standing committee advising the Social Parliament.[1]

---

[1] The tripartite National Board has been suggested for the United States railways (the " Plumb Plan " which commanded, in 1919, so much Labour support); and by the Confédération Générale du Travail, on behalf of the French Trade Union Movement. A similar tripartite organisation seemed to Mr. Justice Sankey, in his Final Report of the Coal Commission in 1919, to afford the best administrative machinery for the nationalised coal-mines. The plan of the Miners' Federation was for one-half the members to be nominated by the Trade Union.

On the other hand, the plan of the Miners' Federation, in agreement with the above-named American and French projects, differed from Mr. Justice Sankey's proposal, which made the District Councils the more influential bodies, and the National Board little more than a consultative organ, in constituting the National Board the controller of policy, with the District Councils as subordinate organs. We think that, on this point, the miners were the better administrators.

District Councils

It need hardly be said that there is no suggestion of the centralisation of industrial administration. Every national industry or service requires a certain measure of central control ; and, on the other hand, the most centralised service calls for a certain measure of district organisation. It would clearly be hopeless to attempt to conduct the administration of the coal-mines, any more than that of the harbours and ports, from a London office. It would be equally undesirable to have anything like as great a divergence between different districts in the matter of postal or railway policy, as between different ports or different coalfields. Accordingly, the amount, the nature and the conditions of decentralisation must necessarily depend on the circumstances of the industry or service. In all cases there should be District Councils, to which various functions, and more or less autonomy in local management, should be entrusted by the National Board. And these District Councils would presumably be constituted on similar lines to those on which the National Board is formed, namely, with the principal executive officer for the district as the chairman, and a tripartite representation of the various vocations concerned, the heads of the chief branches of the local administration, and the various kinds of local consumers ; these appointments being in the hands of the National Board.

Works Committee

We lay great stress on the inclusion, as of right, on the National Boards and District Councils, of independently chosen representatives of the vocations of manual workers concerned in the industry, and sitting, as full members, side by side with the managerial or scientific technicians, and the representatives of the consumers. But the wage-earners' claim to participation in management, which is so distinctive a note of the present century, will not be satisfied by the mere presence of vocational representatives on the National Boards and District Councils by which the course of administration is nationally or locally decided. The management in which the mass of the workmen are more intensely concerned, and that from which exclusion is most bitterly resented, is the management which most obviously affects the circumstances of their working lives. Part of this sphere, the whole range of the standard conditions of employment, may be regarded as covered by the national and district agreements as to rates of pay, hours of labour and many other matters, concluded between the management and the Trade Unions concerned, as presently to be described. But part of the day-by-day management, notably that of the foreman and the works manager, is not and never can be made the subject of formal agreement ; and it is to secure the participation of the wage-earners themselves in this part of management that Works Committees, Shop Committees, Pit Committees or Office Committees, one for each distinct establishment, are as essential as National Boards and District Councils.

The constitution, functions and procedure of these committees will plainly vary from industry to industry, and sometimes from district to district. It is clear that they must always be fully and independently chosen by all the various sections and grades of workers in the establishment or other convenient unit. They must have their own chairman and secretary, and be free to settle their own meetings and their own agenda. It may perhaps be desirable that they should not be composite bodies, including management or consumers' representatives, but exclusively workmen's committees. On the other hand, they should have the right to confer with the management whenever they wish to do so ; and a wise manager will not only make a point of consulting such a committee about any proposal for a change before it is finally decided on, but will also habitually communicate to the committee everything of interest to them industrially, and discuss it with them in all its bearings. But it will be plain that, in a national industry or service, no committee of this sort, and not even the whole body of workmen in the establishment, can enjoy complete local autonomy. The extent to which any particular establishment could possibly be allowed to have its own peculiar arrangements must always be doubly limited. Throughout the whole range of what has been specified as the standard conditions of employment in national or district agreements, no variation would be permitted even by the Trade Union itself. At most the Works Committee would make any needful adaptation of the agreements to local circumstances, and this would require to be sanctioned by the district or national authority. Similarly throughout the whole range of administration governed by rules or decisions of the District Councils and the National Board of the industry or service, no variation by a particular establishment could be permitted ; and even any adaptation to local circumstances would presumably be reported for ratification. The sphere of the Works Committee would be primarily the discussion of grievances and the making of suggestions. It would be valuable in bringing to light, and therefore preventing, any cases of victimisation, of tyranny, and of the hardship more often caused by ignorance or heedlessness than actually by caprice or malice. Above all, it should afford an opportunity for " taking counsel together," for which the removal from industrial administration of capitalist autocracy ought to open up a wide field of usefulness. Moreover, other functions or duties may be confided to the Works Committee by the District Council or National Board, particularly where this is desired by the Works Committee itself; such, for instance, as the arrangement of piecework prices or conditions of Collective Piecework, where this is desired by the workmen, subject always to ratification in conformity with the district and national agreements.

The Recruitment of the Staff

It is plainly impracticable to lay down in advance how all the appointments will be made to all the various grades and sections of the staffs in all the nationalised industries and services. The vital point to be aimed at is the constant recruiting of the staff from the persons best qualified for the duties required from them. How far the plan will prevail of prescribing a definite qualification as a condition of entrance to a particular vocation ; and how and by what authority the qualification will be determined, is discussed in our subsequent chapter on "The Reorganisation of the Vocational World." It may be suggested that, as there indicated, the plan should anyhow be that of determining first how many persons of each vocation, section or grade are required for the needs of the public service ; and then of choosing from among the applicants for the advertised vacancies those who appear best suited to the position. No one has any right to an appointment in any particular service ; and those applicants who were not selected would simply have to seek another opening. The greater part of the work of recruiting the staff, under the conditions laid down by the National Board and the District Councils, would fall naturally to the heads of departments in the various establishments, or to special Appointment Officers to whom they might depute the taking on of boys and girls for manual working occupations, aided by the counsel of Juvenile Advisory Committees connected with the schools, and under conditions providing for apprenticeship or suitable technical instruction. Additions to the manual working staff would be made in an analogous way. First appointments to the clerical service should be made on the results of open competitive examination. For promotions, and for the selection of those best qualified for positions of management and direction, or as technicians of any kind, resort should be had to standing Appointment Boards or Selection Committees, such as have been already described, on which, according to the circumstances, there should sit representatives of those from whom the person to be appointed will receive orders, of those to whom he will give orders, and, in the case of technicians, also of the vocational association concerned with the work. The appointment of principal officers of the District Councils would presumably be finally made by these bodies on the recommendation of such a Selection Committee or Appointments Board. The most important appointments of all, those of the heads of departments under the National Board, including its principal technicians, would naturally be finally decided by the National Board itself, in consultation with its own officers, having before it the recommendation of a Selection Committee constituted on the lines laid down. It may be suggested that all officers should be appointed, after a probationary period, on incremental salary scales ; and that promotion from grade to grade should be made exclusively on the ground of capacity for the higher post, not " merit " or seniority. We state all this to avoid ambiguity or misunderstanding ; but the proposals themselves amount to no more than the common practice of the best industrial undertakings of magnitude—a technique of recruitment which, though already greatly developed, is doubtless capable of further improvement.

DISCIPLINE BOARDS

In all large undertakings " personal questions " account not only for a considerable expenditure of time by the administrators, but also no small part of the friction which impairs both the efficiency of the enterprise and the happiness of those concerned. Especially when employees are charged with offences for which they are liable to fine or degradation, or even to dismissal, is it necessary to provide definite machinery to ensure that there shall be no suspicion of injustice, carelessness or personal tyranny. For these reasons experience has shown the advantage, in the organisation of extensive staffs, of dealing with what are called " discipline cases " by a special Board. It has been found useful to constitute such a Board in such a way that, with a chairman of high position in the industry, half the members represent the element of management (not being themselves personally concerned), and half the wage-earners, in each case taking employees belonging to the same grade and section of labour as that to which the defendant belongs.[1] Discipline Boards of this kind, high or low, great or small, according to the circumstances, should adjudicate in all cases in which workers of any grade are charged with offences warranting their being fined, degraded or dismissed.

[1] Examples of Discipline Boards are afforded by the New South Wales Railway Department, the Municipality of Lyons, and other large organisations. See *The Works Manager To-day*, by Sidney Webb, 1917.

Collective Bargaining

There are certain matters of industrial administration for which the machinery of National Boards, District Councils and Works Committees, just because this machinery is devised for the administration of industries as wholes, is inappropriate and inadequate. It would not, for instance, be proposed that these bodies should themselves settle either the pay, or the hours or the other conditions of employment of the workers in the industry. By the very nature of the case, every industry includes workers of different kinds, varying considerably in relative numbers, labouring under different conditions, with different degrees of skill, and of different grades. No such group or kind of workers would be satisfied to have its conditions of employment settled for it by a composite body on which its particular variety could only be minutely represented, even if it were represented at all. Further, however liberal might be the representation on the National Board of the workers as a whole, the Trade Unions, comprising particular sections of these same workers, would not be disposed —nor could the economist advise them to consent— to give up their right, in strict accordance with their agreements of service, to withdraw their labour in concert or, in other words, to strike for better terms. There is, in the long run, no other way of adjusting the conditions of the industrial employment of free men than by bargaining ; and the constitution of each national industry or service should accordingly provide specific machinery for ·Collective Bargaining. For this there seems nothing more satisfactory than the Joint Boards, in which representatives of the management (nominated by the National Boards) meet in prolonged argument and discussion an equal number of representatives of the Trade Union of each separately organised grade or section of the persons employed. It may be pointed out that what gives a special acerbity to Labour disputes to-day is the fact that what is not conceded in wages merely enlarges the share of the landlord or the capitalist profit-maker. With the expropriation of the landlord and capitalist, this source of contention disappears. What is left is a twofold issue. No more can be shared among the producers than is produced, but there remains to be determined how a given annual product should be divided between common needs (including provision for the future) and individual pay ; and—a more likely cause of quarrel—at what rates this individual pay should be allocated to different grades and sections of the producers concerned. In the Socialist Commonwealth the Joint Boards would be very greatly assisted in their negotiations by being supplied by the Employment Department, the Health Department and the Education Department, with full and authoritative information as to (a) the effect of the condition of employment upon the health and education of the workers concerned and their families ; (b) how the several industries and services compare with each other in such matters, and also in amount of pay ; and (c) how each industry or service stands in the order of preference or choice by the young people, and whether each is attracting its proper quota of recruits. In fact, with an ever-growing submission to the arbitrament of public opinion in such matters, any intractable labour disputes ought to be brought to an amicable compromise, after argument, by a full use of the essential instruments of Democracy, Measurement and Publicity.[1]

[1] By " Measurement" and " Publicity," words which will be found re-appearing at many points in this book, we mean more than may at first appear. Included in " measurement " is of course a determination of kind and a valuation of quality, as well as a mere quantitative enumeration. Included in " publicity " is not merely the issue of a bluebook, but every

Advisory Committees

Another function of importance for which, in the administration of each national industry or service provision must be made independently of the National Board, District Councils and Works Committees, and apart altogether from the machinery for Collective Bargaining, is that of suggestion and criticism on the one hand, and of scientific investigation and research on the other. This criticism and initiative is required both from the consumers and from the producers. On the side of the consumers the germ of the necessary organisation exists, but only the germ, in such a body as the Advisory Committees of Telephone Users which the Postmaster - General has instituted in the various districts, on which (through Town and County Councils, Chambers of Commerce and similar bodies) the principal users of the telephone in each locality are enabled to formulate their complaints and suggestions, to confer with the administration upon their grievances, and to bring their views authoritatively before the department concerned. Similar organisations have sprung up without official sanction among such users of the railway service as the commercial travellers, the season-ticket holders and the frequenters of workmen's trains. The cyclists and the owners of motor cars have, in much the same way, exercised a useful influence on the road administration. We suggest that there would be every advantage in a multiplication of such voluntary organisations, the formation of which should be officially instigated and facilitated, so that, by their expert representatives in each case, the users of each of the principal services,

---

method by which knowledge can be brought home to the average citizen, as well as to the persons particularly concerned. The reality of Democracy is, in our view, dependent to a vastly greater extent on the adoption of Measurement and Publicity than on any choice between one method of voting and another.

and the consumers of each of the principal commodities should, in constant friendly communication with the administration concerned, sift all the popular complaints, formulate every promising suggestion and press for the redress of every substantial grievance, whether relating to quantity, quality, method or price.

Still more essential to progressive efficiency is, we think, the voluntary co-operation of the producers. This is at present most successfully exercised by the " Subject Associations " or scientific societies in the brain-working professions, notably in medicine and education. Whether the form be that of the various societies for the study of different branches of medicine and surgery, which are confined to professionals, or of such bodies as the Classical, Historical, English and Modern Languages Associations, or that of the Teachers' Guild, which admit amateurs of the subject as well as professional teachers ; or that of the Society of Illuminating Engineers, which combines in one body such varied professionals as architects, gas and electrical engineers, surgeons and opticians, with such influential " consumers " or users as the directors of education under the Local Education Authorities, may be left in each service to be determined by experience. It is indeed not easy to overrate the beneficial influence in this way of such bodies as the five great institutions of engineers on the one hand, or, on the other, of the mixed organisation long known as the Engineering Standards Committee, now the British Engineering Association, to which reference has already been made. We have already mentioned the fact that the vocational organisations of the manual workers have, so far, done very little in this way, and have, in fact, never been encouraged to render the same sort of service in connection with their vocations as the doctors and teachers, the engineers and the chemists have done. Trade Unions which have sought to do so have, in fact, been officially rebuked and obstructed.[1] With the greater diffusion of education, and especially with the frank admission of the manual workers to participation in management, we see no reason why " Subject Associations " or scientific societies should not become as noted a feature of the Trade Union world as they are among the combinations of the brain-working professionals. We look to see all such bodies, whether arising among the producers or among the consumers, accorded full and cordial recognition as a valuable, and though entirely voluntary and unofficial, indeed an essential part of the machinery of administration.

The Sphere of the Social Parliament

We can now survey in due perspective the whole scheme that we propose for the administration of each of the national industries and services, from the Works Committee and District Council up to the National Board, with the accompanying Joint Boards for Collective Bargaining, and the voluntary associations for criticism and original research. We must now revert to the Social Parliament and define more precisely in what relation it will stand to the industry or service.

The Social Parliament must, it will be clear, control but not administer ; decide such great issues of policy as may present themselves, but not interfere with management ; safeguard the interests of the community as a whole, but keep its hands off the actual working of the machine. In the main the control will be exer-

---

[1] When the Post and Telegraph Clerks' Association attempted to study the methods by which the Post Office could increase the efficiency of its service of the public, and began to publish studies upon the postal cheque system, which is successfully in operation over the greater part of Europe, the Postmaster-General made it known that any such investigation, which might be held to imply criticism of the backwardness or apathy of the British Postal Administration, was regarded as a breach of official discipline ; and steps were taken to prevent the study being proceeded with.

cised by the ultimate " power of the purse." Thus the National Board will present to its particular Standing Committee an annual budget, specifying both the receipts and the outgoings expected for the ensuing year ; involving, accordingly, its proposals as to expenditure on salaries, wages and costs of all kinds, as to works of development contemplated, and as to the prices to be charged for the product. Such an estimate can be approximate only ; but it will enable the Standing Committee on the industry, with the concurrence of the Standing Committee on Finance, to advise the Social Parliament to sanction the budget, and therefore the general policy thus outlined, for the year to come. Any important change in system or in policy that the National Board recommended— such, for instance, as the electrification of the whole or part of the railways, or the development of a new coalfield—would probably be separately reported. Once the sanction of the Social Parliament had been given, the National Board would have authority to carry out the whole administration, and, in particular, to use its own discretion as to such changes in price as may be required, without requiring to submit to the Finance Department, or to its particular Standing Committee, any item of proposed expenditure or any administrative act, for approval or sanction.

It will be the duty of the Department under the Standing Committee to keep itself constantly informed of what the National Board is doing ; and to be always inspecting, costing, auditing and researching, in order that it may at all times be able to inform the Standing Committee how the policy prescribed by the Social Parliament is being carried out, and with what results. But this Department will have no right to interfere with the National Board, or to give it instructions. It will be for the Standing Committee itself, from time to time, to confer with the National Board as to the results of its administration, but the Standing Committee will not be empowered to interfere with its discretion. What the Standing Committee can do is to report to the Social Parliament its judgment as to what is going on.

We may suppose that the standing committee for each nationalised industry or service, which the Social Parliament will appoint at the opening of every session, will attract to its membership those in the Social Parliament who are specially interested in the subject, and in any case the constant occupation of the members of each committee with the affairs of one particular industry or service will soon render them acquainted with it. We may visualise that other standing committees may, from time to time, have proposals or objections bearing on each other's sphere ; and there will be consultations between the respective chairmen, conferences between committees, and occasionally joint reports—it may even be conflicting reports—to the Social Parliament itself. For the standing committees will not be entitled themselves to prescribe policy or give decisions, but merely to ascertain and communicate to the administrations concerned the policy authoritatively laid down by the Social Parliament itself.

In order that the standing committees may be able to inform the Social Parliament how the several industries and services are actually being performed, and to give responsible advice as to what decisions should be come to, it will be necessary, as already explained, for them to have the assistance of an adequate staff. They will need at all times to know, statistically and comparatively, what is the output and what are the results at the various points of the service ; they will require to ascertain, by all the devices of costing and audit, how the service compares with analogous services elsewhere, and with its own previous record ; they will be always having studies made and researches conducted in university laboratories and experimental model establishments, into possible improvements and developments. Without all this, no standing committee can exercise that continuous supervision over the service which alone can enable it to ensure that the policy of the Social Parliament is being, in fact, put wholeheartedly and effectively into operation, or give any informed or useful independent advice as to future policy. The elaboration of such embryonic departments as now exist at the Home Office (for mines), at the Board of Trade (for railways and canals) and at the Ministry of Labour (as regards wages and other conditions of employment) into departments adequately staffed and equipped, as regards each of the national industries and services, for all the manifold duties indicated, may accordingly be assumed. To what extent each standing committee will need to have its own department (such as exist at present in respect of mines and railways), and to what extent the work of all the standing committees can be best done by a single department for each function (as, for instance, in costing and audit), may be left to experience to decide.

How the Administration will Work

But these control departments will be wholly unconnected with the administration itself. This will be directed for each national industry or service by its own National Board. It is to the National Board that the Social Parliament must look for the adoption and execution of the policy that may from time to time be prescribed for the industry in the interests of the community as a whole, and it is accordingly the National Board that must give directions to the District Councils, and, through them, for the entire

working of the industry.   It is therefore to the
National Board that must be entrusted the selection
and appointment of the principal executive officers
and the prescription and control of the plans upon
which the industry will work, whether technological
or financial.   To the National Board will also come
complaints and appeals of all kinds, and it is the
National Board that will be responsible, in the last
resort, for the redress of personal grievances.

The National Board should not, any more than the
District Councils, sit in public, at any rate normally.
But the secrecy which now characterises Capitalism
even more than it does government administration,
will be frankly abandoned.   The utmost practicable
publicity should therefore be given, as a matter of
regular routine, to the proposals and proceedings of
the administration, not merely for the continuous
information of the Sócial Parliament and especially
of the Standing Committee concerned, but also for
the education of the producers, the consumers and the
citizens.   We suggest, for instance, that each national
industry or service should have its own monthly or
weekly journal, published at the lowest possible price,
made as informative as its editor knows how, and
supplied gratuitously, not only to the newspaper press,
but also to every public library and every Trade Union,
Professional Association, consumers' organisation or
scientific society connected with the industry or service.

The District Councils will be responsible to the
National Board for the execution, within their respective districts, of the policy and plan of operations that
they will from time to time receive from the National
Board, to which they will be always reporting their
proceedings and their achievements.   The number
and character of the districts will, of course, vary from
industry to industry.   It is impossible to decide, for
instance, whether the coal-mining districts should be

6 (as now arranged by the Mines Department of the Home Office) or 22 (as prescribed in the Coal Mines (Minimum Wage) Act, 1912 ; or 14 (as proposed in Mr. Justice Sankey's Report of the Coal Industry Commission, 1919) ; any more than by how many separate operating districts the existing couple of hundred separate Boards of Directors of the present railway companies will be superseded.

INITIATIVE AND PUBLICITY

We hope to have made it clear that, whilst each establishment, each Works Committee, and each District Council must necessarily conform to the general plan of operations for the time being laid down by the National Board, and whilst the National Board itself must necessarily carry out any policy prescribed by the Social Parliament from time to time, each of these executive authorities, from the highest to the lowest, will be also taking the initiative within its own sphere, and continuously making suggestions for the development and improvement of the service. But in this direction we go further than anything of which the community has yet had experience. Besides the suggestions from within the administration—from the Works Committee and establishment manager right up to the National Board itself—and besides those emanating from the standing committees of the Social Parliament, it should be officially recognised as part of the function of all the vocational organisations connected with the industry or service—the Trade Unions no less than the Professional Associations ; of all the " Subject Associations " or scientific societies, of which a great development is to be expected, and of all the various organisations of consumers or users of the product which the industry or service exists in order to supply, to be continuously furnishing

criticisms and suggestions upon any part of the policy
or administration to which, as a matter of course,
publicity should be given in the official journal of the
industry or service, and elsewhere ; and to which
the National Board should be required to give at
least the consideration of an authoritative report.
All such criticisms and suggestions will, in fact, constitute part of the material (though only a part) upon
which the organised department of investigation and
original research, already referred to as operating
under the direction of the standing committee, will
be independently at work.   Under any genuine
Democracy it is, in the last resort, public opinion
that decides ; and the more effectively we can educate
public opinion, the greater will be the success of
any administration.   In place of the jealous secrecy
in which the 1400 separate colliery companies at
present enshroud their operations, and of the bureaucratic concealment which to-day marks alike the
Post Office and the railways, we visualise the administration of each national industry and service, no
longer concerned for magnifying the private gains of
particular capitalist groups, or enhancing the net
revenue of the Exchequer, but merely for increasing
the efficiency of the service to the public, in the glare
of a whole series of searchlights, impinging at different
angles upon what is essentially the same problem,
namely, how to obtain for the community as a whole
the greatest possible efficiency in relation to the efforts
and sacrifices involved.

The Transformation of Authority

Let us pause to consider how this continuous
bringing to bear, at every stage, of organised knowledge and the " acid test " of comparative statistics, emanating from diverse centres of disinterested

research—one of those silent improvements in industrial administration which are already imperceptibly
transforming the business world—will, under any
genuine Democracy, affect the supreme issue of the
exercise of authority in its relation to personal freedom.
To-day it seems, in the Labour and Socialist world,
that the vital question is who should give orders and
who should obey them—whether the government of
industry shall be " from above " or " from below."
In the ensuing years of ever-increasing socialisation
this controversy will become largely meaningless.
Paradoxical as this may seem to-day, we venture on
the prediction that, from the standpoint of personal
authority, it will matter far less than at present exactly
how the executive command is apportioned. In
industry no less than in political administration, the
combination of Measurement with Publicity is to-day
already undermining personal autocracy. The deliberate intensification of this *searchlight of published
knowledge* we regard as the corner-stone of successful
Democracy. The need for final decision will remain
not merely in emergencies but also as to policy ; and
it is of high importance to vest the responsibility for
a decision, according to the nature of the case, in the
right hands. But a great deal of the old autocracy,
once deemed to be indispensable in government
departments and capitalist industry alike, is ceasing
to be necessary to efficiency, and will, accordingly,
as Democracy becomes more genuinely accepted,
gradually be dispensed with. A steadily increasing
sphere will, except in matters of emergency, be found
for consultation among all grades and sections concerned, out of which will emerge judgments and
decisions arrived at, very largely, by common consent.
This common consent will be reached by the cogency
of accurately ascertained and authoritatively reported
facts, driven home by the silent persuasiveness of

the public opinion of those concerned. The Works Committee, the District Council, the National Board, the Social Parliament itself, will have before them, not merely the spontaneous promptings of their members' minds, and not even only the information provided by their own officials, but much more. To such committees and councils there will come, as a matter of course, a stream of reports from independent and disinterested experts, retained expressly for this professional service, which will carry with them no coercive authority, but which will graphically reveal the results, material and moral, of each establishment or of each industry, in comparison alike with its own past, with the corresponding results of analogous cases elsewhere, and with the possibilities opened out by new discoveries great or small. " Gentlemen," the chairman will say, in opening a joint meeting of the Works Committee and the Management, " you will have read the report of the Health Officer showing that our staff has a markedly lower standard of health than it had during the preceding decade, and lower also than the average of the district. Scarcely less disquieting is the Education Officer's report, which has also been circulated to you, reporting that our young men and women come too tired to the Continuation School to be able to get adequate advantage from the costly instruction provided for them. On the other hand, we have the best output return in the whole industry ; and owing to your decision to put at once into practice the new method of operating that was laid before us in the memorandum from the District Council, we have actually the lowest accident rate ever recorded. But it is plain that we cannot stand being gazetted to the whole world as being the most backward in health among all the establishments in the industry, and as depriving our young people of their educational chances. The question that we have to consider is which of the suggestions put before us, or what modification of them, we can adopt for improvement in these respects, consistently with maintaining our good position in other respects." Or we may imagine the District Council of an industry faced with reports giving, with graphic statistics, the result of investigation of the complaints of particular consumers' organisations, that supplies had been irregular or insufficient, owing to some arrangement of holidays, shifts or the hours of beginning and quitting work that proved to result in undue discontinuity of production. There might be no idea of lengthening the working day or of lessening the holidays ; but the problem of how best to maintain continuity of supply would have to be faced, and faced in the light of the reports discussing all the various solutions that had been suggested. To the obstruction of mere disgruntled criticism, there would always be the challenging reply, " What are your alternative proposals ; let us discuss them."

The proposed new feature is that, in every case, the disinterested professional expert who invents, discovers, inspects, audits, costs, tests or measures— in supplement of the initiative in all these respects of the administration itself—will have no power of command, and no right to insist on his suggestions being adopted. His function is exhausted when his report is made. His personality will find expression, and his freedom will be exercised without limitation, in the process of discovery and measurement, and in the fearless representation of whatever he finds, without regard either to the *amour propre* of the management or to the rebellious instincts of any grade of employees. It is the special function of the directors of industry, acting through their respective committees, to get understood and adopted such parts of the expert reports as are applicable to a particular establishment, district or industry. The real authority will more and more be exercised by the public opinion of the successively enlarging circles of persons concerned—a public opinion which the practice of wide and gratuitous publication of the reports will make both well-formed and all-persuasive.

CO-ORDINATED INSTEAD OF CHAOTIC COMPLEXITY

We can imagine that readers unfamiliar with the actual organisation and working of capitalist industry to-day, and even those capitalists and managers who have not realised its complexity, may be appalled at the complications unfolded. As a matter of fact, the scheme propounded is, compared with what exists under Capitalism, one of simplification. In the coal-mining industry, for instance, the nationalised industry would, on the lines suggested, work under no more committees than at present, with fewer separate units of administration, with fewer meetings for discussion, and fewer opportunities for debate upon what should be done. The 4000 separate owners of coal as a mineral in the earth, periodically consulting their several solicitors as to how to get the utmost royalties, would be replaced by a single National Board, advised by a single staff of mining engineers and legal experts. The 1400 separate Boards of Directors of colliery companies would be replaced by a score or so of District Councils under that National Board. The Pit Committees which now exist, in one or other form, in many collieries, and informally among the miners themselves in all of them, would become generalised and have an official status. Instead of the debates in the House of Commons, controlled by the Home Secretary primed by his Mines Department, there would be those of the Social Parliament advised by its Standing Committee on the Mining Industry, which

would be itself equipped with an independent department of knowledge and research. Much the same
may be said of the other great industries. Those who
declaim against the absurdity of " government by
committees " do not realise the extent to which every
great industry is, even under Capitalism, already
" governed by committees "—by boards of directors
(of which there are, in 1920, over 66,000 in Great
Britain), and their committees and sub-committees,
by managerial committees of all kinds, by stores
committees and contract committees and what not.
Can any one compute among how many separate
boards and committees the management of the score
or more of distinct railway systems under the couple
of hundred separate railway companies in this country
is at present shared ? Nor does amalgamation dispense with the committees. Every trust, in Britain
or the United States, is run by a whole series of
committees. In other industries under present-day
Capitalism the bewildering chaos of management,
or more correctly of lack of management, transcends
all possibility of description. Who can estimate, for
instance, among how many different boards and committees, partnerships and combinations, in how many
entirely unco-ordinated centres of management, unaware of each others' proceedings, and constantly in
conflict or in confusion, the direction of all the innumerable establishments in the British engineering
industry is dispersed ? The difference between what
is now proposed and what already exists under Capitalism is not any increase in the complication of the
machinery of administration, but its simplification and
rationalisation on the one hand, and on the other the
dragging of it into light. What we wish to substitute
for the present chaos is systematic co-ordination.
What we propose to end is not simplicity but secrecy.

THE PRICE OF LIBERTY

It is, however, true that the machinery of administration of any national industry or service—covering an area nation-wide, supplying a thousand separate needs, impinging on ten million families—is and must necessarily be complicated. It is true, moreover, in a certain sense, that this complication is a characteristic of Democracy. The simplest of all governmental systems—so at least it seems at first sight—is that of uncontrolled autocracy. The unrestrained Dictatorship of the Capitalist achieves in industry a similar simplicity—so, at least it appears at the outset—by the identity of the ubiquitous motive of private profit, and by the ruthlessness of competition in the struggle for existence. Neither autocracy nor the Capitalist System long retains, as a matter of fact, its assumed pristine absence of complications, but is found, in practice, to become a whole mass of complications, cycles upon epicycles and wheels within wheels, only concealed from the ordinary citizen by business or bureaucratic secretiveness. But however this may be, Democracy cannot afford to dispense with complication in its administrative machinery, because only by an extensive variety of parts, and a deliberately adjusted relation among those parts, can there be any security for the personal freedom and independence in initiative of the great mass of individuals, whether as producers, as consumers or as citizens. It is only by systematically thinking out the function that each person has to perform, the sphere that must be secured to each group or section, the opportunities in which each must be protected, and the relation in which each must stand to the others and to the whole, that in any highly developed society the ordinary man can escape a virtual, if not a nominal, slavery. Those impatient democrats who will not take the trouble to understand the problem, and who petulantly demand, at the same time, the elaborations and refinements of civilisation and the anarchy and simplicity of the primitive age, cannot in the nature of things ever be gratified. The condition of any genuine Democracy, of the wide diffusion of any effective freedom, is such a systematic complication of social machinery as will negative alike the monarchical and the capitalist dictatorships, and prevent the rise of any other. The price of liberty —of individual variety and specialisation " in widest commonalty spread "—is the complication of a highly differentiated and systematically co-ordinated social order.

CHAPTER IV

THE REORGANISATION OF LOCAL GOVERNMENT

IT is usual to underrate the magnitude, the range and
the social importance of the part of government and
administration which is not organised nationally, but
is entrusted to the Local Authorities. Solemn treatises
on the British Constitution scarcely mention the form
or the power, the functions or the activities, of the
Councils of Parishes, Rural and Urban Districts,
Boroughs and Counties, and, indeed, the thousands
of local governing bodies by which, in fact, the
greater part of British public administration is conducted.

In the first part of this book we dealt with the
Local Authorities in their economic aspect as obligatory
associations of consumers supplying the inhabitants
of their several areas with an ever-widening range of
commodities and services, and incidentally as having
directly on their pay-rolls something like one million
families, or nearly one-tenth of the whole population.
We refrained from describing the chaotic state into
which British Local Government has got, alike in
areas of administration, in constitutional structure,
and in confusion of powers and finances. We did so
deliberately, because we foresaw that, when we came
to our constructive proposals, we could neither explain
nor justify them except in close connection with an
explicit account of the need for local, as distinguished

from national, administration, and of the deplorable
condition into which the whole organisation of local
government has been allowed in Great Britain to fall.

THE DECAY OF CIVIC PATRIOTISM

When the indictment of capitalist profit-making
comes to be formulated with any completeness there
will be no count more serious than its destruction of
local patriotism as an incident in its heedless defilement of urban life.   Alike in ancient times and in
Mediaeval Europe, the patriotism of the City State
was one of the finest enthusiasms of human society.
Even in the sixteenth and seventeenth centuries there
lingered in Britain—among the citizens of London
and Norwich, the burgesses of Bristol and Liverpool,
for instance—no small degree of public spirit and of
local pride in the community of which they felt themselves part—a communal consciousness which claimed
the right of self-determination in resistance to the
autocratic fiat of King or Lord.

But with the silent extension of a profit-making
Capitalism, and the shrinking up of the Mediaeval
Guilds and Municipal Corporations into close bodies
of non-labouring capitalists and owners of ground-
rents and market monopolies, Local Government fell
into disrepute.   The powers of the nineteenth-century
Municipality in Britain — arising, as elsewhere explained, for the most part out of those obtained by
voluntary associations of consumers formed among
neighbouring property-owners—were devised and exercised, not in the interests of the great mass of poverty-
stricken inhabitants, but primarily to minister to the
health and comfort of the richer residents ; and whilst
they incidentally reduced the extravagantly high death-
rates of a century ago in the slums as well as in the
residential quarters of the wealthier inhabitants, they

did practically nothing for the restoration of municipal patriotism among the people at large. The majority of the denizens of the urban areas remained, after 1835 as before that date, devoid of any emotional pride in their city, and without any aspirations to promote its corporate interest. It is significant that such spasmodic impulses of local patriotism as stirred, here and there, during the greater part of the nineteenth century were almost entirely confined to the fortunate minority of prosperous business men, by whom the greater part of the city, its trade and its accumulated wealth, were individually and privately owned.. The shipowners and merchants of Liverpool, who watched the coming and going of their fleets of ocean ships to and from their own great docks and warehouses ; the millionaire warehousemen and manufacturers of Manchester, whose cotton goods reached the markets of all the world ; and, later in the century, the proprietors of the great Birmingham combinations in hardware and machinery, who felt themselves able to undersell any smaller manufacturers elsewhere, could develop an honest pride in the rapidly growing urban aggregations which were at once the means and the mark of their capitalist domination. In their leisure hours, and from their surplus income, these public-spirited citizens sought to build up the corporate life of " their " city ; to enrich it with public buildings, with picture-galleries, with open spaces, with technical colleges, and finally with a university. But in the slums of Liverpool and Manchester and Birmingham—even in the crowded cottages of the artisans and clerks, who together made up two-thirds of the population—anything like municipal patriotism or civic pride remained almost unknown. In the last decade of the century the establishment of the London County Council gave an opportunity for a municipal revival among the formless aggregation of four and a half millions of people who were called, collectively, London ; and, with really heroic efforts, the Progressive Party sought to galvanise the Metropolitan masses into a feeling that they belonged to " no mean city." But this use of what was essentially the instrument of the myth achieved no lasting success. In spite of energetic and enlightened administration of the exiguous powers conceded to the Council, and of striking but costly improvements, London was, and remained, to the great bulk of its inhabitants, emphatically a " mean city " ; and within a couple of decades the faint flicker of popular municipal life in the Metropolis was quenched in a successfully organised capitalist reaction.

With the upgrowth of the Labour Party in the twentieth century, under Socialist inspiration, a renewed assault has been made, throughout all Britain, upon the whole series of Parish, District, Borough and County Councils among which the powers and functions of Local Government are now scattered ; and with the election of thousands of Labour Members to these councils—occasionally in an actual majority—a fresh impulse has lately been given to municipal administration. But there is a significant difference between the impulse to take part in Local Government of the Labour Members of to-day and that which inspired the rulers of the mediaeval city, or that which created, among the wealthy citizens of the Liverpool or the Birmingham of the past century, what passed for municipal patriotism. The Labour Members do not seek election to the local council of to-day because they are proud of their city, but because they are ashamed of it. Unlike the fourteenth-century citizens of Florence or of Bruges, they are striving, not for municipal magnificence or even utilitarian efficiency, but rather for the removal of municipal degradation. So low has fallen our conception of municipal life in Britain to-day that what even enthusiastic reformers

are concerned about is not the glory of the utmost
development of communal life, the widest possible
extension of the civic functions, or the outshining in
municipal achievement of any other city, but merely
the scavenging of the slum, the mitigation of scandalous
overcrowding, the arrest of preventable sickness, and
the stopping of the collective neglect that we now
know to be virtually infant murder. Municipal enterprise has, in our degradation, come to mean little
more than rescuing our own neighbourhood from the
material and moral defilement and pollution to which
Capitalism has condemned it. We are so obsessed
by the necessity, lest worse things happen to us, of
enforcing merely " the National Minimum of Civilised
Life "—alike in water supply, in paving and cleansing,
in housing, in education, in the provision for maternity,
infancy and old age, in the care of the sick and the
physically or mentally infirm—that the larger aspects
and purposes of Local Government, the limitless promotion in all directions of the activities, the faculties
and desires of the citizens, by the creation of the best
possible material and mental environment for them,
almost escape our attention.

The Chaos in the Constitution and Powers of existing Local Authorities

The century-long municipal atrophy that we have
referred to, in conjunction with the contemptuous
indifference with which the predominantly " political "
Cabinet and Parliament have successively tinkered
with social problems, has left Great Britain cut up into
multifarious, incongruous and often mutually conflicting areas, of very unequal size and population,
within which all the functions and powers of Local
Government are entrusted, with every variety of
restriction, senseless or rational, to an extraordinary

medley of boards and councils, large and small, sometimes directly elected by the people, sometimes formed partly by co-option, sometimes partly by appointment from above, sometimes indirectly elected on a federal plan, sometimes created and empowered to exercise only a single function, and sometimes authorised to carry out, within prescribed limits, whatever the inhabitants desire. The complication is such that not even the most skilled cartographer can display in one map, or even in a series of maps, the whole tale of these anomalies, in such a way as to enable any enquiring citizen completely to understand the Local Government organisation under which he is living. Like the capitalist organisation of industry, its complications and varieties are so chaotic and senseless as to defy analysis and almost to baffle description.

AREAS

To begin with the question of areas. In only an insignificant proportion of cases are the areas of the several Local Authorities determined with any reference to the functions now entrusted to them. Since the division of England, possibly a thousand years ago or more, into counties for one set of purposes, into manors for another set of purposes, and into parishes for yet another set, all the circumstances have changed, the population has shifted, industry has been transformed, the means of communication have been revolutionised and the functions of the Local Authorities have been entirely altered. Upon the older divisions there have been superimposed from time to time, all down the centuries, new districts for particular purposes, from Municipal Boroughs, Commissions of Sewers and Surveyors of Highways to Boards of Guardians, Port Authorities and Joint Asylum Committees, often without any regard to the

older divisions. So frequent and extensive have been
the revolutions in industry and communications, and
so greatly has population shifted, that it would have
been miraculous if any one of the thousands of separate Local Authorities now existing found its historic
area best suited for its modern functions. But, for
the most part, the sentimental value of the historic
area has been lost. During the past three-quarters of
a century Local Government areas—not excluding in
many parts the immemorial county—have been cut
and carved about in a series of insufficiently considered
attempts to deal with urgent difficulties ; at some
points extending boundaries out of all recognition,
at others creating brand-new authorities with districts
differing from those formed for other purposes, at
others, as it is said, "cutting the heart out of the
county" for some immediate local advantage, without
regard for the effect of this surgical operation on the
remainder of the organism. The confusion, brought
about in the first three-quarters of the nineteenth
century by the long series of separate and sometimes
inconsistent statutes, has been increased by the efforts
of the more powerful municipal authorities to extend
their jurisdiction over growing suburbs, as well as by
the attempts by energetic minor authorities to raise
themselves in the official hierarchy. Parish Councils
have thus become Urban District Councils, Urban
District Councils Non-county Boroughs, Non-county
Boroughs County Boroughs, in each case gaining
powers, and usually extending boundaries, at the
expense of some other body or bodies, below or above
or beside them in the strange medley of authorities.
Nor is the distribution of functions among all these
boards and councils any more logical or sensible than are
the areas over which they preside. The overlapping
and confusion of functions are seen at their worst
in the co-existence of the Poor Law Authority with

those responsible for what we may call municipal administration.[1] Up and down England there are everywhere duplicate Local Governing Bodies—in some cases as many as five or six different authorities within the same area—dealing, at the expense of one and the same fund of rates and taxes, but on antagonistic principles, with the children, with the sick, with the mentally defective, with the aged and with the able-bodied unemployed. In the greater part of England more than one Local Authority will be found responsible for health, for housing, and for the organisation of medical services. The financial waste involved in this overlapping and confusion, even more than the inefficiency that it causes, has at last convinced the Government Departments concerned, and even the Cabinet, that a thorough reorganisation is required, involving the complete abolition of the Poor Law, and the merging of all the services of the Boards of Guardians, rooted in a " deterrent " relief of destitution, in the ubiquitous municipal administration, based on the supply of public services to all who need them. But although the Government has specifically pledged itself to this reform, and although the House of Commons only assented to the Ministry of Health Bill of 1918 on the faith of that pledge, the hypertrophy of business that, as we have seen, characterises the Political Democracy, has hitherto prevented its

[1] This chaotic overlapping of functions and duplication of services led to the unanimous recommendations of the Royal Commission of the Poor Law, 1905-9, in favour of the abolition of the Poor Law Union area and Board of Guardians. The confusion and waste was described in detail in the Minority Report of that Commission, which recommended the abolition of the Poor Law as a separate system, the complete merging of the functions of the Poor Law Authority in those of the general County and Municipal administration, and the rearrangement of all these services in a single organisation, divided into branches according to the nature of the service to be rendered—all provision for the sick and bodily infirm to be one service, all provision for the mentally defective to be another, all provision for the healthy aged to be united, and equally all provision for the able-bodied unemployed. This recommendation was adopted, in substance, by the Reconstruction Sub-Committee on Local Government, 1917, and accepted as the policy of the Government, but has not yet been carried out.

fulfilment. Whether or not there is to be any extension of public administration, the reform of Local
Government is the most urgent need for the British
government of to-day.

The Inefficiency of the " Great Unpaid "

This senseless complication and confusion in the
constitution, areas and powers of British Local Government, for which Parliament and the Cabinet are
directly responsible, is at once the cause and the
result of the governing authority in each locality
remaining in the hands of a myriad of unpaid representatives. The slum landlords, the public-house
keepers, the building contractors, the pawnbrokers,
who, especially in the urban areas, are good enough to
give their unpaid services on the council that determine the environment in which the people spend
their days and nights, are, to use an American expression, " not there for their health." The morality
and good manners of these bodies may be improved
by the scraps of time and attention which the leaven
of public-spirited business men, fervent Labour
representatives, or intelligent *rentiers* may spare from
their daily avocations and personal pleasures to attend
the multifarious meetings ; but these attendances
cannot make up for the absence of men and women
who can devote to the service of their fellow citizens
the whole of their working hours, and all their professional skill, in return for a livelihood. We do not
undervalue the long-continued and devoted service
which many public-spirited property-owners have,
in all parts of Great Britain, for two or three centuries
given to Local Government without fee or reward.
It is very largely to their influence, especially in the
counties, that we owe the tradition of personal integrity and incorruptibility by which British Local

Government, in spite of much calumny, is, on the whole, distinguished. But especially in the great urban aggregations characteristic of the Britain of to-day, the task, as these gentlemen themselves complain, has got beyond the spare time and energy of persons with other avocations. Every proposal for increased activity of the County Councils meets with resistance from those who feel themselves overwhelmed by the existing work. The survival of the unpaid representative is, in fact, to-day, one of the bulwarks of the society of capitalists and landlords, by means of which it instinctively manages, in a nominal Democracy, to keep Local Government from taking on the full measure of the duties now required from it. Not until the representation of the electorate and the execution of its desires has been made a vocation by itself, as distinctive, say, as that of a surgeon, a nurse, an engine-driver, or an architect, can any form of democratic Local Government rise to the full height of which it is capable.

The Principles on which Reconstruction
should proceed

Municipal government, itself merely a particular form of socialisation, presents essentially the same problems of a co-ordinated Democracy as those already dealt with in our chapter on nationalised industries and services. In the reorganisation of Local Government the three main aspects of man in society—man as a producer, man as a consumer and man as a citizen—have to be considered and provided for.

But local self-government as distinguished from national presents problems of its own.

THE PRINCIPLE OF NEIGHBOURHOOD

There are, it is clear, obvious reasons why many industries and services have to be municipalised rather than nationalised. The case for a local administration of industries and services rests primarily on the consciousness among the inhabitants of a given area, of neighbourhood and of common needs, differing from those of other localities ; and on the facility with which neighbours can take counsel together in order to determine for themselves what shall be their mental and physical environment, and how it can best be maintained or improved. All this is greatly intensified in the modern urban society. The residents in a given area have necessarily to make use of the same drainage system, the same water supply, the same artificial sources of light and heat, the same educational and medical institutions, the same libraries, the same parks and open spaces, and the same organisation of local transport. And the tie of neighbourhood influences in a thousand unforeseen ways the nature of the administration. In the characteristic municipal industries and services producer and consumer are very near together, and automatically aware of each other. The railway - engine driver has no contact and no consciousness of solidarity with the myriads of unknown passengers whom he transports. The miner in the bowels of the earth can form no picture of the destiny of the coal that he is hewing for unknown consumers. But the teachers in the municipal schools, the doctors of the municipal dispensary, the sweepers of the municipal streets live and move and have their being among the very people whom they serve. Even the motor-men or the conductors of the municipal tramcars get to know at least the faces and the destinations of their daily passengers, and, like the stokers in the municipal gasworks, realise that it is their own families who are inconvenienced by any interruption of the service.

This sense of solidarity among neighbours, living in the same environment and using the same complex of local services, is a valuable social asset which Socialism aims at preserving and intensifying. Its impairment by the segregation according to degrees of personal riches, and by the geographical separation between the masses of rich and poor households, has been one of the worst results of the Capitalist System. The very differences among localities, with the different local administrations that they involve, provide an increase in the scope for individual choice, a widening of personal freedom, and a safeguard against a monotonous uniformity and a centralised tyranny over the individual. In the very nature of the case the democratic control, which must be exercised by the Citizen-Consumers, is facilitated and strengthened by the opportunities for taking counsel together that municipal life affords. It is an advantage that the municipal electorate can know personally, and keep constantly under observation, the representatives whom it elects to administer its local affairs. It will be remembered that Rousseau thought this tie of neighbourhood to be indispensable to Democracy.

THE PRINCIPLE OF A DIFFERENTIATION OF NEIGHBOURHOODS

But one locality requires quite a different complex of public services from those demanded by another. A city on the coast or traversed by a broad river has very different environmental needs from a densely crowded inland aggregation, in the midst of other aggregations of houses. The schools and colleges, the picture galleries, the halls for public meetings, even the books in the public library in a new industrial centre will rightly differ from those of an ancient university town or well-endowed cathedral city. Moreover, all the industries and services constituting the economic and social environment of each locality—differing in the complex that they make from those of other localities—are so intimately interwoven one with another that they cannot effectively be dealt with except as a whole. The health of the town depends very largely on its drainage system, but this itself depends on its water supply. The infantile death-rate and the prevalence of tuberculosis may both be governed by the paving and scavenging and by the degree of overcrowding ; whilst these are themselves very largely influenced by the housing arrangements, and these again by the local transport system. The distribution of schools and colleges has to be governed by the spread of the population, which again depends on housing and transport, and upon the development of the local industries. Each particular urban or rural district needs, in fact, to be planned as a whole and administered as a whole, neither dividing areas which are homogeneous in their needs and ideals, nor completely isolating the administration of the several services. This, in fact, is the philosophy of what has latterly been known as " regionalism."

The Principle of Direct Election

We do not escape, from time to time, a controversy as to the merits, in communal as well as in vocational organisation, of direct as compared with indirect election—whether the representatives of the people should be chosen directly by the electorate concerned, or by electoral colleges or other elected bodies to which the choice is entrusted. It is impossible to enter here into this controversy, which is as old as Democracy itself. We can only give the conclusion to which a study of the innumerable examples of both methods of selection has led us. If by democratic government is meant not merely government by the people's nominees, but also the largest practicable measure of continuous control over their nominees by the people themselves, then there can be no doubt that, for any legislative or administrative body having to decide issues of policy, the system of direct election is incomparably the superior. Only by the direct choice of the person who will have to decide the issues of policy, can the electorate, as a whole, take the decision into its own hands. Other devices may secure more efficient or more economical administration, but it is by the direct contact between the member of the administering body and the electors to whom he is responsible that experience shows that this continuous consciousness of consent can best be obtained. It may be that where it is only the execution of policy that is in question, and especially where the administration is mainly a matter of routine, raising no questions in which public interest can be stirred, this continuous consciousness of consent can (without detriment to anything but the political education of the elector) be safely dispensed with, and possibly a higher degree of expert efficiency secured. But, at any rate, wherever issues of policy are at stake, and wherever public interest can be aroused, it can hardly be gainsaid that direct election—especially where it is illumined by genuine publicity and strengthened by frequent consultations between the elected representative and those to whom he is responsible—affords to government a strength and a solidity, and to the whole of the people an education and a satisfaction, that far outweigh any advantage that any known method of indirect election has ever offered. We accordingly propose, as the fundamental basis of democratic Local Government, that, whatever the constituency and whatever the electorate, the representative who is to be a member of the governing council shall be elected directly, and not through the vehicle of an electoral college or other intermediate body.[1]

THE PRINCIPLE OF THE GENERAL REPRESENTATIVE

A more controversial principle is what we may term that of general, as distinguished from " ad hoc "

---

[1] There has been a large and varied experience in English Local Government of indirectly elected bodies of every kind and degree, from Joint Committees of one or more Local Authorities for managing particular institutions up to completely autonomous bodies administering complexes of services. The upshot of this experience is distinctly unfavourable to the principle of indirect election, especially for authorities having wide powers. Joint Committees of County and Borough Councils to manage schools, hospitals and other institutions work fairly well : they are little more than committees of the directly elected bodies—the distinction being that they report not to one but to two or three authorities, whilst it is these directly elected authorities that determine the policy to be pursued. The evil begins when the indirectly elected body does not report to the directly elected authorities, but pursues its own policy uncontrolled by them. When the functions of such indirectly elected bodies are purely routine, and involve only technical considerations, they may work efficiently ; but even with these limited functions they are apt to become corrupt, or to indulge in favouritism in the appointment of officials. Thus, even when indirectly elected bodies are not falsifying the will of the electorate, they are open to the objection, from the standpoint of Democracy, that it is very difficult for the electorate to exercise its right to control the agents who are acting in its name. The electorate cannot, in practice, dismiss these agents, except by the process of dismissing the members of the directly elected bodies by whom these agents are appointed. (It will be noted that the expedient of the Recall, which can only be recall of the person elected, hardly mends matters, as it can seldom in practice become known to the electorate which of the elected persons is responsible for the choice of the particular members of the indirectly elected body.) Experience has shown, in fact, that in-directly elected bodies, which have to decide issues of policy, or to administer extensive complexes of services, become addicted to the characteristic secretiveness of bureaucracy, because they are absolved from the necessity of carrying the electorate with them ; and they tend not only to be corrupt but also to pursue a policy which is contrary to the wishes of the electorate. Further, an indirectly elected body tends to accentuate any characteristic of the directly elected bodies by which it is appointed. For instance, if the directly elected bodies are reactionary and apathetic, the indirectly elected body will be ultra reactionary and apathetic ; or if the directly elected bodies are predominantly Catholic or " Freemason," Individualist or Socialist, with minorities belonging to other temperaments or creeds, the indirectly elected body will be found to belong almost exclusively to the dominant faction. This artificial intensification of majority characteristics in itself throws the indirectly elected body out of harmony with the electorate.

representatives, for the administration of local services.
The history of English Local Government is strewn
with attempts, afterwards abandoned, to set up
separately chosen bodies to administer each of the
congeries of services that make up the complex of
Local Government : Commissioners of Sewers, Boards
of Health, Boards of Highways, Burial Boards, Boards
of Guardians for the Relief of the Poor, Library
Commissioners, Commissioners of Baths and Washhouses, and, most important of all, School Boards.
The argument in favour of these administrative
authorities being separately elected has always been
that in this way, and in this way only, could the elector
control the policy of the representatives. But this
argument ignored the fact that all the services have
to be paid for out of the rates, or have to contribute
to the rates, in making up the local budget, which needs
to be dealt with as a whole. It was, moreover, found
by experience that the objects of one service are so
closely intertwined with the objects of another, that
in practice, education cannot be given properly without
taking into account the prevention and treatment of
disease among young children, whilst the prevention
and treatment of disease cannot be secured without
the provision of houses, open spaces, water, transport
and all the other innumerable developments of Local
Government. Further, it has been discovered that the
multiplying of elections in itself distracts the attention
of the elector from the qualifications and conduct of
the elected persons, whilst the specialised character
of the administration involved leads to candidates
standing who are interested, not in the general question
of maintaining a satisfactory material and mental environment for the citizen, but in some side issue, such
as religious teaching, anti-vaccination, house property,
the maintenance of particular roads, or the prices
charged for gas and electricity. The typical case was

that of the School Board, which was instituted in
1871 as a separate body, because it was supposed that
in this way the organisation of an adequate educational
service would be best promoted. After a generation
of experience the separate School Board was merged,
in 1902–3, in the general governing council for the
locality, with the result, as seventeen years' experience
has proved, of a great development of the educational
service, a valuable widening in the range and quality
of what is provided for the children, and a considerable
advance in the technical efficiency of the administrative staff. Most important of all has been the increase
in efficiency, due to the closer connection that became
possible between education and all the other branches
of municipal work, from health to housing, from
libraries and museums to playing-fields in the parks
and open spaces. No less useful has been the
gradual replacement of representatives interested only
in the narrow issues involved in the management of
elementary schools—often, indeed, only in the maintenance of particular kinds of religious teaching in
these schools—by representatives taking a broader
view, of education as a whole instead of merely
primary teaching, and of child nurture in place of
mere instruction.

The Principle of " Full Time " and adequately paid Representatives

It is nowadays abundantly clear that, in any Socialist
community of magnitude and complexity, with all
the enlargement in scope of the communal activity
that is involved, membership of any but the smallest
local governing bodies must be a " full-time job."
The duty of continuously representing the needs and
desires of the electorate : of weighing in the balance
how the delicate and highly differentiated complex of

public services can be best co-ordinated ; of discovering how the plans of the expert technicians, and the faculties, the aspirations and the initiative of the various grades of workers directly in the service of the local community can be explained to the whole body of citizens ; how the inarticulate *malaise* and incoherent desires of different sections of these citizens can be impressed upon those who in their service are seeking to maximise the utilities and amenities of the communal organisation ; how the " National Minimum " from time to time prescribed by the Social Parliament can be made consistent with the largest measure of local autonomy and the utmost differentiation of the common provision according to local needs—all these functions of the elected representative on a local council taking on the enlarged functions which are now called for, entail, for their adequate fulfilment, a technique by itself, some sort of specialised training, and possibly, eventually, even the requirement, from candidates for the important office of elected representative, of a minimum of manifest qualification for the position. When the whole population enjoys in its life something like the same standard of material circumstances and something like a common comfort and amenity of the home ; from infancy to manhood approximately equal opportunities of education and professional training, it may be predicted that this demand that our elected representatives shall be both trained for their duties and adequately maintained for the efficient performance of them,[1] will be as much a commonplace of Demo-

[1] The introduction of payment of Local Representatives will be highly objectionable to a large proportion of the existing members of Local Authorities, including many of those public-spirited and devoted representatives to whom British Local Government owes so much. It may be admitted that the change from unpaid to paid service will have considerable consequences, some of them unpleasant, and that, like all changes, it will be accompanied by some loss. It is, however, already being made inevitable by the course of events ; and no full and frank acceptance of Democracy in Local Government is possible without it. With advancing socialisation, and the dwindling of a class that " lives by owning," the provision of main-

cracy as the insistence on definite vocational qualifications, along with payment at Standard Rates, for

---

tenance becomes as indispensable for elected representatives as for public
officials.

The change will doubtless come gradually. Already payment of travelling expenses and for the loss of "remunerative time" is conceded to the
members of Insurance, War Pensions and Profiteering Act Committees.
This does not, however, enable the regularly employed wage-earners to
serve, nor does it suffice in the cases, already not infrequent, in which almost
the whole time is absorbed by the public duties. The hard-working chairmen of County Councils, and those of important committees, must (as
many Mayors already are) promptly be provided with substantial salaries
or allowances.

The conventions and prejudices of the property-owning, business and
professional classes, which during the whole of the nineteenth century practically monopolised the duty of representation, make these classes full of apprehension at the very idea of "Payment of Members." But they should not
forget that the practical monopoly of representation that they have enjoyed,
when they have been willing to serve, because the four-fifths of the electorate living on weekly wages could not afford to give the time, has been
itself an evil. When the representation has been genuinely disinterested,
as it has very often been, it has been, far too often, unconsciously biassed
by class characteristics, often to the extent of positively frustrating the desires
and will of the majority of the electorate. No one can imagine, for instance,
that the policy habitually pursued by most Boards of Guardians in Poor
Law Administration, or that by Rural District Councils about Housing, or
that by some County Councils about the provision of land for small holdings
—whether or not it was a wise policy—has been that desired by the majority
of the adult inhabitants of their areas. In this way, the failure to provide a
livelihood for elected members amounts, in fact, to a falsification of Democracy. But the service of unpaid members is not always disinterested. The
crowd of little property-owners, estate agents, publicans and shopkeepers,
who have hitherto been so strongly represented on the smaller councils have,
unfortunately, furnished many instances of essentially corrupt administration ; that is to say, administration in their own interests as property-owners
or traders. Elected persons who are not paid will sometimes manage to
pay themselves, even if only by warding off reforms that would be finan-
cially injurious to their own interests.

The demand made by the Labour Party for the payment of all persons
elected to perform public services is irresistible in a genuine Democracy.
What would be thought to-day of a proposal to restrict election to candidates
who could show that they had a "property qualification" of £500 a year
income ? Yet this is what the refusal of "Payment of Members" means.
When service on a Local Authority, with the enlarged functions that are
proposed, is seen to involve the devotion of full time to the public service—
when, moreover, it is realised that the class of "gentlemen of independent
means" is a dwindling one—we shall wonder why we ever thought it either
honest or practicable to depend for essential public services on the chance
of finding people of competence able and willing to serve without maintenance. It will be seen that there is just as much "honour" in being a public
administrator with a salary, as in being one without a salary. But already
even the most scrupulous country gentlemen do not refuse to receive
payment for service on a public body (as members for the Thames Conserv-
ancy Board, for instance ; and some of the more active members of the

each section of the workers by hand or by brain.[1] When the duties of a member of a Local Authority become so onerous and incessant as to take up practically his whole time (as is already the case for active members on the London County Council, and for many a chairman elsewhere), the provision of a livelihood during the term of service is the only alternative to an altogether undemocratic exclusiveness. When, as our plan contemplates, this continuous work is required from all the Local Councillors, how can proper " Payment of Members " be resisted or objected to ?

The Correspondence of Area and Functions

The supreme importance of maintaining and intensifying the bond of neighbourhood, and local pride in a highly differentiated environment, and of making the body of representatives responsible for the whole complex of services which make up the material and mental environment in which the citizens live and move and have their being, together with the necessity of obtaining an adequately qualified and sufficiently remunerated body of full-time representatives, who shall be directly responsible to and closely identified with their constituencies of citizen-consumers, has become a commonplace with most of those who have themselves served on important Borough or County Councils. What is not always so apparent is the need for combining these fundamental requirements with some elasticity with regard to areas, according to the several services to be rendered. It is true

---

Ecclesiastical Commission) any more than when they attend the meetings of the boards of their insurance, railway, banking or other joint-stock companies.

[1] The whole subject of the prescription of minimum qualifications for employment as a means of maximising individual freedom, will be subsequently dealt with in our chapter on " The Reorganisation of the Vocational World."

that all these services of Local Government, in country and town alike, constitute a single complex of environment ; and that no one among them can be administered so as to secure the maximum efficiency and the largest measure of democratic control, without all the rest of the complex being taken into consideration, at the same time and by the same elected representatives. Yet it is equally apparent, in examining the technical details of the several services, especially the more modern municipal and county services, that some of them imperatively require, alike for their efficient and economical working, and for any effective participation in their management of the vocational workers concerned, areas of very different extent from the areas best adapted to other services. It may well be, for instance, that paving, lighting and cleansing the thoroughfares, the prevention of nuisances, the management of elementary schools and the provision of public baths and washhouses are best administered together, for a group of neighbours resident within a comparatively small area. On the other hand, the obtaining of an unpolluted water supply, the tramway service, the distribution of electricity, the adequate provision of parks, commons and woodlands for public recreation, town planning and housing in garden suburbs, and the provision of the highest technological and university education call for areas and populations of much greater magnitude. The fundamental problem of any democratic reorganisation of British Local Government, which Socialists even more than others are called upon to solve, is how to provide for the administration, as a single environmental complex, of diverse services, retaining and even intensifying the bond of neighbourhood and the consciousness of common life, under one and the same body of directly elected representatives immediately responsible to their constituents—and yet to secure for each of the different public services, as wide apart from each other as local scavenging and the provision of a university, such an area of administration as will permit, in all of them alike, of a maximum of efficiency and economy.

The Local Government of To-morrow

Now, there may possibly be various alternative ways of solving this problem ; but we can only present, for discussion, the one which, after much consideration, most commends itself to us. We suggest that the alteration of Local Government must, in a sense, be a drastic one, in that it should not tinker merely with particular services or particular areas, but be made applicable simultaneously to the whole nation. It is imperative, if only for the sake of affording a common basis for the national Grants in Aid, which must inevitably be continued, that for each great service of Local Government there should be, from one end of the kingdom to the other, everywhere an elected Local Authority specifically charged with that service and responsible for maintaining the prescribed National Minimum, over an area suited to the service. But it is no less important that the bond of neighbourhood, the associations of local propinquity, should become more than ever the basis of the whole.

The Representation of the Citizen-Consumer

For this purpose there should be everywhere a common and approximately equal unit of representation, which we shall call the Ward. We propose, in fact, to extend to the rural areas the system of Wards already existing in the Boroughs. We do not suggest (as it will be at once alleged) the ignoring of existing boundaries or of historical associations. In the vast majority of cases it will be possible to take as the Ward some existing parish or village, or neighbouring group of villages, without alteration of boundaries. It will indeed be necessary, for the sake of economy and simplicity in registration, to make the Wards everywhere non-conflicting with the constituencies adopted for the election of Members to the national assemblies. But the object is to constitute everywhere a self-conscious unit, which might comprise something like a couple of thousand families in the country, and twice or thrice that number in large cities, which could get to know personally the candidates whom it was asked to elect, which could be addressed by them in public meeting, and with which they could reasonably take counsel from time to time over what are, in fact, the common concerns of them all. No improvement (beyond that of the completion of adult suffrage) is suggested in the present method of a register of all adult residents, voting periodically by secret ballot.

Each of the Wards so established would necessarily become, not only an electoral unit, but also a unit for the collection of rates or local taxes. But how far each Ward would become also a separate unit for administration would depend upon circumstances. In a sparsely peopled district the Ward would presumably take over all the functions of any small Urban Sanitary Authority, and manage among other services its own paving, lighting and cleansing. On the other hand, in Boroughs and Cities, where the complex of local services is already administered by a single Municipal Council, the Ward would probably remain —apart from its principal feature of affording an opportunity for constant consultation between the representative and his constituents, a matter to which we attach the greatest importance—merely an area for the purposes of the election of councillors and the collecting of rates.

But the special advantage of the uniform division into Wards, with their direct election of representatives to deal with the whole environmental complex constituted by the services of Local Government, lies in the facility that it affords for an easy grouping of areas. Whenever there is a question of determining the unit of area or population to be adopted for any particular service, the Wards themselves should be grouped—according to the geographical features, character of the population, local means of communication and, above all, the nature of the service—in such a way as to form, for each function, the area in which the administration can be made most efficient and most truly economical. For the area of administration thus determined, the elected representatives of the Wards that were combined would automatically constitute the governing Council for the particular group of functions in question, all of which would be at least so intimately interdependent that they required an identical area, and for which an identical office and one and the same administrative staff could be provided. For another function, or group of functions, a quite different geographical area might afford the most efficient and the most economical service; and for that functional group the Wards would therefore be differently combined; the elected representatives of the Wards thus associated forming the Council for that particular function or set of functions, which would also have its own office and administrative staff. In this way it would be possible to have one area for the administration of such services as paving and cleansing, the management of the elementary school, and the provision of allotments, under its own directly elected Council; and quite another area, *equally under its own directly elected Council*, for the supply of gas, water and electricity and the management of tramways; and yet another, *equally under its own directly elected Council,* for the organisation of medical services, the provision for the sick and infirm and the promotion of the public health. One and the same Local Councillor for the Ward would sit as its representative in each of these Councils, keeping all of them continuously in contact with the people for whom they would be severally administering, and responsible to his particular electorate for the policy pursued in each of them. It is not, of course, suggested that there should be a different area, a distinct office and administrative staff, and a separate council for each of the multitude of services or groups of services now devolved upon, or in future to be entrusted to the Local Authorities. On the contrary, the advantages are great of uniting as many as possible of these services. An existing County Borough, for instance, might well continue to have all its services, or nearly all of them, united in one common area of administration, with a single Town Hall and Municipal Office. But it should always be practicable—without upsetting the general scheme of Local Government, without multiplying elections or rates, and without departing from the invaluable direct election of representatives by the people concerned, to assign, to each service requiring a smaller, a larger or an altogether different area than the others, as nearly as possible the particular area that the efficiency or economical working of the service appears to demand.

The rural districts present problems of their own. In sparsely inhabited areas, a couple of thousand families are spread over a considerable area, in which the units of neighbourhood may be half-a-dozen small villages, each of which has a certain, though exiguous, local life of its own, and may have little knowledge of the residents in the others. This, however, is a difficulty which is lessening with the improvement in the means of communication, and with increasing tendencies towards migration to employment in neighbouring areas. It may be suggested that the 10,000 existing Parish Councils and Parish Meetings, in many of which corporate feeling is being slowly built up,[1] might well be maintained in existence for their present functions, whilst all the newer and more important functions to be assumed by the Ward, or by the aggregations of which the Ward will form part, should not be associated with any smaller area than one containing a couple of thousand families. The difficulty now experienced by such an area (as, for instance, in the election of the Rural District Council) of finding candidates able and willing to afford the time and expense of giving unpaid service on a body meeting outside the village would, of course, not be experienced when the elected representative is assured of a livelihood to enable him to perform his public service.

The Local Councillor

It is impracticable here to work out in detail how many elected representatives there should be for each Ward. There is much to be said, as far as all the larger functions of Local Government are concerned, for having one only. There should, at any rate, be everywhere one man—the Local Councillor—who would become extremely well known in his Ward, whom the local elector would hold responsible for the efficiency of every branch of the local administration. But where the Ward is not only a unit of election and rating, but is itself an administrative district (in supersession of the majority of the present small Urban Districts under 10,000 inhabitants), there might also be elected, along with the Local Councillor (who would form part of the County or other higher Council in which the Ward was grouped) four, six or eight

---

[1] See *Parish Councils and Rural Life* (Fabian Tract No. 137).

other representatives who would sit only on the Ward Council.

With the enlargement of business that any general municipalisation involves, and with the concentration that we propose, it becomes essential that all the Local Councillors (whose function should be frankly that of representatives, quite distinct from that of executive officials of health or education, tramways or drainage, or even from that of the Town Clerk or principal manager) should give their whole time to their duties as Local Councillors ; and should, accordingly, be adequately paid. Their working day would be fully occupied by serving as members of the various Councils and their committees and sub-committees, to which they would belong, from the Councils dealing only with the services appropriately administered in the smallest unit of area, up to those requiring for efficiency and economy areas of much greater extent. They should submit themselves for election in their several Wards, either triennially or quinquennially ; but there would be advantages in their being also statutorily required to meet their constituents regularly face to face at public meetings, to be held annually or even quarterly, in order that they may explain to those whom they represent what is being done in all the Councils on which they sit, answer questions and meet objections, and hear the desires and complaints of their constituents. Once a year, at least, a report of the proceedings of each Council should be forwarded by post to every elector, as well as to all the local newspapers.

There will yet have to be provided, in a manner presently to be described, due participation in the administration of the municipal industries and services of the various kinds and grades of workers concerned in them. It must, however, be noted that the Local Councillors elected by the Wards represent more than the consumers.[1] They are responsible not only for satisfying the desires of the consumers or users of the several commodities or services that the Council provides, but also for maintaining and improving the complex of local services constituting the mental and physical environment of the locality. Further, the Councillor is specially charged with the financial co-ordination of the various public services ; with the question, vital to-day, of the rates to be levied on the citizens, together with the equally important question, possibly more important in the future than it is to-day, of the prices to be charged for the various services or commodities in order to make the municipal income and expenditure balance. Hence it may be visualised that the Councillors sitting on the Management Committees of the various services presently to be described, will occupy a predominant position. In fact, these Local Councillors concentrate, in themselves, the function of representing the consumers of the commodities and services and the citizens of the locality, as well as such other functions of national import which the Social Parliament may delegate to the Local Authority. It seems to follow that the Councillors on all the Management Committees should be in the majority, or at any rate carry the power of exercising a majority vote in the ultimate determination of policy. It may also be suggested that for financial business, such as adopting the annual estimates and fixing the precept, or deciding to incur capital expenditure of magnitude, to be raised by loan, the elected Local Councillors, who represent the interests

[1] We look to see voluntary organisations of the consumers or users of particular municipal services—such as the parents of the children in the municipal schools, the members of the football or cricket clubs using the municipal playing-fields, the readers who habitually make use of the municipal libraries, the regular attendants at the municipal concerts, the frequenters of the municipal tramcars—bringing to bear on the Executive Committee concerned their suggestions and complaints, and being officially recognised as Advisory Committees.

and desires of all the citizens and who are responsible
for the permanent interests of the locality as well as for
the expenditure of the sums levied upon their electors,
should sit alone. The several Councils would have
at their disposal the Grants in Aid allotted to them
out of national funds (which will presumedly represent
a quota of the equivalent of the " rent " of land and
other differential advantages secured from the national
industries). They would also have the receipts from
the various municipal industries and services, which
already make up so large a total sum, and which will,
of course, be steadily increasing. For any balance
that may be required (including the necessary provision for interest and sinking fund on any municipal
indebtedness) they must look, as at present, to their
electors, either in the form of the rates, or by any
other method of local taxation that may from time to
time be sanctioned by the Social Parliament. It may,
however, be observed that, with a general municipalisation of all the public services, together with a steadily
increasing proportion of the industries of local nature,
the final adjustment of the revenue and expenditure
sides of the Council's accounts will be effected, very
largely, by fixing the prices of the several services
rendered ; just as many a British Borough Council
to-day makes a substantial profit on its gas, electricity
and tramways ; something on letting for hire the
pleasure boats in its parks, or even on the graves in the
municipal cemetery ; and supplies the libraries, playing fields and picture galleries gratuitously, whilst
paying half its huge school expenditure out of the
Government Grant and levying rates for the balance.
The amount annually required by each Council in the
shape of local taxes would be levied by way of precept
proportionately on the various Wards which that
Council was serving. Each Ward would receive pre-
cepts from all the various Councils into which, for

the different services, it was grouped ; and the aggregate amount thus required would be collected from the inhabitants on a single demand note. The duty of collecting this revenue in each Ward could probably be conveniently combined with that of keeping the electoral register, and possibly, under the supervision of the Registrar - General, with that of maintaining, in such a way as to prevent their becoming inaccurate,[1] all other registers of the population now required for births, marriages, deaths and various other purposes.

Such a scheme for the representation of the inhabitants in Wards grouped in various administrative councils according to the nature of the services to be rendered, whilst maintaining all that is necessary in the way of uniformity of system, would have the great advantage of permitting of its application to a greater or lesser extent in different parts of the country, and with regard to different services, according to the desires of the inhabitants, the circumstances of the locality and the requirements of the service. Thus, in counties which are approaching the point at which they may most conveniently be wholly apportioned among coterminous County Boroughs—this may possibly be the case in the West Riding of Yorkshire and in Middlesex, and it has been suggested for Glamorgan, if not also elsewhere—it would be quite possible, in supersession of the Council of the Administrative County, to group all the Wards into four, six or ten great County Boroughs, and yet permit of other groupings, equally under directly elected councils, for such purposes as the water supply from a common catchment area, the generation of electricity or the provision of university education. On the other hand, in the essentially rural counties an ever larger aggregation

---

[1] The need for the Central Index Register, by means of which alone the existing local registers can be prevented from becoming always inaccurate, is referred to subsequently in this chapter.

of services might be entrusted to the grouping of Wards that would correspond to the existing Council of the Administrative County.[1]

Vocational Representation

So far, with a view to clearness of exposition, the administration of municipal industries and services has been considered only from the standpoint of the Citizen-Consumer. It goes without saying that provision must also be made, with regard to each of them, for due participation in the administration of the various grades and sections of the persons employed. Indeed, this participation of the workers concerned can, because of the precious bond of neighbourhood, often be more fully developed than in the case of the national industries and services, in which the need for national uniformity of operation and for systematic conservation of the national resources compels a considerable degree of centralisation. It is suggested that, whilst the final responsibility for municipal finance and consequently the supreme control of municipal policy must be reserved for the Council of directly elected representatives of the Wards grouped under it, the current administration of each municipal industry or service undertaken by the Council should

[1] The question arises, by what central authority or department the Local Government areas should be fixed, and the necessary changes (including alterations in boundaries, powers of different bodies and numbers of elected representatives, etc.) made from time to time ? Affecting, as this must, the work of many different services of national importance, such as education, health, transport, electricity, etc., each of which will have its own central department under its own Standing Committee of the Social Parliament, we deprecate the setting-up of a new " Local Government Board." What may be best may be a sort of permanent " Boundary Commission." made up of representatives of all the central departments concerned, and of the federations of Local Authorities, with an office confining its attention strictly to the adjustments of Local Government constitutions and areas that are from time to time called for. Eventually the duty might be entrusted to the federation of Local Authorities that we hope to see developed, in consultation with the standing committees of the Social Parliament that are concerned with the various services.

devolve upon a separate committee or board of a composite character, comprising, along with directly elected Local Councillors, the nominees of the Professional Associations and Trade Unions whose members are engaged in the work.

COMMITTEES OF MANAGEMENT

The relation of these committees or boards to the Council of directly elected representatives itself should be something like that which has, in the most energetic and efficient Borough and County Councils, been worked out in practice for the Education Committee, on which, however, it is at present rare to find genuine vocational representatives of any kind, and practically never any of the Trade Unions of manual workers. What is now suggested is an effective representation, determined by the vocational organisations concerned, of various grades and kinds of teachers on the Education Committee ; of doctors, dentists, midwives and nurses on the Health Committee ; of asylum attendants and mental specialists on the Asylums Committee ; whilst the building operatives, the quantity surveyors and the architects would be represented on the Housing Committee, and representatives of the institutes of engineers and of the engineering Trade Unions would assist the Works Committee. Even the Finance Committee would find it helpful to have the co-operation of the powerful organisations of accountants and auditors, whilst the Establishment Committee would need that of the Trade Unions of clerks and other municipal employees. There may even be an advantage in the addition of a nominee of the Local Trades Council to represent specially the less numerous and humbler grades of municipal employees who cannot all be specially represented.

Machinery for Collective Bargaining

For the purpose of negotiating terms and conditions of employment there must be Joint Boards, in each of which the representatives of a separate vocational group, whether of brain workers or of manual workers, will meet an equal number of representatives of the management, to adjust from time to time the conditions under which the Council employs its staff. The councils should also be supplemented by Appointment and Discipline Boards, such as have been already described in the chapter on Nationalised Industries.

The Practicability of Vocational Self-Government in Municipal Government

It is one of the beneficent results of the precious tie of neighbourhood that it seems possible for the workers, by hand and brain, to undertake, in municipal services and industries, especially in small places, a high degree of vocational self-government. The relation between the producer and the consumer of a particular service, when both of them live in the same locality, are subject to the same public opinion and are in fact frequently personally known to each other, approximates, more than is possible in national industries, to that between the customer and the mediaeval craftsmen associated in their gilds. Already, in Britain, it has been found practicable to refer the whole question of discipline over panel practitioners under the National Insurance Act to Local Medical Committees exclusively made up of the representatives of the medical profession. It is the Local Medical Committee that decides whether a local practitioner has been guilty of professional neglect or of extravagance in his prescriptions, whilst the Pharmaceutical Society exercises somewhat similar privileges in the discipline of the local chemists. There seems no reason why this professional self-government should not be extended to the organisation of " team work " in common dispensaries or joint clinics, or to a much closer co-ordination of the work of the general practitioner with that of the specialist, or of domiciliary attendance with that of hospital treatment. And a similar professional self-determination can clearly be extended, for some part of school management, to the teachers under the Local Education Authority. In the case of the manual working organisations there are many advantages in their being encouraged to carry out, under their own management, any public work within their several vocations of which they proved themselves capable, or of undertaking, if they chose, such a collective contract for labour as is common in Italy. The great difficulty in developing this professional self-government and this collective responsibility of fellow-craftsmen will arise, not from any disinclination on the part of the Local Authority to make experiments in this direction, but from the very imperfect organisation of the vocational world and the low standard of public spirit and vocational initiative which is one of the unfortunate effects of a century-long capitalist wage-system. These defects will be considered in our chapter on " The Reorganisation of the Vocational World."

The Industries and Services of Local Authorities

There seems practically no limit to be assigned to the number and range of the industries and services that might advantageously be undertaken by Local Authorities. A few great industries and services (such as the whole expansion of the Post Office, the railways and canals, afforestation, the supply of coal and oil, the generation of electricity, probably banking and insurance, the smelting of metals and the conduct of lines of passenger steamers) will be undertaken by the national Government. At the other end of the scale is the provision of the innumerable kinds of commodities for household consumption for which the consumers' Co-operative Movement has proved itself to be the most advantageous form of socialisation. Between these two great classes lies an immense field for industrial organisation in the common service, in which the British Local Authorities have yet very partially adventured—at many points, indeed, falling behind the municipal achievements of other countries.[1] It is, of course, easy to contemplate the universal provision by our Local Authorities of water, gas and (so far as its distribution is concerned) electricity ; of such local transport as tramways, omnibuses, ferries and river services ; of the provision of houses of all sorts ; of public baths and washhouses, and burial-grounds and crematoria ; of complete sanitary services, from paving, cleansing and lighting the thoroughfares up to every kind of preventive and remedial treatment for the sick, at home and in institutions ; of a complete provision for the special needs of maternity and infancy, infirmity and old age ; of education of every kind and grade from nursery schools to post-graduate courses available for students of any age ; of parks and open spaces, woodlands and mountain sides, with holiday homes of all sorts. With a revival of civic patriotism, the Local Authorities will find themselves undertaking the responsibility for the whole mental and physical environment of the population which they serve—in town planning, in joint organisation of the rapidly dwindling spaces

[1] For remarkable surveys of the variety of industries and services successfully undertaken by Local Authorities, see *Collectivist State in the Making*, by A. E. Davies ; *State and Municipal Enterprise*, by S. and B. Webb (*New Statesman* Supplement, May 8 1915).

between the towns, in the elimination of hideous advertisements and the prevention of defilement of the ground and streams. Above and beyond all this is the provision of art, music and the drama. How extensive will be the work we cannot compute. Already more than fifteen hundred million pounds' worth of the national capital is being administered in this country by the Local Authorities ; and if these Authorities were all even as energetic and enterprising as the best among them now are, the amount would probably be doubled or trebled. The extent and range of the direct administration will be greatly increased as it becomes the rule for Local Authorities, in their position of associations of consumers, to free themselves from their present subjection to rings and price-agreements among municipal contractors, by producing for themselves, individually or through their federations, like the Co-operative Societies, as many as possible of the commodities that they require. It may well prove to be the case that, in a Socialist Commonwealth, as much as one-half of the whole of the industries and services would fall within the sphere of Local Government.

EMULATION AMONG LOCAL AUTHORITIES

Municipal industries and services enjoy certain advantages in administration over national industries and services which a Socialist community will clearly seek to develop. The bond of neighbourhood and the stimulus of local pride have already been mentioned. But what should become peculiarly characteristic of municipal administration is local emulation and the rivalry in efficiency among the administrators of all local services. Hitherto this local emulation and rivalry in efficiency has been very little evoked, and it has practically never been pointedly appealed to by Ministers or the Government Departments, who have been positively afraid of too much municipal efficiency. Any such emulation necessarily depends, it will be seen, on the full and frank adoption of the two principles to which reference has already more than once been made in this book, namely Measurement and Publicity. Except comparatively recently, and only in a few points, there has been practically no attempt to assess, with precision and authority, how the administrations of the British Local Authorities compare with one another in the relative extent, efficiency, cost and success of their several services. The citizens cannot be, effectively, either proud or ashamed of their city unless they are told, exactly and with authority, how it compares with others. And without either local pride or local shame, local administrations will remain stagnant. It is not mere coincidence that the publication, just a couple of decades ago, of fuller and more precise statistics of infant mortality in the various towns, in comparison one with another, was soon followed, nearly everywhere, by a considerable reduction in the death-rate among the babies. The nation may fairly expect to see in future—perhaps under the direction of a Federation of Municipalities in supplement of the efforts of the national departments—all the Local Authorities regularly compared, in sets, according to their populations, as to the average percentage of children at school, the proportion each year passed forward to higher stages of education, the physical records at each age, the sickness-rate as well as the death-rate—the number, per thousand population, of books in the public libraries, auditors at the public concerts, picture-galleries, recreation grounds, acres of parks and open spaces available—the relation between the total population and the provision of hospitals, convalescent homes, mental asylums, homes for the aged—

the comparative record of literary, artistic and scientific
output of the various local areas—the relative success
of the several administrations in cost per unit of product—the greatest bound onward, during the preceding year, among all the towns in the perfecting of
the thoroughfares, of the medical and educational
institutions, of the parks and open spaces, of the
libraries, the picture galleries and the theatres—
finally by some impartial qualitative assessment of each
town as a whole, as to the success of its efforts during
the preceding year to increase the beauty and general
amenity of the environment that it provides for its
people.   How far this appeal to local emulation should
be conducted by the national departments concerned,
such as those of Health and Education ; how far by
the great and powerful Federation of Municipalities
that will, it may be hoped, develop out of the Municipal
Corporations and County Councils Associations ; and
how far by special " Subject Associations " or scientific societies, possibly international in scope, we need
not seek to distinguish. However conducted, the
appeal to local pride and local shame should be made
a standing feature of the Socialist administration of
the future ; and it should be enforced by distinguishing
marks of national approval conferred on those Municipalities which show themselves to have best risen
to the height of their vast responsibilities.

THE FEDERATION OF LOCAL AUTHORITIES

This emulation among different Municipal Authorities, whether with regard to particular services or to
the whole complex of services that they administer,
will not militate against—on the contrary, it will
help forward—the development of federal institutions
among the various Local Governing Bodies. It is
one of the outstanding advantages of local, as com-

pared with national, administration that it offers an easy opportunity for the development of a freer and more elastic centralisation than is possible in an industry or service nationally administered from a central office. Already this tendency is at work among our present confused and conflicting Local Authorities in the County, Urban and Rural District Councils Associations, and in the Municipal Corporations Association, which are at present organisations for the purpose of mutual service and of a defensive alliance of the different categories of Local Authorities against each other and against Whitehall and Westminster. Under a better-organised Local Government and with the continuous pressure for increased socialisation, these federal institutions will probably become creative rather than defensive, and their growth will be greatly stimulated and systematised.

We do not pretend to forecast the particular directions in which these federations of Local Authorities will develop, or the order in which they will grow, but it may be pointed out that they might with advantage at once unite in a common scheme for the testing by examination of the annual crop of recruits to their clerical service, and in a common scheme of superannuation for the whole of their staffs, making possible a much greater interchange of officials than is now practicable. In another direction they could advantageously undertake, on a federal basis, the whole service of auditing their own accounts, and of establishing a joint department for municipal statistics and the comparative costing of every municipal industry and service—work which would otherwise have to be undertaken under the direction of the Social Parliament. There is, indeed, no reason, seeing that it will be the Local Authorities that will maintain all the local registers of inhabitants for births, marriages, deaths and other purposes, why they should not by a federal organisation relieve the national Government of its task of keeping the General Register Office at Somerset House. They might then do what the national Government has not yet seen its way to accomplish, namely, institute such a Central Index Register, and such automatic relations between it and the local registers, as would keep these at all times free from duplications and " dead entries," and thus enable each Local Authority to know at any time exactly how many persons are residing within its jurisdiction, and, consequently, not merely what are the accurate local birth-rates and death-rates, but also what amount and kind of provision of municipal service will be required.[1]

In other directions, too, the scope for joint action will be great. Such a common service as the insurance against losses by fire in municipal buildings might at once profitably be undertaken co-operatively by the Local Authorities themselves. There is, moreover, no reason why the Local Authorities should not conduct their own banking service for themselves, as the 1500 Co-operative Societies already do, with a turnover exceeding 500 million pounds a year. British Municipalities should note that a considerable number of Italian Municipalities have formed a federation for the mutual exchange of surplus products and the joint disposal of waste substances of various kinds. All the various Local Authorities of Britain

---

[1] This subject was specially investigated by a Departmental Committee of the Local Government Board (now Ministry of Health) appointed January 17, 1918 ; and an important Report was prepared in March 1919, which the Government has not even taken the trouble to publish. In this Report it was shown that, whilst the nation now maintains at a total annual cost of, literally, hundreds of thousands of pounds no fewer than 12 central and 20 local registers of the inhabitants in different aspects, no means are taken to bring these into connection with each other, so as to prevent each of them from being at all times inaccurate both by excess and by deficiency. The Report describes how this evil can be cured, without imposing any new obligation on the citizen, by the formation, at a cost of £15,000 a year, of a Central Index Register, by means of which every one of the existing registers could automatically be kept accurate.

need not individually manufacture the uniform clothing that they now buy for their staffs, or the books and other requisites needed in their schools and libraries, or the stores regularly consumed in their various departments, any more than they need each to set up a printing press for the multifarious printing that they will require. There seems no reason why there should not be a federation of Local Authorities for the manufacture and distribution among themselves of practically all the innumerable articles that are now purchased by them, habitually at full if not excessive prices, from profit-making traders. The Local Authorities have, even to a greater extent than the 1500 Co-operative Societies, the advantages of a known, certain and regular demand ; abundance of capital at the lowest possible rate, and a total absence of bad debts ; and there seems no reason why their productive federation should not quickly be as extensive and as successful as the English and Scottish Co-operative Wholesale Societies, which now manufacture to the extent of 60 million pounds a year, and distribute wholesale commodities of all sorts to the extent of over 120 million pounds a year. It goes without saying that, on the management committees of such federations of Local Authorities, there would naturally be the same sort of representation of the various grades and sections of the workers concerned, the same Joint Committees for Collective Bargaining, and the same sort of Advisory Committees for criticism and suggestions as we have described for the national industries and services.

THE RELATION OF MUNICIPAL INSTITUTIONS TO THE SOCIAL AND POLITICAL PARLIAMENTS

What will be the relation of these various circles of Local Self-government, with their specialised com-

posite executive committees and their federal institutions, to the Social and Political Parliaments respectively?
It has already been indicated that the Social Parliament
will have its separate Standing Committees on Education, Public Health, Transport and Communications,
and on other industries and services which will be
administered, mainly or partially, by the Local
Authorities. It will be the duty of these standing
committees and of the staffs in their service to see
that the National Minimum of Civilised Life from
time to time prescribed by the Social Parliament in
respect of each of these services is maintained intact
throughout the whole community. Further, it has
been suggested that these standing committees will
have departments of organised research and discovery,
and statistical departments for the ascertainment of
the facts of administration by periodical or special
enquiries. The exact amount of supervision by the
machinery of inspection and reports that may be
exercised by the standing committees and their
departments over the Municipal Councils will presumably depend largely on the degree to which these
councils develop their own federal institutions.
Assuming that the municipalities evolve, as it is to
be hoped that they will, energetic and efficient federal
departments for audit, for costing and for comparative
statistics, these functions would not need to be repeated,
so far as Local Government was concerned, in the
central government departments under the standing
committees. In this case the standing committees
would exercise only a general supervision over the
Local Authorities, and would conduct enquiries only
when those seemed to be called for by public opinion,
or asked for by Subject Associations or professional
bodies. On the other hand, we ourselves attach so
much importance to the utmost possible development,
in the Socialist Commonwealth, of research and dis-

covery, that we should urge the retention, under the Social Parliament, of a highly organised central department for this purpose, even assuming that the federated Local Authorities established their own departments of the same kind. The line of demarcation between their respective researches would doubtless come to be analogous to that already suggested between the central Department of Research under its own Standing Committee, and those of the several National Boards administering the national industries and services.

There are, however, two categories of rights, communal and individual, in which the Social and Political Parliaments would need to exercise constant supervision over the Municipal Authorities, the right of ownership and the right of personal liberty. In the Social Parliament would be vested the maintenance of the sovereign right of the whole body of the people in the national resources and the national product, and consequently in the distribution of the national product among localities and individuals. It would not, for instance, be open to a Municipal Council to impose a tax, except in the way and to the degree permitted by law enacted by the Social Parliament ; nor would it be open to a Municipal Council to seize any private property except in so far as this might be authorised by legislation of the Social Parliament. Hence, in devising its local budget, and in framing its plans, each council would have to consider within what limits and in what way they were empowered to deal with private property ; and this would have been determined by the Social Parliament.

Similarly, it is exclusively in the Political Parliament that is vested the exercise of the sovereignty of the people over the life and liberty of the individual. Thus, it would not be possible for the Municipal Council, of its own authority, to make a bye-law creating a new crime. Such a bye-law could not be made the basis of a prosecution in the Courts unless it had already been sanctioned by the Minister of Justice in accordance with the Criminal Code enacted by the Political Parliament. To take a concrete case, the Municipality might, under a statute enacted by the Social Parliament, take over all the public-houses and itself supply or refuse to supply alcoholic drink, but it could not prosecute individuals for brewing beer or distilling spirit unless such an act had been, by the Political Parliament, made an offence against the law. A Municipal Council, in fact, could exercise rights over property and rights over personal freedom only in so far as delegated to it by the legislation of one or other parliament.[1]

[1] *The Local Police Force.*—It is very desirable that the local police force should (as now in Britain outside the Metropolitan area) be administered by the Local Authority. The primary object of " the Watch " is for the prevention of crime, not merely for the arrest of criminals. Scarcely less important is the function of giving information to citizens, one that will need to be much developed. There is also the function of making enquiries of citizens, which should certainly be kept under the Local Councils. Strictly municipal, too, is the function of seeing that the local bye-laws are actually observed, and keeping order in public places, etc. A comparatively small part of the time of the police would, in fact, be taken with the actual apprehension of criminals or other work delegated to it from the Minister of Justice and the Political Parliament. But it would remain for the Minister of Justice to see that this protection of life and property to prevent infractions of the Criminal Law was carried out with efficiency by all the Local Authorities. It may be suggested that the present system of Grants in Aid under which one-half the cost of the police is met from the National Exchequer should be continued. Such Grants would be paid by the Financial Department of the Social Parliament on the precept of the Minister of Justice.

CHAPTER V

THE preceding chapter on the Reorganisation of Local Government will have shown that the gradual establishment of a Socialist Commonwealth does not imply the " nationalisation " of all industries and services—still less any simultaneous transformation of all of them together ; and also that it does not necessarily involve the " centralisation " of administration. It is equally erroneous to assume that Socialism is bound up with the compulsory organisation of citizens in " government," either national or municipal. The only essential feature in " socialisation " is that industries and services, with the instruments of production which they require, should not be " owned " by individuals, and that industrial and social administration should not be organised for the purpose of obtainng private profit. Thus, the consumers' Co-operative Movement—an emanation from the Socialist, Robert Owen, moulded into successful form by the Chartist " Rochdale Pioneers " of 1844—is nowadays rightly recognised as supplying a necessary part of the constitutional framework of the Socialist Commonwealth. As already indicated in the first chapter of Part I. of this book, voluntary associations of consumers are not confined to what is commonly included in the Co-operative Movement, but have also arisen spontaneously with other objects, from the most exclusive social club in Pall Mall to the great network of Friendly Societies among the wage-earners.

THE CO-OPERATIVE MOVEMENT

The consumers' Co-operative Movement, which already includes in Great Britain, as in several other European States, as many as one-third of all the families, first claims attention, and other voluntary associations of consumers may be dealt with subsequently. It should, however, be noted that the task of the constitution-maker must necessarily be different, in the case of these voluntary associations of consumers, from that imposed in dealing with either national or local government. The essential feature of these voluntary associations is that they are voluntary, and whilst it is useful to discuss what may be thought to be their appropriate sphere, and even to examine the constitutional conditions and public safeguards to which the public interest may require them to be subjected, their own organisation and development will necessarily depend, in the main, on the opinions and desires of those who may from time to time constitute their membership.

It will be unnecessary to repeat the description already given of the organisation in Great Britain of the consumers' Co-operative Movement, with its membership of three or four million out of the ten million families; its supplies of all household requisites, already exceeding in value two hundred million pounds annually; its own colossal growth, importation or manufacture of an ever-increasing range of these commodities; its own factories, its own farms, its own ships, its own insurance and even its own bank, run without dependence on capitalist profit or private enterprise. But great and continuous as has been the successful extension of the Co-operative Movement in Great Britain, its administration, measured by the size of the capital employed, amounts at present to no more than five or six per cent of the aggregate of British industries and services. The first enquiry must be, how extensive is the reasonably possible sphere of the consumers' Co-operative Movement in the Socialist Commonwealth ?

THE LIMITATIONS OF THE CO-OPERATIVE MOVEMENT

There are, it will be clear, certain existing limitations on its growth, which may be regarded as, for the most part, transient. At present the Co-operative Store secures the membership neither of the very poor nor of the wealthy. The sweated workers, the vast army of the casually employed, even the men and women existing on the exiguous incomes of the general labourer, find themselves for the most part, largely through the strain upon character that their irregularity of income involves, unable to take advantage of Co-operative membership. At the other end of the scale are the households of the wealthy, and even those of the professional classes, who, largely under the influence of mere class-prejudice, do not care to put up with the rough and ready service now dominated by the needs of artisan families, and are not tempted by its petty economies. With the progressive levelling up and increasing regularity of the lowest incomes—in course of being effected under the still only half-understood Policy of the National Minimum—and the steady scaling down of the higher incomes by taxation and the gradual elimination of private profit-making, which will characterise our progress towards the Socialist Commonwealth, the possible membership of the Co-operative Societies will tend steadily to become more and more nearly identical

with the whole population. The Co-operative Movement can provide whatever kind or quality of commodities and whatever refinement of service its
membership for the time being requires ; and with
a progressive diffusion among all families of all the
essentials of a civilised life ; with an ever greater
community of education, and, be it added, with the
growth of good manners among the relatively rich,
we expect to see Co-operative membership eventually
as universal as the use of the Post Office.

The question arises how far the sphere of the
Co-operative Societies should extend, not in the
distribution of commodities for domestic use, to
which there need be no necessary limit, but also in the
extraction of raw materials, the conduct of agriculture,
the manufacture of the commodities needed by the
households, their importation from other countries,
and the performance of various minor services—all
of which are now being successfully undertaken by
British Co-operative Societies, though in some cases
only to a relatively small extent, for the supply of the
needs of their own membership.

A considerable limitation is at present placed upon
Co-operative manufacture by the need of having
the most economical unit of production. There is
at present much that the Co-operative Movement
sells but does not itself manufacture, merely because
its membership consumes too small a proportion of
the output to enable it to produce that fraction as
cheaply as the manufacturers who supply the whole
market. With every approach towards universality
of membership, and complete loyalty of the members
to the Movement, this limitation, as the actual experience of the past quarter of a century abundantly
demonstrates, is to a great extent removed. We may
say at once that, without pretending to forecast the
future, we see no reason for imposing any rigid

boundaries on voluntary co-operation of this kind.
As will be hereafter indicated, there will always remain
in the Socialist Commonwealth a large, and it may
possibly be an increasing, sphere for the services, not
only of the independent practitioner in the various
professions, " calling no man master " and paid by
the separate fees of a succession of individual clients,
but also of the independent craftsman in all the
manual arts, to whom the customer of distinguished
taste or peculiar requirements may always resort. But
subject to this extensive and possibly increasing
exception, there seems no reason in the nature of
things why the various forms of consumers' Co-
operation should not, in due course, eventually provide,
for practically all the inhabitants, all the household
requisites and objects of common expenditure not
supplied by the national or municipal industries and
services. For experience has shown that no sharp
distinction can be drawn between production and
distribution ; and it would even be quite practicable,
if agriculture, mining, shipping and the manufacture
of this or that commodity were organised as national
services, to permit any consumers' Co-operative
Society, or any federation of such societies, to have
its own mines and farms, ships or factories, for the
supply of its own members, side by side with the
same services conducted by municipalities or National
Boards as already described, and even in rivalry with
these, if the members of the Co-operative Societies
thought such a course expedient. There are many
advantages, not only in the greatest possible freedom
of development in the Socialist Commonwealth, but
also in actual variety of organisation ; and, subject
to the systematic arrangements for accurate costing,
audit and publicity carried out under the supervision
of the Social Parliament (which should be made
universal on all enterprises, by whomsoever conducted),

in the widest possible emulation among the various types of democratic organisation for public objects.

It may, however, be contemplated that in certain industries and services nationalisation or municipalisation will prove to be the better form of socialisation.

In many cases the users or consumers of the service or commodity do not form a practicable constituency, apart from that of themselves as citizens, which could control the administration. The national railway service could hardly be governed by the votes of the incoherent mob of passengers who pour out of the termini of our great cities ; or the characteristic municipal services by any other membership than that of all the municipal electors. The future interests of the community are in other cases so much involved, and so largely in opposition to those of the present generation, that there is no logical reason, and even possible danger, in vesting the administration in the hands of an electorate whose attention is deliberately focussed on the immediate interests of the consumer of to-day. Thus all issues affecting the conservation of national resources—this seems to us important in the case of coal and timber—can rightfully be entrusted only to the community of citizens. Finally, there is in some cases (notably as regards the site value of land and minerals) an economic advantage to be reaped which is equitably the property of the community as a whole, and cannot justly be left to be appropriated even by a municipality, or by any other fraction of the community. On one or other of these grounds certain industries and services fall, in the Socialist Commonwealth, within the sphere of national or municipal rather than of voluntary associations of consumers. But in reality the exact line of demarcation to be drawn between voluntary and obligatory Democracies of Consumers is only of theoretic interest. It is significant that, subject to consideration of marginal cases (of which may be instanced the provision for domestic uses of coal and milk),[1] great and growing as is the development of Co-operative enterprise, it is everywhere practically non-conflicting with the parallel development of national and municipal enterprise.

But what about the export trade? The critics of the Co-operative Movement are always pointing out that the very origin and purpose of Democracies of Consumers is production for use and not for exchange, and it is to this all-important characteristic that they owe alike their practical success and their theoretical justification. That being the case, is not the Co-operative Movement, or for that matter any Democracy of Consumers, obligatory as well as voluntary, conclusively debarred from manufacturing and trading in goods to be bought and consumed, not by their own members, but by non-members inhabiting other countries, and living under other governments? Recent developments have, however, discovered that Democracies of Consumers, far from being limited to

---

[1] Enthusiastic co-operators, confronted with the problem of the present chaotic state of milk distribution, have suggested that the local Co-operative Society should take over the distribution of milk to all households within a particular area, as has been actually done successfully by the Basle Co-operative Society. But the distribution of milk, it has been contended by the advocates of the rival plan of municipalisation, is largely a public health question, so much depending on its purity, and an adequate supply being necessary, irrespective of their affluence, to the life of infants, nursing mothers and invalids. It is even urged that the service ought to be connected with the Local Authority's health clinics. An analogous suggestion with regard to the Co-operative distribution of coal is also objected to, because household coal for domestic use forms only a sixth of the whole. The Municipality, with its tramways, gasworks, schools, hospitals and other institutions, is itself one of the largest consumers of coal—the Glasgow Town Council already buys, for the use of the Municipal Departments, about as much coal as all the households in the city put together—whilst it is feared in some quarters that the requirements of another important class of consumers, the manufacturers, might be neglected by an association of consumers representing predominantly the interests of housekeeping women. It does not seem objectionable that different localities should pursue different policies in these marginal cases, in accordance with the relative popularity and efficiency of the Co-operative and the Municipal bodies. There is positive advantage in experiment in such cases.

the supply of their own members, may be found to be the one and only solution of international trade on Socialist principles, independent either of the capitalist importer or exporter, or of both of them. Thus the Co-operative Wholesale Societies of half a dozen European countries, besides themselves obtaining directly from abroad an increasing part of the supplies that they severally require, have begun to exchange with each other their surplus products or those for which they possess exceptional advantages. And during the Great War nearly all the governments themselves acted as collectivist importers on a gigantic scale, purchasing abroad—often directly from other governments—not only every kind of munitions, but also enormous quantities of metals, wool, cotton, wheat, meat and other requirements of their own people. To the extent to which either of these movements develops, the export trade of the world, conducted by capitalist merchants for private profit, will have been transformed essentially into a reciprocal exchange of imports, conducted by the paid agents of the consumers and citizens, to the exclusion of capitalist profit. There seems no reason why this demonstrably practicable " collectivisation of international trade "—in which the Co-operative Movement would play an ever-increasing part—should not become the predominant form between civilised communities. In a world in which all industry was socialised, all speculative exporting for private profit would cease : in its stead there would be reciprocal imports, organised by Democracies of Consumers for use instead of for exchange. And seeing that the Democracies of Consumers (whether they take the form of Co-operative Movements or of nationalised or municipalised industries) of one country, might become constituent members of similar bodies in all other countries, there would cease to be any production for exchange or any " profit on price." The whole world would become one vast complicated network of associations of consumers, starting from different centres, penetrating continents and traversing oceans, without exploiting for private profit either the faculties or the needs of any section of the human race.

It must, however, be contemplated that the export trade to nations not themselves adopting Socialism or Co-operation and unprovided with governments with which other governments can deal in a corporate capacity—and with it, possibly the bulk of the shipping and banking, and perhaps of the manufacture, that this export trade necessitates—will remain longest within the sphere of the private capitalist, subject to whatever conditions of control and taxation the community may find it expedient to impose.[1]

Constitutional Changes in the Co-operative Movement

With the progressive elimination of capitalist profit-making, and the frank acceptance of the principles of Socialism, the present constitution of the consumers' Co-operative Movement would naturally undergo some change. We hesitate to offer any elaborate scheme for the reform of what must remain essentially voluntary associations, but certain considerations may be suggested.

It will not be gainsaid that the British Co-operative Movement has shown itself at once more conspicuously democratic and also more completely satisfactory in the constitution of the autonomous " store " or local Co-operative Society than in those of the federal institutions of the Movement, the Co-operative Union

---

[1] The problem presented—not to Socialists only—by the evils accompanying capitalist trade with barbarous or savage races is referred to in the subsequent chapter on "The Transitional Control of Profit-making Enterprise."

and the English and Scottish Wholesale Societies.
From the standpoint of political education and of
popular control the most valuable element in the
Co-operative Movement is the local society's quarterly
meeting of members, and its directly elected Committee of Management. The regular meeting of all the
members and their special meetings for particular
purposes provide a close and continuous connection
between the management and the consumers, so that the
management gets to know the needs and aspirations of
the consumers, whilst these gain alike confidence and
control. Some difficulty arises when the membership
of the store is so numerous—in a few cases amounting
to more than 75,000—or is spread over so large an
area that the quarterly meeting either becomes too
large for the transaction of business, or fails to provide
a practical opportunity for more than an insignificant
fraction of the members. This drawback is being
overcome by the multiplication of district meetings
connected with local branches. A like difficulty has
arisen from the choice of the committee out of a very
numerous membership, when it often comes to mean
election by small cliques of persons who habitually
attend. This has been provided for in some societies
by the members of the committee, after facing the
members at a quarterly meeting, being elected by ballot
on a given day, after the fashion of a municipal election.
It is, indeed, not always easy, so long as the society's
affairs are proceeding satisfactorily, to induce any
larger proportion of the members to vote than is
customary at a municipal election ; or even to attend
the members' meetings. Hence these reforms of
the electoral machinery might well be accompanied, in
large societies, by the adoption of the German system
of a distribution of the whole membership into small
geographical blocks, with a regular house-to-house
distribution of the local Co-operative journal by a

member appointed for the purpose, who, at the same time, advertises the forthcoming meetings and asks for any complaints, so that the members may be given a genuine opportunity of expressing their desires, and also induced to take a livelier interest in the concerns of the society. It is unnecessary, however, to exaggerate the shortcomings in the working constitution of the autonomous local Co-operative Societies in Great Britain. The fact that the constituency is localised and easily accessible, and one of neighbours, themselves actually consuming the commodities which are provided, gives the Co-operative Society, so far as the supply of household requisites is concerned, no small advantage over the Town Council.

In the constitution of the federal institutions, the English and Scottish Co-operative Wholesale Societies and the Co-operative Union, the Co-operative Movement has had to rely on indirect election, the directors of both Wholesale Societies and the members of the Central Board of the Co-operative Union being elected by the committees of management of the affiliated stores or local societies. The working of these federal institutions exhibits some of the usual features of indirect election. The three or four million members constituting the rank and file who are served have, in practice, no more control over their administration than the customers of the great joint-stock companies of "multiple shops," or than the citizens of London have over the Metropolitan Asylums Board or the Port of London Authority. The very names of the governors and directors of these great institutions are unknown to the members ; and as they are practically never displaced once they have found seats on the Board, control of policy and administration by the four million co-operators themselves must be regarded as being at a minimum. By comparison, indeed, with the capitalist enterprise which it supersedes, the Co-operative Wholesale Society is effectively democratic in character. The criticisms of the members of the local societies as to the quality and price of the commodities supplied are focussed in the committees of management, and make themselves heard at the quarterly delegate meetings held simultaneously in half a dozen different cities, which are attended by the directors. The fact that the directors have, very largely, been selected from among leading administrators of local societies, and that they are not separated by any difference in social class or affluence from the members of the local committees, facilitates a useful intercourse between them. Much more detailed information as to the current administration is laid before these quarterly meetings, and more lucid statistics, than any joint-stock trading company ventures to publish to its shareholders. It would be unfair to make it a matter for blame that the Co-operative Wholesale Society—exposed as it is, to the strongest and sometimes the most embittered competition of capitalist enterprise—should think it necessary to keep its own counsel as to new projects, and to maintain a discreet silence about its business methods, its successful purchases or its occasional losses. But if we ask how far this great democratic organisation exhibits the characteristics of the ideal Democracy of popular aspiration, it is difficult to ignore the allegation that it has some of the weaknesses of an honest but somewhat impervious bureaucracy—secretiveness, a dislike of publicity, an impatience of criticism, and, it is commonly alleged, a certain amount of favouritism in appointments and promotions. All this is the more dangerous in that the whole administration is wrapped in obscurity, without the publication of salary lists, details of costing, or anything beyond a bare minimum of comparative statistics enabling the members to watch for themselves the relative expense or efficiency of the various departments. The directors of the English Co-operative Wholesale Society (and the same is true in a slightly less degree of the Scottish Co-operative Wholesale Society) habitually regard themselves as personally directing the administration as well as deciding the policy ; and though they cannot quite ignore any definite decision of the delegate meetings to which they present their reports, they claim that the right to decide executive issues, even in matters of policy, is, and must be vested in themselves, to the exclusion of the members of the affiliated local societies, who are collectively the owners of the concern.

On the other hand, the English Co-operative Wholesale Society, in particular, has evolved, in its board of directors, a piece of administrative machinery unlike anything existing elsewhere, which has proved to have notable advantages. The thirty-two directors (who are, in practice, recruited by election only at the rate of one or two a year on the occurrence of vacancies by death or retirement) do not resemble, in character and in function, either the boards of large joint-stock companies or the councils of boroughs or counties. In the first place, they are all " whole-timers," giving their entire attention to their duties as directors, for which they receive a fixed salary, of an amount negligible by a capitalist captain of industry, but sufficient, in the Co-operative Movement, to attract the ablest of its local administrators. In the second place, they are almost invariably trained for their work by long and conspicuous service in the administration of the local Co-operative Society (which may have, it must not be forgotten, an annual turnover running into hundreds of thousands of pounds, and its own manufacturing departments) either as manager, or as secretary, or as chairman of the committee of management. Belonging all to essentially the same social stratum, and nurtured in the same atmosphere of Co-operation, with much the same business experience, the members of the Wholesale Board evidently make a highly efficient committee. The Board, as a whole, meets weekly, and there are three standing committees of about a dozen members each ; but a more intimate touch is kept with the administration of the hundred different establishments, not only by sub-committees of half a dozen members, but also by each establishment being assigned to a particular director, who makes a point of visiting the place once a week, not merely to inspect, but principally for a prolonged and intimate consultation with the manager (who, as a technical expert, is often in receipt of a higher salary than the director) about the difficulties met with, the policy to be pursued and the progress of the enterprise. Decisions as to policy naturally rest with the Board, but the directors, we gather, habitually refrain from interfering with the business or technical details of any manager who retains their confidence. The personal consultations between directors and managers are supplemented by a large number of written reports, in which managers submit proposals to the committees, to the meetings of which they are frequently summoned for discussion of the new projects and of the changes of policy that are continually being made. There may be, on the Wholesale Board, no great captain of industry, no Napoleon of commerce, no administrative genius ; but these plain men, almost entirely of working-class extraction, with a formal education limited usually to that of the primary school, have managed to create, and to maintain in efficiency, an extraordinarily successful administrative organisation ; having behind it a couple of generations of continuous success, in a business now exceeding in turnover of commodities a hundred million pounds a year ; comprising a hundred different productive enterprises in a dozen different countries ; with a specially constituted Research Department, in which over fifty specialists are always at work on testing what is done and elaborating new schemes ; and an aggregate staff of 40,000 persons. What the directors contribute, besides judgment, experience and knowledge of the great community which they have to serve, is, most conspicuously, the cement that keeps all the establishments and departments together, preventing overlapping, securing mutual service and maintaining continuity of policy. We suggest that the constitution and working of this remarkable body lends some support to the proposal that, when their business becomes sufficiently large to call for all their attention, the councils directing Local Government should be made up of salaried " whole timers." We should like to see made a detailed intimate comparison, in point of efficiency of organisation of the whole complex of departments, and as to the actual services rendered by the directing council, between the English Co-operative Wholesale Society and the Municipality of Manchester or Liverpool.

The Co-operative Movement is, at present, subject to the same general supervision by the Board of Trade, and the same kind of conditions as to incorporation and registration as the capitalist trading joint-stock companies with which it competes, though it furnishes to the Chief Registrar more detailed statistics than are required by the Registrar of Joint-Stock Companies ; and a later chapter will deal with the nature and extent of the control over them that should be exercised by the Social Parliament. But as already indicated for the Municipal and other Local Authorities, the privilege might well be offered to the Co-operative Movement of developing its own federal institutions which should secure, for the local societies as well as for the Wholesales, the same degree of publicity, the same development of independent inspection, test audit and costing ; the same reports by professional experts, the same wealth of comparative statistics, throwing light on the development of every corner of the enterprise, alike as regards output, efficiency, quality and expense, in comparison with all the others, with its own past, and with analogous undertakings under different forms of organisation, as would otherwise have to be instituted in the public interest by the departments acting for the committees of the Social Parliament. It is, however, essential in the Co-operative as in the Municipal world, that any such federal departments for comparative statistics, for audit, for costing or for research and experiment should be wholly unconnected with and entirely independent of the organisations, whether local or themselves federal, upon the efficiency of which the proposed department is called upon to report. Moreover, it should always be open to any important section of Co-operators to petition the Social Parliament for a special enquiry into the methods and results of any part of the Movement, to be conducted by the national departments under the standing committee concerned.

The most serious drawback to the British Co-operative Movement at the present time is, perhaps, the complete absence, alike in the local societies and in the two Wholesales, of any machinery for the participation in the management of the extensive staff, now approaching 200,000 in number, which is employed under conditions not essentially different from those of Joint-Stock Capitalism. There may be good reasons for the customary explicit disqualification—now beginning to be waived in a few societies—of any employee being elected by the members to the Committee of Management, on which even the manager does not sit as a member. There are objections to employees canvassing the members for votes, and perhaps being tempted to do some of them small favours to the detriment of other members. It is, however, not easy to see why a Co-operative Society, and even the great Wholesales, should object to allowing a seat on the Committee of Management, not only to the principal manager, but also to a nominee or nominees of the Trade Union or Trade Unions to which its staff belongs. The Co-operative Movement needs too, it is clear, the same sort of Joint Boards for Collective Bargaining, and, it may be suggested, also the same sort of Appointment and Discipline Boards, and even of Advisory Committees of various kinds, as we have described for the national and municipal industries and services. It is, however, essential that the voluntary character of these organisations should be maintained, and, under present circumstances, it must accordingly be left to the Co-operators and Trade Unionists concerned, among whom the question is now being hotly discussed, to fight the matter out, and to effect the necessary reforms in whichever way is mutually agreed upon.[1]

OTHER VOLUNTARY ASSOCIATIONS OF CONSUMERS

As already indicated, the principle of organisation by voluntary associations of consumers has been applied in Great Britain, with success, to much more than the Co-operative Movement. We need only mention the network of mutual Building Societies, which are really analogous, as regards the one purpose of purchasing a dwelling-house, to the Co-operative Credit Societies, which have had a much less important development in this country than in Germany. Even more extensive are the various kinds of Friendly

---

[1] We shall recur to this controversy in our chapter on " The Reorganisation of the Vocational World."

Societies for mutual insurance of cash benefits during sickness, or for funeral expenses or in other emergencies, together with medical attendance, admission to hospitals and convalescent homes and other advantages. The Trade Unions themselves are, on one side, mutual benefit societies of this nature, providing also for their members a weekly payment when thrown out of employment from any cause whatsoever, insurance against loss of tools by fire, and sometimes also a superannuation allowance. Of like nature are the thousands of social clubs, organised by local societies of workmen and federated in the Club and Institute Union, which has no fewer than half a million affiliated members ; and which provides for them, among other advantages, a series of convalescent homes in different parts of Great Britain. Of the almost innumerable other societies of a similar nature we have not space to speak ; from book clubs and societies for playing every sort of game to musical societies of various kinds, from holiday clubs and societies for organising foreign tours up to groups and associations providing for their members the amenities of a country house or a joint shooting or fishing. We may include in the same general category all the innumerable societies of amateurs of special kinds of music or drama, perhaps also the various churches and chapels outside the Established Church and—though here another element enters—the societies existing for the propaganda of a particular creed or policy by their own members. The aggregate membership of all these various voluntary associations of consumers must approximate to the entire adult population ; the capital under their administration amounts to many millions, and their total annual expenditure to possibly as much as a hundred millions sterling.

It is often not understood that, far from objecting to such voluntary associations of consumers, Socialists look for a great extension of this form of organisation in the Socialist Commonwealth, facilitated by the most convenient arrangements for a simple form of registration or incorporation (which should, however, remain entirely optional), and subject, as at present, to the very minimum of legal technicalities or governmental control. In various ways such voluntary associations may be aided by the national and Local Government and actually made use of (as is already the case with Friendly Societies and Trade Unions under the National Insurance Act) as part of the constitutional machinery of governmental services. Some possible developments may be indicated.

ADULT EDUCATION

In the matter of adult education, which will certainly occupy much of the attention of the Standing Committee on Education of the Social Parliament, it may be expected that a large and ever-increasing part of the organisation will be left to voluntary associations of the scholars themselves, who are in this case the consumers, on the lines successfully laid down by the Workers' Educational Association and the various Labour Colleges. Incidentally the travelling libraries of circulating book-boxes, long organised by the Fabian Society and other agencies, will become a huge enterprise, in supplement of the national and municipal library service, bringing a continual supply of books, old and new, to readers in every corner of the kingdom.

THE FUTURE OF THE COUNTRY HOUSE

Socialists are sometimes pityingly asked by opponents what would become, in a Socialist Commonwealth, of the pleasant but expensive country houses of the wealthy. Unfortunately, the 20,000 or so of such mansions as are at present maintained out of rent, interest and profit will be far from sufficient to supply all the needs of a Socialist Commonwealth. Some of the largest of them will doubtless be maintained as convalescent homes in connection with the Local Health Authorities. Others will become colleges and residential hostels for the varied new developments of the nation's educational system. Others, again, will furnish comfortable homes for little communities of the superannuated workers without friends or relations of their own. But for the most part we look to see these pleasant residences becoming, under various forms of voluntary association, the holiday homes and recreation grounds of the urban toilers by hand or by brain. Every Trade Union, Friendly Society and Professional Association will need such accommodation for its members in every part of the kingdom. It may be foreseen that the annual and other conferences of these bodies, or of their local branches, will often be held in stately mansions taken over four hundred years ago from the religious communities, or erected from their ruins ; and since adapted, with every refined luxury, to the amenities of social life. It may be hoped that every technical college, even every group of elementary or secondary schools, will have the use of such premises for its rural excursions, and periodical holidays. A very small annual subscription, through their various voluntary associations, from all the adult workers by hand or by brain, coupled with a payment for each week's sojourn, would easily suffice for the upkeep of the premises and the maintenance of the necessary domestic staff of all the 20,000 country houses in the kingdom, as, with the gradual scaling-down of private incomes and the progressive elimination of both large wealth and an idle class, these country houses, one by one, come into the market, or are taken over by public authorities.

The Extension of Personality

It will be seen that the Socialist Commonwealth will have available, in the development of voluntary associations of consumers, independent of capitalist profit-making, opportunities for a vast and incalculable expansion of personal freedom. To this opening up of opportunities for the satisfaction of particular desires, and the initiative and variety thereby promoted, Socialists attach the greatest importance. The national industries and services—to some extent even the municipal industries and services—will naturally provide in the first place, as the Post Office does, what is required by the citizens in masses, the commoner needs of groups of substantial magnitude ; though much more may thus be conveniently done in fulfilment of special desires, sometimes for extra fees, than is usually realised. In the provision of household requisites it would be the aspiration of the various Co-operative Societies, whilst beginning with the requirements of the common run of members, to go on to respond, on terms strictly proportionate to any extra cost involved, to the demands of minorities, and even of distinctive individuals among them. There is indeed practically no demand within the range of its service, however exceptional in quality and refinement, to which the Co-operative Wholesale Society is not already, given reasonable notice, prepared to respond. But there will always be peculiar tastes and exceptional aspirations ; there will be the continuous stream of novel demands, many of them purely experimental and certainly transient ; there will be all sorts of cravings—inventive, artistic, emotional, religious, and what not—for which people will want to find expression and gratification ; above all, there will be, in Great Britain at least, an imperative desire to do whatever one feels inclined to do, and to get whatever one fancies, whether or not any of the National Boards or any of the Local Authorities or any of the Co-operative Societies has already foreseen and provided for it. We shall certainly preserve in Great Britain, whatever may be done in countries more accustomed to the " Police State," the enormously valuable principle that whatever is not expressly declared to be an offence against the law is permissible to the individual, without leave or licence from any department or official. Some legal prohibitions there must of course be, but between what is for the time being actually provided by the various forms of collectivist organisation, and what is specially prohibited by the criminal law, there will necessarily always be a considerable uncharted ocean into which individuals must be free to dive at their own peril. Socialists desire to stimulate this individual initiative, and facilitate this satisfaction of personal cravings, by preserving the utmost freedom to groups to combine in voluntary associations of consumers for any purposes not specifically prohibited by the Penal Code. Such associations, catering only for their own members, will be on the footing of the existing social clubs on a basis of mutuality ; their members may accumulate their own joint capital, jointly engage their own freely serving staffs, and supply themselves, within the wide liberties allowed by the criminal law, with whatever they desire. There need be no limit to the possible developments of this corporate extension of individual personality.

All developments of this kind will of course be watched by both the Social Parliament and the Political Parliament ; and it will be necessary, from time to time, to guard against abuses. It will need to be determined in which classes of cases registration should be required, and in which legal incorporation should be permitted. Membership may sometimes have to be restricted to adults. In some cases special provisions may be required to prevent evasion, or at least avoidance, of taxation. The Policy of the National Minimum will call for an enforcement of the standard conditions prescribed under the laws relating to public health, education, employment, etc. ; and the principle of Measurement and Publicity must be applied in these as in all other forms of social organisation. Finally, it may be observed that Parliament may possibly think fit to draw two separate boundary lines, prohibiting to capitalist profit-making the provision of some things which, even if not made the subject of national or municipal enterprise, it may allow to non-profit-seeking voluntary associations of consumers, uniting only for the supply of their own needs, especially when these (like the consumers' Co-operative Societies) remain always open to additional members without premium or limit. We get here an incidental illumination of the respective spheres of the Social and the Political Parliaments. It will be for the Social Parliament to decide what enterprises it will conduct or refuse to conduct as national services ; what municipal enterprises it will forbid ; and under what conditions or limitations either voluntary associations of consumers or the profit-making capitalist shall be permitted to engage in them. It may be imagined that the Social Parliament will always have a bias in favour of its own enterprises, and that it may sometimes be thought to be unfriendly to what it may think of as rival concerns. But the Minister of Justice, responsible to the Political Parliament, will be the guardian of personal liberty ; and it will be his duty to advise the Political Parliament whether any particular class of acts should be prohibited by being made offences under the criminal law. It will be for the Political Parliament to see that the whole expanse between national or Municipal provision on the one hand, and prohibition by the Penal Code on

the other, shall remain open for individual initiative
and associated action.

THE PROBLEM OF THE PRESS

We hazard the suggestion that here may be found
the solution, in the Socialist Commonwealth, of the
difficulty presented by the newspaper press. Although
Socialists foresee a great development of official
journals of every sort, in all the arts and sciences,
industries and services, and in different parts of the
country (published by authority, national, municipal
or co-operative, vocational or university, and often
posted gratuitously to those to whom the information
is important), probably no Socialist proposes that the
community should have nothing but an official press.
At the same time, the conduct of a newspaper with the
object of obtaining a profit—even more so the conduct
of newspapers by wealthy capitalists with the object
of influencing the public mind ; or the purchase by
such capitalists, with ulterior objects, of one newspaper after another—appears open to grave objection,
and obviously leads to very serious abuses.[1] Especially during the stage of transition from a predominantly capitalist to a predominantly Socialist society, it
may be necessary to prohibit the publication of newspapers with the object of private profit, or under
individual ownership, as positively dangerous to the
community. But this does not mean that there should
be no unofficial journals. All that would be for-

[1] A recent case in the Chancery Division of the High Court of Justice,
in which the executors of the late Lord Rhondda sued the directors of the
Western Mail, lends point to this proposal. It was complained that certain
proceedings of the directors had placed " the Rhondda interests " in the
newspaper " in a minority, and caused damage to them," estimated at
£70,000. " Lady Rhondda gave evidence, saying that her father bought
shares in a number of newspaper concerns. He did not buy them for
investment purposes, but to secure control, that being his only object. . . .
He was a strong individualist, and was desirous of obtaining publicity for
those views. She would not admit that it was to help his operations in
coal." (*Westminster Gazette*, March 17, 1920.)

bidden would be individual or joint-stock ownership and commercial profit. The greatest newspaper enterprises could be converted into consumers' Co-operative Societies, in which every purchaser, or at any rate every continuous subscriber, thereby automatically became a member, casting one vote only, periodically electing a managing committee by ballot taken through the newspaper itself ; and the managing committee exercising (with due participation in the management of the vocations concerned) entire control over the enterprise, but being required to devote any surplus of receipts over expenditure to the improvement of the newspaper itself, and being forbidden to distribute any part of it, either in dividends or in excessive salaries, or to individuals at all, otherwise than by way of reduction of the price for the future. It would certainly not be the wish of Socialists to prevent any group of readers from having (within the criminal law) any newspaper that they desired ; and the form of a consumers' Co-operative Society seems to make possible the utmost variety in independent journalism without dependence on capitalist ownership or the unwholesome stimulus of private profit. With periodicals limited to those owned, either by public authorities of one or other kind, or by consumers' Co-operative Societies—ownership by individual or joint-stock Capitalism being entirely eliminated—the transformation of journalism into an organised and largely self-governing profession, enjoying not only independence and security but also a recognised standard of qualification and training, and a professional ethic of its own, would be greatly facilitated.

THE SAFEGUARDING OF THE PUBLIC INTEREST

It will be seen that in these suggestions for Co-operative reconstruction and Co-operative expansion

no proposal has been included for any direct representation on the governing bodies of these voluntary
Democracies of Consumers, of the community as a
whole, or of men and women as citizens. As already
implied, the reason for this omission is that these
voluntary associations of consumers will not own
instruments of production which are of unique value
to the community, or which cannot be replaced ;
they freely admit additional members without premium ; they will not have a legal monopoly of any
trade or service, and the services which they will
administer will not be such as to involve issues of
policy on which there will be a cleavage of interests
between this generation of consumers and the permanent
welfare of the community, or the interests of future
generations. But it goes without saying that if an
association of consumers were to be given a monopoly,
or were to be charged with a service of public rather
than individual importance, some provision would
have to be made for the inclusion in the committee of
management of representatives of the community of
citizens—probably on the nomination of the Local
Authority for the same district. For the rest we rely
on the enforcement of the " National Minimum "
conditions of employment, education, public health
and public amenity ; on participation in the direction
of the service by the vocational organisations concerned,
and last, but not least, on the full and continuous
application of the principle of Measurement and
Publicity, by the Social Parliament, through its
standing committees and central departments.

CHAPTER VI

THE REORGANISATION OF THE VOCATIONAL WORLD

In the foregoing proposals for the reconstruction of the national Government and the administration of the nationalised industries and services ; for the reorganisation of Local Government, with its municipalised industries and services, and for the progressive development of the sphere of voluntary Democracies of Consumers, we have attempted to forecast, in some detail, the participation in the administration of all these industries and services of the workers by hand and by brain. But this necessarily disjointed description of the sphere of the Democracies of Producers as part and parcel of the various types of socialised administration, has given no vision of vocational organisation considered as a whole—as a world by itself, with its own laws of life, its own scope for the enlargement of human personality, and its own sphere for the development of faculty and satisfaction of desire. On what basis will the several vocations be organised in the Socialist Commonwealth ? How will one vocation be marked off from another ? By what method will each vocation be recruited ? What provision will be made for the rise of new vocations due to the emergence in a progressive humanity of new faculties and desires ? By what means shall we secure the necessary elasticity among the vocations, the desirable freedom of migration from one to another ?

What will be the character of the activities of vocational organisation ? And, finally, will there be, as part of the constitution of the Socialist Commonwealth, a national assembly based on a vocational franchise and co-ordinated with the Political and Social Parliaments ?

THE TRADE UNION MOVEMENT AS THE ORGAN OF REVOLT AGAINST THE CAPITALIST SYSTEM

Let us first clear away from the field of controversy a possible misunderstanding. In this chapter we shall discuss, not the immediately urgent question of a successful struggle with a dominant Capitalist System, but the structure and function of vocational organisation in a society that has become predominantly Socialist in character. Under the present Dictatorship of the Capitalist the community is divided into two warring sections, the nation of the rich and the nation of the poor. On the one hand are the few hundred thousand men and women who own or who organise the bulk of the land and capital of the country, who take for their income more than one-half of the entire national product, and who are now combining for the protection of their privileged position. On the other hand is the " class-conscious proletariat " of those who have to depend for their livelihood on wages and small salaries, amounting in the aggregate to less than one-half of the national product, who are now increasingly enrolling themselves in the Trade Union Movement as the organ of revolt against the existing order of society. This sharp division of our community into a party of the " haves " and a party of the " have nots " (a division defiantly proclaimed in this very year 1920 by the present Prime Minister in his appeal to all property owners, whether Conservative or Liberal, to combine against the Labour Party) has been immensely emphasised by the Great War. The sudden and awful searchlight thrown on the Capitalist System by the war itself, and by the nature of the peace which has succeeded it, has revealed to the great mass of manual workers the essentially predatory character of the Capitalist State. The minor brain workers — minor not in capacity or training, or in the social value of their service, but in their exiguous incomes and semi-servile position — the clerks, the teachers, the lower grades of public officials and professional men—are slowly but surely perceiving that if they are to maintain even their pre-war standard of life and liberty they will have, for the struggle, to throw in their lot with the manual workers. This state of war, a war not less real because it is carried on by passive resistance, by periodical stoppages of production by employers or by the employed, and by a chronic refusal on both sides to serve the community to the best of their ability when this seems to conflict with their private gain, is distorting to an ever greater degree the structure and function of society ; not of the political government alone, but also of capitalist enterprise, and of the political and industrial organisation of the manual working class. For the purpose of a successful struggle against capitalist dictatorship in the workshop, in the public press, in electoral organisation, in Parliament and in the Cabinet itself, it naturally seems of vital importance to generate, among the manual workers and the allied brain workers, the most extended and intense class consciousness. This class consciousness, it has been urged by the technicians of revolution, emerges most easily in the workshop, where men and women toil in concert day by day for so large a part of their waking life. It is best accumulated and strengthened by combining all the workers in each industry, and in all industries, in gigantic amalgamations or federations. We need not here enquire whether this subordination of all the separate interests and aspirations of innumerable vocations in one disciplined army will be most rapidly and effectively carried out by the formation of strictly demarcated and all-inclusive unions of all the persons employed in the several " industries," or in all the enterprises of united groups of employers ; or by huge amalgamations of labourers on the one hand, and of skilled mechanics on the other ; or by federations of autonomous unions, such as the Triple Alliance or the Transport Workers' Federation ; or by the larger federation of a reorganised Trades Union Congress with a " general staff," in close connection with an equally disciplined political Labour Party. Broadly speaking, what is desirable for the battle with Capitalism, whether fought on the industrial or on the political field, may well be " one big Union," so organised and so directed that the whole of the manual working class and the whole of the allied brain workers may move at one time with one will, and for one purpose. The more homogeneous and the more highly disciplined the force, the quicker and more complete may well be the victory.

Now, it would be misleading to press unduly the analogy between a war between races and a war between classes. But the world has been taught by bitter experience that an organisation devised for carrying on war to the bitter end of victory or defeat does not teach us, in fact tends to disable us from learning, how best to organise society if the purpose be not fighting but co-operation ; not uniform discipline, but diversified freedom ; not identity of faculties and desires, but the utmost range in variety from group to group ; not repression of individuality in the battle between one herd of human beings and another, but the largest enjoyment for each citizen of the widest possible personal liberty. It follows that, in an attempt to forecast the vocational organisation of a Socialist Commonwealth, we must rid our minds of battle cries and turn our backs on battle formations. In a society in which all adults will be workers so long as fulness of health and strength lasts, and in which all will have equal chances, from birth to death, of enjoying a civilised existence, there will be no room, so the Socialists recognise, for class consciousness and the class struggle.

With this foreword we sweep out of our conception of vocational organisation in a predominantly Socialist Commonwealth all the unlovely requirements, all the inevitable distortions of the class struggle of to-day. We start on our quest of the laws of life that will govern vocational organisation in the future, with two clues—two dominant principles of social expediency —the right of self-determination for each vocation, and the right of free enterprise for every type of socialised administration.

The Right of Self-Determination for each Vocation

Let us interpret the principle of free association in its application to vocational organisation. The spirit of corporate freedom that struggled for expression in the mediaeval guilds of craftsmen, and that was seen at work in the courts and companies, ancient and modern, of the learned professions, as in the colleges and faculties of universities in all countries, has always assumed the form of a continuous and an insistent demand, on the part of groups of persons who feel that they possess a common craft or mystery, a common art or science, that they should be allowed, unhampered by other sections of the community, to determine the conditions under which they render their peculiar social service. These specialised groups feel that they have an inherent right to define, not only the material circumstances of their work, but also how best they can perfect their art or extend their knowledge. Moreover, they feel themselves to be, as a corporate entity, peculiarly fitted to participate in the determination of the nation's policy, so far as their special subjects are concerned. The final cause of vocational organisation, as distinguished from the organisation of citizens and even that of members of the Co-operative Movement, is not the promotion of objects which all men, or most men, have in common, but, on the contrary, the promotion of exactly those characteristics and purposes which differentiate a particular group of workers from the general body. That is to say, vocational organisation is, in the most literal meaning of the term, functional.

WHAT CONSTITUTES A VOCATION

The practical bearing of this conception of the origin and purpose of vocational organisation—once the community is free from the class struggle against capitalist dictatorship—lies in the fact that, when freedom of association is permitted, men and women will spontaneously form groups on the basis of a common technique and the fulfilment of a special type of social function. In each of these groups it will be a matter of secondary importance to its members whether they find themselves at work in the administration of a National Board or of a department of Municipal Government, or of one of the innumerable voluntary Democracies of Consumers ; or, indeed, whether they are employed by some remnant of capitalist enterprise, or are working as individual producers, supplying the needs of individual clients. The bond that will unite them in their vocational organisation will be the complex of needs and desires, faculties and aspirations

which men and women pursuing the same calling feel
that they have in common. It is exactly this specialised
complex that distinguishes them from the rest of their
fellow-citizens, even in their own town ; whilst the
same complex actually unites them with persons of the
same calling belonging to other races or at work in
other countries. It is through the intensification of this
tie of a specialised vocation, knowing no geographical
limits, that man as a producer gains the maximum
freedom to express his personality in production.
On the other hand, any attempt to merge in a single
Democracy of Producers, defined otherwise than by
vocation, men and women who belong to different
vocations, having different needs and desires and
different faculties and aspirations, will lessen alike the
quantity and the quality of their control over their
peculiar calling. For example, the professional self-
determination of the trained nurse is not developed
by the inclusion of nurses in a vocational organisation
dominated by doctors and dentists ; nor would the
professional self-government of medical men be increased by their inclusion in a single Democracy of
all the workers in a National or Local Health Service,
in which the nurses and hospital attendants, the
sanitary inspectors and the sewer-men would form a
majority. In like manner the self-expression of the
carpenters and joiners, or of the skilled engineering
craftsmen, or of the boilermakers, would not be promoted by their being all included in an organisation
of all those engaged in the shipbuilding industry, in
which the conditions under which they exercise their
several crafts would be partly determined by shipyard
labourers and warehousemen, clerks and typists, naval
architects and draughtsmen, or any combination of these.
Any control that the teachers may win over the curriculum of the schools, the size of the classes that they
instruct or the methods of their teaching, would be

nullified by compelling them to gain the consent, in every step of this professional self-determination, of the school caretakers and school attendance officers, of the school nurses and the school doctors, or of the clerks in the offices of the Local Education Authority, all of whom are equally workers in the school service. Hence, whatever arguments may be found in favour of a large and inclusive organisation for the purposes of the class struggle, or in resistance to the capitalist, it does not seem that the essential purpose of vocational self-government will be promoted by any form of organisation that includes in one and the same body masses of men and women of different callings, whose functions in social service are almost as varied and multifarious as those of the whole body of citizens. Each vocation or calling must stand on its own feet and retain its own autonomy.[1]

THE RIGHT OF FREE ENTERPRISE FOR SOCIALISED ADMINISTRATIONS

But in asserting the claim of each vocational group to its own freedom of self-determination, we must not forget that there is also another freedom that Socialists seek to maximise—that of citizen and consumer to determine how he will satisfy his varied and constantly changing needs and desires, and by what measures he will safeguard the future of his community. Thus, whilst provision must be made for freedom in self-determination for each vocational group, provision must equally be made for freedom in self-determination of each communal organ. It is plain that the

---

[1] This does not of course exclude the possibility of federations of allied vocations, which may or may not coincide with " industries " or " services," or with Co-operative, Municipal or national administrations, for any purposes that they may feel themselves to have in common ; nor yet that of temporary and shifting alliances among vocations for particular objects, referred to at the end of this chapter.

community, in its Social Parliament and the administrative boards of the nationalised industries, the
Local Authorities and the voluntary Democracies of
Consumers, must be free (subject, of course, to the
criminal law and to the due application of the Policy
of the National Minimum, and also to the participation
of the workers by hand and by brain in the management of their services already outlined) to extend and
to vary its several enterprises in any direction that
seems desirable. The exercise of this freedom in the
organisation of industries and services will necessarily
involve a wide scope for what has been called by the
economists " the integration of processes." There is
no finality, and indeed but little stability, in the way
that industries and services happen at the moment
to be grouped for purposes of administration. For
example, the Standing Committee of the Social Parliament and the National Board for Transport must
certainly be free to set up hotels, to run omnibuses and
steamers and motor-lorry services radiating from any
railway station or harbour ; to provide not only wait-
ing-rooms, but also baths and restaurants ; to publish
time-tables, guide-books and other literature suitable
for travellers, and, in short, to engage in any other
enterprise that from time to time may be found to be
convenient for the fullest development of transport.
In like manner the Local Authorities should be free
to provide not only individual homes but also various
types of communal homes, including, therefore, restaurants and hotels ; local systems of transport by land,
water and air, with all their appurtenances ; every
description of education and recreation, of medical
and mental treatment, and any factories for the supply
of any commodities or services which it needs in its
work, or for which it sees a demand among its citizens.
Similarly, any voluntary Democracy of Consumers,
whether or not included in the federal institutions of

the Co-operative Movement, will be equally free to carry on, for its own members, any form of production or distribution, in which it chooses to engage, whether what its members thus seek to provide be some highly specialised means of transport, some peculiar kind of housing, some particular form of recreation, some special brand of food or clothing, or some new form of light or heating. We see no reason why federations of municipal authorities should not undertake their own banking and finance, as the federations of Co-operative Societies already do ; why they should not send their buyers into other countries to purchase anything they require, as Co-operative Societies so successfully do ; or, for that matter, why they should not sell their produce to the municipal and Co-operative federations of other nations. Common sense and the automatic check of expense will of course limit any such wild orgy of experiments—a form of dissipation of productive energies which is not usually made a matter of reproach to socialised enterprise—in the direction of pushing to the point of waste this emulation among the various types of socialised administration ; and any such experiments will have to be conducted under the laws and bye-laws already referred to, prohibiting any positive misuse of the instruments of production or the deterioration of the mental or physical environment of the citizens. Why we here emphasise this freedom of all types of socialised administration is to lay bare the fact that each of these administrations will necessarily have to deal not with one vocation only, or even with any unchanging group of vocations, but with each separate vocation that it will find engaged in the new service, or the production of the new commodity, which comes thus to be undertaken in some new connection. We must accordingly visualise the principal vocational organisations, and perhaps the great majority of all of them, finding themselves participating in the management, not only of one, but of all the various forms of socialised industry. For instance, it is clear that civil, mechanical and electrical engineers, medical men, librarians, scientific technicians of every description, accountants and auditors, and craftsmen of every kind and sort, will be engaged alike by the National Boards, by the Local Authorities and by the innumerable voluntary Democracies of Consumers, according to the particular service or commodity that it is their vocation to produce, irrespective of the form of communal administration by which it may be directed. The vocation, in short, cuts across, not only all geographical, but also all administrative boundaries.

VOCATIONAL ORGANISATION AS A STRATIFIED DEMOCRACY

This vision of an endless series of Democracies of Producers as a stratification of persons according to the particular specialisation of their productive faculties — a stratification running right across the vertical divisions among citizens and consumers according to their position on the earth's surface, and penetrating to one community after another, even into the utmost recesses of semi-barbarous countries, varying its intimate character according to the civilisations through which it passes—raises the question of the lateral boundaries between vocations. How rigid will these boundaries be ? By whom will they be determined ?

(a) QUALIFICATION FOR EMPLOYMENT

It may be assumed at once that the Socialist Commonwealth will recognise no claim to entrance into a vocation, still less to monopoly of a vocation, based on royal grant or other personal privilege, on favouritism or jobbery, or on heredity or patrimony. The only justification for a claim to enter any vocation can be the public need for the service and the producer's capacity to render it. It is interesting to speculate how far it will be found expedient in the public interest to require of every aspirant some prescribed test of capacity, by way of qualification for entrance. One of the most attractive features of the mediæval guild was the guarantee of skilled craftsmanship assumed to be given, not only by the enforcement of apprenticeship, but also by the requirement of a masterpiece, as a condition of admission to the privileges of the craft. In the modern world the old professions of law and medicine have managed to retain for themselves an absolutely precise line of demarcation between those who are legally qualified to practise and those who are not ; and the newer brain-working vocations mostly aspire to a similarly authoritative registration of qualified practitioners. Even among the manual workers the old qualification of a prolonged apprenticeship during youth lingers in many crafts, though it finds its sanction no longer in law, but in the rules of some Trade Unions and in the workshop customs of particular localities. Meanwhile other groups of manual workers, like the plumbers and the enginemen, are asking for the more modern test of certification after an examination in technical proficiency. Yet another device is suggested by the example of various branches and grades of the public service, which have, for nearly half a century, been recruited on the basis, not of a qualifying examination, but of the far more searching and restrictive test of an open competitive examination for a prescribed number of vacancies.

Now it would be, in our present state of knowledge, the height of unwisdom to dogmatise as to the devices by which the Socialist Commonwealth would define either the boundaries of the vocations or the conditions of their membership. But the world has enough experience to foresee that some tests and qualifications there must be for particular occupations. There can be no effective self-determination for any vocation without some organisation of its practitioners ; and the first condition of effective organisation is an exact identification of the persons to be organised. It is accordingly unlikely that the rule and practice will be universal that any person, however technically unqualified, may at any time enter upon any occupation that he chooses ; or that any administrative authority, individual or corporate, may engage any person for any service. It is equally apparent that the decision as to who shall be permitted to enter a vocation, or the exact character of the qualifications to be insisted on, cannot properly be entrusted to the final and exclusive arbitrament of any organisation of the existing practitioners. The existing body of medical men cannot safely be given a completely free hand to prescribe the curriculum for medical education, to determine the examination or other tests, or to select the recruits who shall be allowed to practise ; because this would enable the present generation of doctors to limit the numbers ; to stereotype the professional attainments at what was customary when they themselves were trained ; and by requiring an unnecessarily expensive schooling, even to set up a class monopoly of the profession. Nor could the teachers be permitted to settle, as they might choose, the vexed question of whether technical subjects, such as engineering or accountancy, should be taught by trained teachers having some acquaintance with the subject, or by expert technicians with a gift for teaching.[1]

---

[1] " There arises the fundamental question not yet authoritatively settled, whether the instructor in a particular speciality should normally be drawn from the ranks of skilled executants, and taught how to teach, or recruited from among trained teachers, and practised in the subject. This draws in its train the secondary problem of how the curriculum, or the

These considerations point to the tests of competency, where such tests are required as a condition of employment or independent practice, being framed and administered by Joint Boards, including expert representatives of (*a*) the existing body of practitioners; (*b*) those engaged in teaching the aspirants to the profession; and (*c*) the Co-operative, Municipal or national administrations employing the practitioners. We may visualise these Joint Boards working under the searchlights of Measurement and Publicity, emanating not only from the statistical departments, but also from the research laboratories of the psychologists and biometrical workers, engaged on the investigation of all possible methods of discovering and testing human character and capacity. But besides such obligatory testing as may from time to time be prescribed for particular vocations, there would of course continue to be optional tests and distinctions, of higher or more specialised grade, which may be left to be independently organised by the universities or by the vocational scientific societies or Subject Associations, or by such general bodies as the Royal Society itself—tests and distinctions which will carry only such weight as public opinion may concede to them, and which may or may not be insisted on as qualifications for particular appointments.

---

syllabus of instruction in the subject, should be drawn up. In the realms of elementary and secondary education the struggle on this point is a simple one; the issue is between those rendering the service, who think they know how it can be best done, and those representing the community needing the service, who think they must determine what is required. In the realm of the specialist teacher this struggle tends to be a triple one—the skilled executants and the skilled teachers both arguing before the representatives of the community in favour of their respective claims to delimit the speciality and dictate the method of instruction." (*The New Statesman* : Supplement on *English Teachers and their Professional Organisation*, by S. and B. Webb, Part II., Oct. 2, 1915, p. 13.)

(b) The Rise of New Vocations

So much for vocations that already exist and have already secured the recognition of their right to self-determination. But our experience of the last century has proved that, with the perpetual emergence of new needs and faculties, the progress of invention and the continuous development of science and art, there will arise new groups of men and women, having in common a new complex of faculties, aspirations and functional needs, and claiming for their own members the right to vocational self-determination. Indeed, it must not be ignored that one of the advantages of the era of the free enterprise of the profit-maker, relatively to periods of history dominated by vocational organisation (as, for instance, the caste system of India or the gild system of the Middle Ages), was exactly this progressive differentiation of human faculty shown in the rise of new specialisations. As examples, may be cited the emergence of the pharmaceutical chemists, who secured their emancipation from the medical profession in 1844, and the upgrowth of such completely new types of human faculty, grouping themselves in institutes and societies, as the actuaries, the accountants, the quantity surveyors, the sanitary inspectors, the trained nurses and, as a revival of the most ancient of all vocations, the midwives; whilst even more modern specialities in all the sciences, various types of municipal experts, managers and secretaries, and particular grades of civil servants, are now organising themselves independently to resist the Dictatorship of the Capitalist or the bureaucratic autocracy of governmental institutions. Hence, in the Socialist Commonwealth, there must be some machinery for the prompt recognition of new vocations. This is all the more necessary if existing vocations, whether manual workers or brain workers, are to be given any effective measure of self-government in the determination of their conditions of employment and the character of their service. For it must always be remembered that the main toxin developed by the self-government of an existing body of practitioners is its dislike of heterodoxy—its fear of the new generation knocking at the door and claiming to carry on the old service in some other way, by new processes, by new machinery, or even by new types of human talent and training. It is the realisation of this inveterate tendency to a scientific or an industrial conservatism among each successive generation of a vocational organisation—one of the most pregnant facts of Sociology—that makes it imperative to refuse to concede to any group of producers the complete control of the instruments of production with which they work, or unfettered power to organise their industry or service in the way that happens to suit the undeveloped technique of the main body of existing practitioners. But this does not mean that, in any revolution of mechanical processes, or in any new application of science, or in the development of any new art, or in the satisfaction of any new needs or desires, the "established expectations" of any old vocation should be ignored. On the contrary, in the new social order aimed at by Socialists, as was proposed in vain by John Stuart Mill three-quarters of a century ago, one of the first obligations to be recognised will be that of taking generously into consideration the claims of workers of every grade whose services are, in the public interest, superseded by new developments of technique—either by patiently teaching them at the public expense the new methods and processes, or by enabling them to transfer to new fields of work, or by a generous superannuation. The practitioner whose technique has been superseded will receive at least as much consideration as the citizen whose "property rights" are held to be no longer consistent with the

public welfare. At present there is no such consideration shown for the sufferers by industrial revolutions,
small or great ; and equally no provision for the recognition of the emergence of new vocations, it being
assumed that, in a predominantly capitalist society the
employer should be free to exploit and the worker to be
exploited. But even to-day there is, in the lobbies of
Parliament, perpetual intrigue on the part of old vocations to prevent the emergence of new vocations, or on
the part of the new vocations to secure the right to
public employment at the cost of the old vocations ; an
intrigue which results in casually passed statutes sub-
ordinating one vocation to another (for instance, the
dentists, the midwives and the trained nurses to the
medical profession), and in stealthy clauses of other
statutes which give to certain favoured institutes or
societies a monopoly of government posts.[1] In the
Socialist Commonwealth there will have to be some
disinterested and impartial authority, which cannot
therefore spring from either the older or newer vocation, charged to discover and determine under what
conditions any particular group of workers claiming to
have a specialised technique and specialised vocational
needs may liberate itself, as a group, from the jurisdiction of other professionals, and set up for itself as a

---

[1] " A legal monopoly of practice may be given without any statutory
registration of the profession. The two leading societies of public
accountants of England and Wales, the ' Chartered ' and the ' Incorporated '—together with the ' Chartered ' Societies of Scotland and Ireland
respectively—have managed to get clauses inserted in various Acts of
Parliament, both public and private, confining certain appointments (such
as auditors), in particular enterprises of public character or joint-stock companies, to members of these particular voluntary societies. And passing
from law to administration, the great Institutes of Engineers have latterly
come to exercise great influence in favour of a monopoly for their own
members in the appointments to important engineering posts, whilst during
the war the recognition by the Government of these great Institutes in the
selection of men for commissions in the Army and places in munition works
is virtually handing over to the members, associates, or students of these
Institutes the monopoly of certain grades of engineering." (*Professional
Associations*, Supplement of *The New Statesman*, by S. and B. Webb,
April 28, 1917, p. 43.)

new corporate entity, to exercise for itself its own share or participation in the administration of the particular industry or service in which its members are concerned.

(c) How will each Vocation be recruited ?

The actual recruiting, year by year, of each industry or service, as distinguished from the testing or registration of those who desire to join it, needs further consideration. It cannot be assumed that any young man or woman has any right to employment in the particular occupation that he or she may prefer ; or that all those who qualify will be taken on, still less that they will be chosen for the particular posts to which they may aspire. It must clearly be the community's needs that will decide. Approximately how many vacancies may be expected in each branch of industry or public service, in comparison with the number in previous years, will be published by the Department of Employment into which the present Ministry of Labour will develop ; and this information will be supplemented by similar approximate statistics in each locality, which will be always under the consideration of the Local Education Authority. Each administration, local, national or co-operative, will, from time to time, announce publicly the number and character of the new appointments that it proposes to make ; and then proceed to select, from among those who apply, the persons who, possessing any minimum qualifications that may have been prescribed, are judged, after the most effective examination or other tests that can be devised, to be the most competent for the particular service required. The unsuccessful candidates will simply have to apply for vacancies in some other service.[1] There seems no objection to any

[1] We cannot here discuss with the Malthusians " the Population Question " (see Fabian Tract No. 131, *The Decline in the Birth Rate*); but it

number of persons obtaining a legal qualification to practise, at their own risk of obtaining employment or gaining clients. There would indeed be many advantages in every competent citizen voluntarily qualifying himself in more than one occupation, notably in every brain-working professional becoming proficient also in a manual craft, and every craftsman obtaining some intellectual qualifications. Moreover, there are some posts (such as that of Coroner) which are best filled by persons with double qualifications.

The most exhilarating vision of Democracy is, in fact, not that of a drab uniformity either of faculties and desires, or of education and qualifications, but one of an infinite divergence of line and colour, with a constantly increasing number of specialisations and experimental variations. One of the social values of vocational, as compared with communal, " self-deter-mination " is exactly this sorting out of men and women into distinct groups in such a way that varieties in productive faculty are multiplied and heightened by fellowship in thought and action. Nor is this confined to what are commonly thought of as the brain-working professions. It is a mistake to assume that the manual working crafts, which have their own infinite variety in specialisation, demand no intellectual qualifications. On the contrary, they will be increasingly combined with mental training. It is plain that no self-respect-ing Commonwealth will allow such a degradation of its citizens as is implied in the perpetual lifelong repetition of an exclusively mechanical operation.

---

is clear that any problem that arises, whether of excess of population or of deficiency, is not one to be dealt with by any one industrial administration. Any such problem will need to be grappled with by the Social Parliament acting for the community as a whole. For the prevention of unemployment, which will be part of the functions of the Employment Department (the present Ministry of Labour) under its own Standing Committee see *The Prevention of Destitution* by S. and B. Webb, ch. vi., " How to Prevent Unemployment and Under-employment "; and the Labour Party's detailed Unemployment Bill, introduced into Parliament in 1912, 1913, 1914, 1920, etc.

Thus the ideal of the Socialist Commonwealth will be the progressive assimilation of the " nation of the poor " with the " nation of the rich," the abolition of all class-distinction based on pecuniary means, and even the obliteration of any fundamental cleavage between the brain-working professions and the manual working crafts. All occupations call, in different measure, for both muscular dexterity and intellectual skill ; and both these need to be developed to the utmost. In particular, the contemptuously regarded mass of " unskilled " or general labourers will cease to exist as such. With an educational system keenly intent on developing all the faculties of all the students, irrespective of the wealth or social position of their parents ; and on supplying to each of them all the training for which he or she proves himself fit, the minimum level of attainments—now represented by little more than elementary reading, writing and arithmetic — will not only be greatly raised, but will also be of considerably greater range. Practically all the young men and women—apart from the mentally deficient—will be found to possess the minimum requirements for many kinds of work. And it will be part of the obligation of each vocation, from the highest down to the simplest, to see to it, not merely that the candidates are suited to the work, but also that the work is suited to the candidates. The conditions of employment should be such as to permit not only of the worker's progressive development in character as a citizen, but also of his progressive increase of capacity as a producer. Even if, when he begins as a youth, his occupation at the outset may fairly be regarded as unskilled, there will be something wrong in the organisation if, after five or ten years, he has not become at least so far proficient in some specialisation as to have greatly added to his productive capacity.

(*d*) The Relative Position of Obligatory and Voluntary Organisation in a Vocation

The question arises, how far will the organisation of each vocation be dependent on the universal and obligatory registration of the persons legally ntitled to exercise the vocation, in so far as this may be adopted, and how far upon the voluntary association of members of each vocation in a Trade Union or Professional Society? It is undesirable to dogmatise on such a point. But it seems to us that obligatory registration and voluntary organisation will co-exist; and that the former will be employed for what may be called the organ of government, whilst the latter will be the basis of the organ of innovation or of revolt. Thus, assuming that the principle of registration and prescribed qualification spreads, as we anticipate, to one vocation after another, it will be the registered practitioners as such who will elect representatives of the vocation to any statutorily authorised national bodies determining the qualification, the methods of training to be prescribed, and the keeping of the vocational register. Assuming that it comes about that all the various kinds of workers employed have attained this high stage of vocational registration, it might possibly be the duty of all the registered practitioners of these vocations to elect the vocational representatives on the National Board administering a nationalised industry or service. In like manner, in the sphere of Local Government, and in that of the Co-operative Movement, it might, in such cases, be the registered practitioners of the locality or of the department who should be asked to elect the representatives of the vocation on the bodies conducting the management. But, in all these cases, of course, so long as the vocations concerned are not completely registered, the vocational representation, national or local, must spring from the voluntary organisation, whether Trade Union or Professional Society. Moreover, even when a vocation is registered, and confined to persons with prescribed qualifications, it will remain the function of voluntary associations arising within the vocation to maintain and improve, by negotiation and suggestion, the conditions of employment and the technique of the occupation. It seems to us essential, however much the vocation may participate in administration, that it should maintain also an independent organisation of initiative and defence. Accordingly, the vocational representatives on the Joint Boards for negotiating the conditions of employment would naturally be the nominees, not of all the registered practitioners of the vocation, but of the Trade Union or Professional Society. In like manner it would be the " Subject Association," or scientific society of the vocation, who would presumably be asked to nominate representatives to Advisory Committees or other bodies concerned with improvements in administrative or scientific technique. Thus, in the medical profession to-day, it is the registered practitioners themselves (and not any voluntary association of them) who elect representatives to the Local Medical Committee, and the Local Insurance Committee that administer the National Insurance Act ; and (together with others) to the General Medical Council, which keeps the register, prescribes the curriculum and determines the qualifications. A more difficult question is that involved in the formulation of the code of professional ethics. It is the General Medical Council which determines what shall be regarded as " infamous conduct," to be punished by exclusion from the profession. On the other hand, the British Medical Association, and other voluntary bodies within the profession, not only meet the administrators of medical services for negotiation of the conditions of employment, but also formulate their own views of professional ethics, which they can enforce only by any extra-legal sanction that their members are willing to support. This seems to suggest the proper line of demarcation. In any industry or service so highly organised as to have all the practitioners in all the vocations concerned authoritatively registered, any obligation which is to be authoritatively imposed and legally enforced, should emanate from an authoritatively established body, on which the vocations will be represented by persons elected by all the registered practitioners. In so far as this obligation involves the creation of a punishable offence, and thus interferes not only with the rights of persons outside the vocation but also with the personal freedom of the would-be practitioner, it would, under the constitution that we propose, require the sanction of the Minister of Justice responsible to the Political Parliament. At the same time, it would be open to any voluntary association of the vocation to make any additional rules and pursue any policy—assuming this to involve no infringement either of the criminal law or of other persons' legally recognised private rights—that might seem to the members of such an association desirable.

(e) THE FUNCTION OF VOCATIONAL ORGANISATION

It is possible at this point to summarise the activities of this highly diversified and all-pervading vocational organisation, some of it obligatory on the practitioners and some of it optional to them, by which each craft or profession can participate in the control of its own working conditions, and develop its own particular service to the community. How will these activities differ from the activities of the Trade Union and Professional Society of to-day? Foremost in the thoughts of the common run of those engaged in the vocation will be the election of representatives on the various boards, joint committees, district committees of the socialised administrations, whether these be of nationalised industries and services, of municipal industries or services, of voluntary Democracies of Consumers, or of such capitalist enterprise as may at any particular time survive.

How will pay be determined ? It may be foreseen that the question of the material conditions of employment, which now looms large as the main issue, not only among the manual workers but also among the medical men and the teachers, and other brain-working professionals, will not be so absorbing in the Socialist Commonwealth as it is under the Dictatorship of the Capitalist, with its inevitable division of the community into a nation of the rich and a nation of the poor. There will be an assumption of the principle of substantial equality—not necessarily any pedantic identity—of income and material circumstances among all sections of citizens, though differences in the functional needs of this or that vocation, from the typist to the Local Councillor, from the craftsman to the Prime Minister, will require a certain measure of inequality in the allowance for functional expenses, the hours of labour, the accommodation for work or residence and the provision of holidays.[1] All this will be the subject of enquiry and of report to the administrations and the vocations concerned by the Department of Employment under the Social Parliament, into which the present Ministry of Labour may be expected to develop. The Education Department may call attention to injurious effects on training, the Health Department to adverse results in the way of

---

[1] An analysis of the principles on which rates of pay should be fixed, as well as those which should decide the vexed question of sex differences, will be found in the Minority Report of the War Cabinet Committee on Women in Industry; largely reproduced in *Men's and Women's Wages—Should they be Equal?* by Mrs. Sidney Webb, 1919.

health, and even the Productivity Department to improvements in productivity that an alteration of conditions might produce. There will even need to be variations in the attractiveness of the employment offered by the various administrations of diverse types, merely in order to maintain a due adjustment between the number of vacancies that the needs of each service require to be filled, and the number of persons who press forward to enter it—an adjustment that may be made mainly by alterations in the attractiveness of each service in the way of conditions of work, hours of labour, provision for holidays, exceptional privileges of one or other kind, and allowance for functional expenses, much more than by mere changes in the rates of remuneration, though such variations (subject always to the basic standard set by the Policy of the National Minimum) need not be absolutely excluded. Whatever may be required in times of national peril, voluntary service will certainly be the rule, in all occupations and all grades. Hence, wherever there was found to be any shortage in the supply of candidates for appointment, in comparison with the vacancies, the occupation would necessarily have to be made more attractive, relatively to other occupations. All this would be the work of negotiation and conference in the committees representing the several vocations and the administrations of the services concerned.

The right to strike—that is to say, of concerted refusal to renew contracts of service—could not be denied to a vocation, any more than the right to suspend the service if it became too onerous could be withheld from any administration. It is, we think, highly improbable that matters would often come to such a pass. Once the community starts from an assumption of substantial equality, the relative conditions of employment between one vocation and another will be determined by public opinion, on the basis of the facts made known by Measurement and Publicity ; and any attempt to make use of a position of economic advantage possessed by any section of producers will be fought down, not by the method of political suppression but by the more natural expedient of public disapproval and, in the last resort, of a similar withdrawal of service on the part of other sections of producers. In the Socialist Commonwealth the legitimate retort to " Direct Action " is " Direct Action." Should the miners refuse to hew coal, the other crafts, if after reports from all concerned and widespread publicity they think the miners unreasonable, will refuse to supply them with spirits, beer, picture - palaces and tobacco. Each vocation will, in fact, once the distorting influence of profit is out of the way, be kept in order by all the other vocations, so far as concerns any claim to an unfair share of the national product. Looking back on the long history of vocational organisation, from the mediaeval gilds and colleges to the modern Trade Union and Professional Association, it seems probable that the chief cause of dissension and lengthy proceedings in the Courts of the Socialist Common- wealth will be not the relative conditions of employ- ment of different vocations, but the claim of one vocation to perform a particular service required by the community, as against another vocation. The arguments adduced will concern the superiority of one set of processes over another, the justification for one type of talent and training superseding an older type, together with the conditions of compensa- tion to be afforded to the superseded profession. Fortunately for a quarrelsome world, generations of men pass quickly ; the old can be pensioned and the young can be educated. In the great majority of cases the change from one process, one material or one product to another can be made, assuming common recognition of the duty of inflicting no unnecessary harm on any section of the community, merely by a diminution or suspension of recruiting for the enterprises in process of supersession, and, if need be, by a lowering of the age of pensionable retirement for those of longest service who may desire to leave.

(f) SUBJECT ASSOCIATIONS

The most noticeable development in the vocational associations, whether Trade Unions or Professional Societies, will, it may be anticipated, be the growth of intellectual activity in the science and art of their vocations. In such professions as medicine ; civil, mechanical and electrical engineering ; naval architecture ; industrial chemistry, and insurance, it seems already to absorb more of the attention of the practitioners than anything else. An analogous growth of intellectual interest may be expected in the technique of work in every industry and service, equally among those who mainly use their muscles as among those who mainly use their brains. At present it is true that, as a result of the suppression, under the Capitalist System, of the old " instinct of workmanship " which characterised the mediaeval craftsman, the artisans and labourers of the machine industries in particular have fallen terribly behind the older and more independent brain-working professions in their interest in the technique of their work. How natural and, under the circumstances, how inevitable this has been, every student of Capitalism will appreciate. So long as any improvement in their industry enures, in the main, to the capitalist proprietors—so long as even mechanical inventions are made, by legal patents, the instruments of profit-making monopolies so long, indeed, as the remuneration of labour is assumed to be governed by " supply and demand," with the inevitable logical inference that " restriction of output " defers the period of unemployment and increases the market rate per unit of effort—it is difficult for the Trade Unions to feel that thinking about the development of their several vocations is at all their business, or that anything which they might contribute will not be used to the disadvantage of their own members. But with the elimination of the capitalist profit-making and the competitive wage-system, with security against loss of maintenance through unemployment and against any degradation of the Standard of Life, there is no reason why the extraction of coal, or the making of sewing-machines, or for that matter the shifting of logs of wood from ship to wharf, should not become as truly an art, and be as much consciously based on science, as, horticulture or surgery. In a Socialist community it may be expected that those who now become Trade Unionists will, without abandoning their organisation for safeguarding their Standard of Life, also develop the same sort of " Subject Associations," or scientific societies, for the study of the art and science of their occupation, as exist among actuaries or doctors, or among the players of football or golf. To give one example among many, the whole development of " Motion Study " has so far been vitiated, and (in this country at least) kept back, because the investigation and the experimentation have not taken place at the instance of, or among the bricklayers or yard labourers, or female factory operatives, whose motions have been studied—not even with their participation or concurrence—but have been made by quite another class of persons, whose object was, not the development of character or capacity of the operatives whom they studied, but the extraction from their labour of a larger profit for the owners of the instruments of industry upon which they worked.

The doctors are conspicuous for the way in which they have, by their own studies, developed and improved both the science and the technique of their particular vocation. But imagine the indignation with which the physicians and surgeons would receive a proposition that the technique of their profession should be determined by the investigations and studies of a set of people who had no practical training in medicine, and had no intention of practising it, but sought merely to discover, for the profit of another individual or another class, how to make the doctors treat a larger number of patients per hour ! Yet this is what the " Efficiency Engineers " of the United States have, in their Motion Study, tried to do to the manual-working wage earners. When in Great Britain, Motion Study becomes an effective instrument of progress, it will be, we suggest, because it has been taken up and developed, in a Socialist community, by the workers actually concerned, for pure love of the progress of their several arts. There may then be, in each manual-working vocation, the same emulation, the same zeal for training, the same high proficiency, perhaps even the same sort of friendly contests, as was developed in a Huxley or a Tyndall ; or, to vary the comparison, as is seen in such a boxing champion as Carpentier, or such expert golfers as Ball and Vardon.

(g) The Development of Professional Ethic

One of the most characteristic aspects of vocational organisation is the development of specialised rules of conduct to be enforced by the organisation on its membership. Owing to the persistent pressure of the Capitalist System on the standard of life and personal liberty of the manual workers these rules of conduct have, in the Trade Union Movement, been, in the main, of the nature of restrictive regulations preventing one member from undercutting another. Even in the brain-working professions a large portion of what is termed " professional ethic " has a similar aim—for instance, the rules forbidding competition in price and criticism of procedure among members of the same organisation or the same profession. These rules, whether of Trade Unions or Professional Associations, tend to maintain a high standard of honour between one member of an organisation and another : it is a moral gain when one man voluntarily foregoes his own pecuniary self-interest, and in some cases even his livelihood, for the sake of fellowship. But they may easily militate against desirable innovations, and they sometimes positively restrict the output of the industry or service. There is, however, another, and a higher development of professional ethic, directed towards the good of the community as a whole. In the most highly organised brain-working professions we watch professional ethic seeking to raise and standardise the conduct of the members of the profession towards the public. The most universal of these requirements is the distinction set up between what is permitted to a professional man, and what is customary in the business world. According to the accepted canons of commercial enterprise, business men are permitted and even encouraged to compete with each other in price and quality, and to use the arts of a frequently mendacious advertisement to promote the sale of their respective wares. They are assumed to make their profit by exploiting the labour of mind or body of whole armies of employees. They enter, without scruple and without reproach, into secret understandings with other business men, with regard to sharing the profits of common undertakings. Above all, it is taken for granted that a business man will keep for his own profit any new invention or discovery that he makes, or of which he obtains control ; and that he will attempt, whether by secrecy, by trade mark or by patent, to prevent any one else from making use of this advancement of knowledge in the service of the public. All this is prohibited by professional ethic to the members of the most highly organised brain-working professions. The lawyer, the doctor, the architect, the consulting engineer, is forbidden by his professional organisation to take contracts in which the labour of other people—except as regards a certain narrowly limited class of assistants in his own profession—is exploited for his own profit. He is always assumed to gain his livelihood solely by the use of his own faculties. He is prohibited from having any pecuniary interest, direct or indirect, in the materials, plant, processes, establishments or institutions which he recommends to his clients. Any receipt of commissions from other professionals, or from business enterprises, is against professional etiquette. In his private relations with individual clients the professional man is prohibited from using the influence that he gains as a professional man to obtain from his client anything beyond his recognised remuneration. Any attempt to use his professional relationship as an opportunity for impoverishing his client is condemned as infamous conduct. So long as he is professionally engaged, the member of a brain-working profession is required to think only of the advantage of his client, and not of his own pecuniary interests. In the higher ranges of professional ethic he is expected to risk, and even to sacrifice, his health or his life in the performance of his professional duty, an obligation which is not recognised in business.[1]

In the remarkable monograph on *The Sickness of an Acquisitive Society*, by Mr. R. H. Tawney, it has been pointed out that the alternative to the crushing

[1] See, for all this, *The New Statesman*, Supplement on " Professional Associations," by S. and B. Webb, April 21 and 28, 1917.

discipline which was exercised in the past by the Dictatorship of the Capitalist, and which is now, through the rise of vocational and communal Democracy, patently breaking down, is the spread to the manual working class of the nobler part of professional ethic. " The essence of a profession," remarks Mr. Tawney, " is that its members organise themselves for the performance of a function. . . . Once industry has been liberated from its subservience to the interests of the functionless property-owner, it is in this sphere that Trade Unions may be expected increasingly to find their function." [1] When the service rendered by the different kinds of manual labour, even by those now termed " unskilled," has taken on the characteristics of a professional technique —a matter of common training, common skill and common responsibilities—is it too much to anticipate from those whose work is predominantly manual, as from those whose work is predominantly mental, a new development of professional ethic, more especially in that part of it which emphasises the responsibility of the vocation to the community as a whole ?

(h) VOCATIONAL ADMINISTRATION OF INDUSTRIES AND SERVICES

It must not be forgotten that there is no reason to assume that, in the Socialist Commonwealth, every adult citizen will be engaged, at salary or wages, in some vast administrative machine. The one economic sin to be condemned in the healthy adult will be " living by owning " ; whilst living by the aid of the employment of other people's labour, even if this employment be accompanied by valuable organising capacity, will be regarded as a method of livelihood,

---

[1] *The Sickness of an Acquisitive Society*, by R. H. Tawney, 1920, pp. 59, 78, etc.

presumably transient only, and fraught with some peril to the community ; requiring, in fact, as will be indicated in the next chapter, to be kept specially under public control, and as soon as practicable superseded. But it will have become manifest, in the foregoing proposals, that there is nothing in Socialism that requires, or even makes probable, the suppression of the independent craftsman or brain-working practitioner, pursuing independently his own vocation, managing his own affairs and offering his personal services to a succession of clients. The constitution for the Socialist Commonwealth outlined in this book, not only leaves room for, but actually relies on the continuance of a class of independent professionals—in medicine and law, in accountancy and costing, in engineering and architecture, in physics and chemistry, and many other vocations—from whom the various public departments, the Local Authorities, the Co-operative Societies of different kinds, the vocational organisations, the surviving remnants of Capitalism and, last but by no means least, the private citizens may be able to get disinterested and impartial expert advice and assistance in return for a fee. There are, it will be seen, great advantages in not having all the experts engaged in the salaried employment of great administrations, in favour of which they would be supposed to be biassed, even if they were not. In Part I. of the present book it was shown that there is a vast gain in personal freedom in every citizen, as well as each separate administration, being able to get the service of the expert professional who is desired. It has proved to be advantageous, in protecting the freedom and status of those members of the profession who hold salaried offices, and in keeping the profession united, that the Professional Association should include both the independently practising and the salaried members.

To what other vocations this form of organisation may extend we do not pretend to say. The artist, the artistic craftsman, the instructor in any of the arts or crafts, the executant in all forms of music, the country carrier, the agriculturist, even the jobbing carpenter or gardener may all continue to practise independently their several vocations. Moreover, they may all strengthen their position, and mutually assist each other, not only by vocational associations, but also by joining together in Co-operative Societies, either for their common purposes as producers, or for their common needs as consumers.

Another conspicuous field in which an essentially vocational administration may be expected to prevail in the Socialist Commonwealth is that of the universities, and, in fact, of all the manifold institutions for higher education and research. The organisation of learning, whether on the side of teaching or on that of research, cannot, indeed, be effectively done in any other way. The community must be represented on the governing bodies of the institutions, and notably in their financial administration, presumably by the nominees of the national and local Education Authorities ; and as public money will need to be provided, in far larger amounts than at present, the fundamental conditions under which it will be expended must receive the sanction of the Education Department responsible to the Standing Committee on Education of the Social Parliament. But subject to these general conditions the universities and institutions for research must clearly be allowed a free hand in administration, which cannot practically be placed in any other hands than those of the vocation concerned, that is to say, those who serve as professors or lecturers or researchers or writers on the whole range of subjects dealt with. There are, however, dangers to be guarded against. It is the vocation as a whole that should be repre-

sented in the various governing committees and councils, not exclusively the holders of the principal pro-
fessorships. Each subject of study should have its
own Board of Studies, representative of teachers, researchers and writers of various grades, which should
be enabled to have an effective participation in the
administration. Care must be taken to prevent the
exclusion of unpopular subjects, or of unorthodox
views. Subject, however, to a suitable constitution
being drawn up for each institution, in which all these
considerations are given due weight—there is much
to be said for an impartial Court or Board of Trustees
or other laymen to hold the scales even between rival
faculties—there seems no reason why, in this vast
and important field, the actual work of administration
should not be committed to the vocation.

And who can tell what the Future hides in it ?
It is unnecessary to fetter the Socialist Commonwealth
with all the limitations and frustrations that have been
burnt into us under the Capitalist System. In a world
of vocational organisation such as has been fore-
shadowed, in a community adopting the principle of
socialisation, experiments in delegating the particular
functions of management, or the administration of
particular establishments or even of particular services,
to groups of professionals in any vocation, even to all
those engaged in the vocation, would clearly be permissible, so long as there was effective freedom to the
National Boards or Local Authorities to terminate the
arrangement whenever they thought that the community might be better served in another way. This
liberty to experiment in any form of administration is,
in fact, a necessary inference from the principle of
Freedom of Enterprise for socialised administrations.
The necessary instruments of production could be
provided on lease, with proper covenants and at a
suitable rent. A group of teachers might, in a city

where there was a choice of schools, undertake to manage one of them, as well as teach in it ; but they would have to come up to the prescribed National Minimum of education, and administer according to the desires of the parents, or of the general body of citizens, for a certain type of education. A group of medical men and nurses, including, for that matter, also the hospital attendants, could undertake the administration of one of the hospitals of the city or county. It would be absurd to exclude arrangements in workshops of the nature of a Collective Contract with the operatives concerned, under which they would produce what was required at a concerted price, so long as the operations of such a group did not result in any lowering of the vocational Standard Rate or fall below the National Minimum. There need even be no theoretical objection to an entirely self-governing establishment, so long as it paid its rent, did not descend below the prescribed National Minimum in the conditions of employment of any of the persons engaged, and produced its commodity in the same quantity and quality, in return for the price, as that produced by the National Board, the Local Authorities or the voluntary Democracies of Consumers. There will certainly be, in the interstices of the great industry, groups of craftsmen and of agriculturalists, and also individual craftsmen and small-holders, setting up as independent producers ; paying to the community a proper rent for any instruments of production that they employ, when they do not themselves provide what they require ; and supplying commodities or services for sale, in competition with the socialised enterprises. There may even be imagined local communities of persons, at once producers and consumers, who might segregate themselves in self-supporting societies, and perhaps inaugurate a new social order. What would be indispensable in all cases would be a universal application of Measurement and Publicity. Any form of organisation which did not descend below what was for the time being prescribed by the Policy of the National Minimum, and which depended entirely on finding voluntary customers or support, might, in the Socialist Commonwealth, take its chance and find its place. Room can be left for infinite variety. Whether any such forms of organisation could survive in competition with the advantages of communal direction from the standpoint of the consumers' demand ; whether it would not often prove necessary to intervene in order to protect their members, or at least the non-adult among them, from a socially injurious degradation of the standard of life, may be left to the event to decide. It would be the object of the Socialist Commonwealth to proceed as little as possible by the method of prohibition. With complete Measurement and Publicity, and the ever present alternative of socialised provision, each vocation, even every citizen and every producer, might safely be left free to " prove all things," in the assurance that he or she would, in the end, hold fast only to that which was good.

(i) Is there any Place for a National Assembly of Vocational Representatives ?

There remains the question whether, in the reorganisation of the vocational world herein adumbrated as part of the Socialist Commonwealth, there is any place or function for a national assembly of vocational representatives. Frankly, we do not see that there is. So far as experience affords any guide, there is the very smallest indication in Great Britain of the practicability of such an assembly, or of any possible function that it could perform. There is, as has already been mentioned, at present no sign, in any

country, of any common national assembly of representatives of the brain-working professions even among
those employed at salaries. Among the manual
workers, even with the common bond of resistance
to the capitalist employer, the Trades Union Congress,
after more than half a century of existence, cannot be
said to have manifested any very intense corporate
life ; or — apart from the purely political issues,
not affecting the trades or the Trade Unions
as such, which are now dealt with by the conferences of the Labour Party—to have discovered
any purpose that it can serve other than that of defend-
ing the institution of Trade Unionism against attack.[1]

It has sometimes been suggested that there is a
part to be played in the Socialist Commonwealth,
when the Dictatorship of the Capitalist has been eliminated, and when Trade Unions are no more exposed
to attack than are the Institutions of Civil, Mechanical
and Electrical Engineers, by a national assembly
elected by the producers as such, voting in their several
vocations, as a counterpoise to, and sometimes in
substitution for, the national assembly elected by the
citizens, voting in their geographical constituencies.
We see great difficulties even in constituting such an
assembly.[2] With such a complete national register

---

[1] See *History of Trade Unionism*, by S. and B. Webb, edition of 1920.

[2] We may remind the reader that what is usually called the " Soviet
franchise " of the Russia of 1919–20, so far as our information goes, is,
strictly speaking, not vocational at all. As regards industrial employees,
it rests on the aggregation of persons employed in a particular factory,
whatever may be the vocations that they practise or the Trade Unions to
which they belong ; as regards the rural districts, it rests on the geographic-
ally defined village or commune : in both cases those only are excluded who
" live by owning," or who employ labour at wages. The " Soviet franchise,"
in fact, may be said to have its own peculiar geographical basis, namely, that
of a strictly determinate place in which the electors are working, as distinguished from the place in which they are living. Further, it has its own
peculiar method, in contrast with the secret ballot, of voting by show of
hands in a public meeting. It must be remembered that, in a huge country
like Russia, not provided with any register of local inhabitants, or with
any machinery for taking a ballot, the " Soviet franchise " may have been
the only practicable way of ascertaining the opinions of the majority of the
people.

as may be contemplated, in which the actual vocation
and current address of every person would be recorded
it would, indeed, not be impossible to arrange (except
perhaps in the case of the sailors, firemen, stewards, etc.,
of sea-going vessels) for an election, though the preparation and revision of the vocational registers would
be expensive ; but the obstacles in the way of even
an approximately " Proportional Representation "
would be great. The masses of miners and of agriculturalists, with something like a million workers each ;
the three - quarters of a million persons, comprising
not a few distinct vocations, employed in the various
engineering workshops ; or the like number, with at
least as many distinct vocations, engaged in the textile
industry, would be difficult to represent at all pro-

There are those who have advocated the adoption in Western Europe
of the " Soviet franchise " ; meaning, as we believe, essentially the ascertainment of the Common Will likely to be generated in a public meeting, held
at a place where the electors are united in work. As the workers in any one
establishment of modern industry, or the inhabitants of any British village,
do not belong to a single vocation, or to any one Trade Union, such a
franchise and method of voting could not be correctly described as affording
representation of vocational organisations. But even if the British people
were prepared to resort to another form of exclusive electorate (the Russian
exclusions, by the way, amounting numerically to far less than those of the
British franchise prior to 1918) ; and to an abandonment of the protection
afforded by the secret ballot, any organisation of the British electorate on
the " Soviet system " would be found impracticable. In Great Britain, the
industrial workers by hand and by brain are not, as in Russia, aggregated
in a comparatively small number of factories, but dispersed among, literally,
millions of separate workplaces, such as factories and workshops, mines and
quarries, shops and offices, docks and warehouses, of every size and kind.
The rural and semi-rural populations are not, as in a Russian village, almost
exclusively peasant cultivators, but of an extraordinary heterogeneity, from
the agricultural labourer and independent craftsman to the village shop-
keeper and the resident government official or professional man ; from the
wholesale trader's outworkers to the public works contractor's shifting mass
of skilled and semi-skilled labour, not to mention the innumerable types of
itinerant traders, petty carriers, commercial travellers, brokers, insurance
and other agents, who may live in the rural village or the garden suburb, but
who spend their working lives perpetually travelling on highway and rail-
road, or in standing in market-places, exchanges or on the doorsteps of
innumerable homes. The " place of work," in Great Britain, neither
coincides with any vocation nor provides any practicable machinery for
taking the votes of the whole people ; even if it were determined to exclude,
as in the Russian version of " paupers and criminals," those who " live by
owning," or by the employment of others at wages.

portionately to the 40,000 medical practitioners or ministers of religion, the 20,000 solicitors or public accountants, the six or eight thousand architects, or the thousand or two of practising barristers. Indeed, without making intolerably large an assembly that will have to represent something like 20,000,000 active producers, no vocation numbering fewer than 30,000 members could, on any arithmetical basis, claim as much as a single representative, whilst the miners and agriculturalists would want as many as thirty apiece.

What is more important is, however, the consideration that, even if a National Assembly could be formed by election from all the several vocations among which the twenty million producers would be divided, there would be, as it seems to us, no interest that the representatives would, as members of their several vocations, have in common. *To have interests in common, even when there is disagreement about them, appears to be indispensable for any effective assembly.* If it were a question of an assembly of wage-earners face to face with an aggregation of capitalist employers, there would be at once the common interest, which to-day to some extent unites the Trades Union Congress, of obtaining a universal rise of wages, or other improvement of the conditions of service, at the expense of the profits of the capitalist employers. But if the capitalist employers are assumed to be eliminated, and the producers, together with their families and their sick or infirm or superannuated relatives, to constitute the whole community, jointly disposing of the entire product of their collective labours, there would be no outside party to attack or to despoil. There would be no more to divide than was already being appropriated ; and any attempts to raise above the common level the conditions of any one vocation could, in practice, only be made at the expense of the other vocations. Even if the active workers in the several vocations felt tempted to improve their own conditions at the cost of lessening the amount appropriated to the children, the sick, the physically or mentally defective, the superannuated aged or the involuntarily unemployed, such temptations would be checked by the realisation that the persons thus injured were, after all, only members of the families of their own electors.

The fact is that, whilst a vocational constituency offers advantages over any other basis of election, *when what is to be discussed and decided concerns peculiarly the vocation in question,* the case is reversed when what is to be dealt with concerns not the vocation as such, but the community. When what is in question is mining or agriculture, medicine or accountancy, there is much to be said for those who are engaged in the occupation voting as miners or agriculturalists, doctors or accountants, and choosing representatives of these several vocations. When, however, what is in question is how the future interests of the community as a whole are to be safeguarded, or what is to be done to maintain us all in health or to train the young, or how the national taxation is to be levied, or what shall be the nation's policy in foreign relations, it is neither necessary nor desirable for men and women to vote as members of particular vocations, accentuating the feelings distinctive of those vocations, rather than as citizens, accentuating their consciousness of a common interest as members of one and the same community, in the future well-being of which they are all involved. The very argument which is used in favour of vocational representation against the manner in which the House of Commons is to-day chosen— namely, that among the electors in a geographical constituency there is and can be no common will that it is possible to represent on any vocational question — is equally applicable against the election of representatives by vocations as such, when what is to be represented is no will that all the members of the vocation have in common. If it is the vocational will, not the civic will, that ought to be represented when vocational issues are involved, it is equally the will of the citizens as such, not that of carpenters or engineers as such, that needs to be represented when the questions at stake touch their feelings and emotions as citizens, and not as carpenters or engineers. And this theoretical objection to the use of vocational representation, where what is to be dealt with is not the interest of the vocation itself, is supported by such experience as we have of assemblies chosen on a vocational basis. What happens in a vocational assembly, having no common bond of interest, may be seen in the way in which, in the Trades Union Congress, notwithstanding the common tie of a revolt against the Capitalist System, the representatives of the several vocations are always engaged in what the Americans term log-rolling—each vocation trying to get passed the particular resolution which concerns itself alone by exchanging promises of support for other resolutions in which it takes no interest whatever ; and in securing the election of its own candidates to any electoral offices by bargaining in votes with the representatives of other vocations. It is, in fact, to this effect of vocational representation that may be attributed the greater part of the failure of the Trades Union Congress to become an effective governing body for the Trade Union world. Our own conclusion is that, where what is in question is anything beyond the distinctive interests of the vocation as such, vocational representation, far from being an advantage, is a positive impediment to any ascertainment or formulation of the General Will of the community and to any ensuring of its execution. Vocational representation seems to us, therefore, in the literal sense, undemocratic.

Nor is the prospect made brighter by the proposal that the national assembly of producers' representatives should be elected, not by the 20,000,000 producers themselves, arranged in vocational constituencies, but by the Trade Unions and Professional Associations, or their executive committees. The inherent disadvantage of representation by vocations when what is to be dealt with does not concern the vocations as vocations is not removed by this election by highly selected samples of each vocation. It is difficult to imagine a national assembly of the delegates of Trade Unions and Professional Associations proving any more capable of formulating the General Will of the nation as a community of citizens on essentially national or civic issues than the Trades Union Congress is. On the contrary, the inclusion in the Trades Union Congress of representatives from the various Professional Associations of teachers, doctors and dentists, from the General Council of the Bar and the Law Society, from the different institutes of engineers, and the rival societies of accountants and architects, to say nothing of the hundreds of other Professional Associations, would make confusion worse confounded. But this suggestion brings us face to face with the dilemma set up by the alternative of the vocational associations being either voluntary organisations, independent of any authority, and free to have what members and what constitutions they please ; or else organisations of universal and obligatory membership exercising public functions, and forming an essential part of the administrative structure of the community, in which their membership and constitution could hardly escape statutory definition. Our own view inclines to that commonly held, that the Trade Unions and other vocational associations had better remain free, independent and voluntary bodies, from time to time waxing and waning in membership and changing in relative strength according as one grouping or one form of association or another commends itself to various sections of producers. But in that case it would be difficult to entrust a national assembly formed on such an indefinite and such a shifting basis—much the same in fact, so far as the manual workers are concerned, as that of the Trades Union Congress—with any legal authority or statutory power.

This is not to say that there cannot be any room, in the reorganisation of the vocational world, for general assemblies on a vocational basis. Whilst there seem no place and no function in the Socialist Commonwealth for a national assembly professing to formulate a General Will of all the several vocations as such— a national assembly which would represent, if not exactly the same aggregate of individuals, at any rate precisely the same aggregate of families as the members elected by the adult citizens in geographical constituencies—there is no need to deprecate assemblies of delegates of various vocational associations, any more than those of delegates of the membership of a single association, for dealing with any matters in which they feel that they have, as representatives of distinctive vocations, any common interests. The most important type of such an assembly might be one representing a number of distinct vocations that felt themselves allied to each other, and separated from the rest of the community, in respect of some distinctive common needs in vocational education, or in their conditions of employment, or in their terms of service. For instance, all the seafaring vocations might meet together with advantage ; or all those connected with rural life ; or all those requiring an exceptionally prolonged intellectual training ; or all those needing exceptional allowances for functional expenses. We might see persisting the present tendency for the employees of different vocations engaged in the service of a particular type of administration, whether national or local authorities, the Co-operative or the Friendly Society world—including some grades of brain workers—to form federations for discussing, with the associated managements, the questions concerning their service. " Subject Associations " and scientific societies already meet each other, and will certainly continue to do so in the much greater development of their work that will mark the Socialist Commonwealth. It is hard to foresee any matters in which all the vocations in the community would feel that they had a common interest, separating them from the rest of the community, because their aggregate membership would, in a Socialist Commonwealth, itself be co-extensive with adult citizenship.

CHAPTER VII

WE do not foresee any sudden and simultaneous termination of the Capitalist System. History does not describe any form of social structure being entirely and universally superseded. What is seen to occur, in one century and in one country after another, is one or other form of organisation becoming predominant, though not to the complete exclusion of other forms ; and then this predominant form, with its dominating consequences, being superseded by another form gradually becoming predominant, though again without eliminating all vestiges of the older system. It took the Capitalist System several centuries to become the dominant form in British industry. The process of transition from profit-making industry to public service, which has during the past quarter of a century made such great strides, and has been accelerated by the Great War, will clearly continue for some time, and may at no one moment ever be completely accomplished.

This lesson of history is reinforced by observation of social psychology. The genius of the British race does not take to catastrophic changes, involving an immediate alteration of the whole social structure and entailing a violation of the habits and established expectations of large masses of people. Moreover, large sections of the British manual workers, not to mention the whole of the professional brain workers, have already achieved an appreciable standard of " life, liberty and the pursuit of happiness," and feel, rightly or wrongly, that they have a good deal more to lose than their chains. Further, thousands, and indeed tens of thousands of the leading members of the Labour and Socialist Movement in Great Britain, unlike those of most other countries, have had practical experience of the working of public adminis-tration, not only in the gigantic business of the Trade Union and Co-operative Movements, but also as members of Local Government bodies directing such important public enterprises as tramways, the supply of water, gas and electricity, housing, drainage and paving, as well as such vital social services as education and public health, in which thousands of brain-working professionals are serving. Not a few have sat in the House of Commons and some have formed part of Ministries, where they have perforce realised the interaction of foreign and home affairs. No wage-earning population in the world—with the possible exception of the Australians—has so effectively as that of Great Britain learned the difficulty of com-bining administrative efficiency with popular control. All this knowledge leaves the British manual-working class sceptical about the possibility of any sudden and simultaneous social transformation, especially when the revolution is unaccompanied by any deliberately thought out and generally accepted alternative scheme of organisation. It is not a matter of a merely " poli-tical " revolution, in which a sudden wave of irresist-ible popular feeling might upset the Government, upset the Law Courts, upset Parliament itself, and instal in the seats of authority, national and municipal, with complete power to do what they thought fit, the leaders of the most insurrectionary " Industrial

Unionism." There have been such revolutionary upheavals of " illegal " and unconstitutional " Direct Action," in this country as elsewhere, not without a certain measure of success, for their own purposes and in their own way, and it is not to be supposed that there will never be any others. But the drawback of every such sudden and simultaneous upheaval is that even its success leaves the job still to be done. Whoever gets into power, and whatever the instrument and circumstances of the revolution, the transformation of the social and industrial machinery of a whole nation takes time. It cannot be improvised. It is in the very nature of things that the transformation can be effected only piece by piece. If it is not done on a systematically thought out plan it will presently be found, whatever orders and commands have been promulgated, that it has not been done at all.

For all these reasons it is plainly imperative that any constitution for a Socialist Commonwealth—at least for Great Britain — must include provision, not for socialisation alone, but also for the democratic control, in the public interest, of whatever industrial and social activities may be, for the time being, in the hands of private owners of instruments of production, whether individuals or groups, isolated producers or employers of other persons for the purpose of private profit. No less incidental is the decision of the conditions under which the process of the gradual extension of socialisation will be conducted, including the terms upon which particular industries will be taken over, as they successively become ripe for transformation into public services.

THE POLICY OF THE NATIONAL MINIMUM

Let us first consider the character and methods of the democratic control that, in the interests of the community as a whole, it is necessary to exercise over those undertakings which, at any particular time, have not yet been promoted to the status of a public service. Experience has now abundantly demonstrated that it is impossible to allow any enterprise, inspired by the motive of pecuniary self-interest, and carried on for the purpose of private gain, to remain autocratically controlled. The Policy of the National Minimum, for a long time ignored by the economists, and even in the twentieth century rejected by the Liberal and Radical Parties as incompatible with their Shibboleth of " Freedom of Enterprise," has now become a commonplace, though still without being whole-heartedly carried out. Its universal application will be the foundation of any Socialist Commonwealth.[1] The whole framework of the Factory Acts, with their logical extension in the Trade Boards Acts, securing a Legal Minimum Wage—transformed by a much more effective participation in their administration by the vocational organisations of the workers concerned, and immensely strengthened by the scientific prevention of unemployment which is now practicable, and by adequate provision for the involuntarily unemployed—will ensure that no worker, however defenceless, shall fall below the " National Minimum " of subsistence and leisure for the time being prescribed by the Social Parliament. It will be the function of the Local Authorities to see to it that a corresponding " National Minimum " in housing and public health is everywhere secured. No less essential is the enforcement, through the whole community, of a similar " National Minimum " of educational attainment and educational opportunity effectively opened to every boy or girl, from the bottom to the top of the educational scale, irrespective of the means of the

---

[1] See the very significant detailed programme of the Labour Party, entitled *Labour and the New Social Order*, 1918.

parents. All this has been made, by a generation of principally Socialist investigation and almost exclusively Socialist propaganda, " common form," so far as thinking folk in Great Britain are concerned; although the half-instinctive resistance of the propertied classes, and the intellectual *sabotage* of the administrators, have so far prevented any honest and generally effective carrying out of what is ostensibly adopted. But there is another, and in the long run a supremely important field for the application of the Policy of the National Minimum, in which scarcely a beginning has been made. Not as a producer, nor as a member of a Trade Union or Professional Association, but as a citizen, every person has a vital interest in the maintenance, undefiled, of an environment that is both physically and mentally healthful, invigorating and refining. Under the dominion of the Capitalist System, there exists, so far, only the germ of this application of the Policy of the National Minimum, in the law against nuisances, the Rivers Pollution Acts, the Smoke Abatement Acts, and a very faint-hearted regulation of public advertisements. It may be assumed that, in a Socialist Commonwealth, one of the constant preoccupations of the Social Parliament—one of the points on which it will be perpetually pressing the Minister of Justice— will be to put a stop to the scandalous destruction of the beauty and amenity of the mental and physical environment upon which the lives of the citizens finally depend. It is inconceivable that any intelligent Democracy should continue to permit the capitalist manufacturer, merely in order to increase his profits, wantonly to defile what is not his but our atmosphere with unnecessary and really wasteful smoke from his factory chimneys ; to pollute the crystal streams that are the property of all of us by the waste products of his mills and dye-works ; to annihilate the irreplaceable beauty of valleys and mountain slopes by his quarries and scrap-heaps ; to leave a whole countryside scarred and ruined by the wreckage which he fails to remove when one of his profit-seeking enterprises has exhausted its profitableness, or becomes bankrupt. In so far as any industry is left to capitalist profit-making, the community must at least see to it that the greed for private gain is not allowed to rob the citizens of their common heritage in a land of health and beauty. This control of private enterprise with a view of safeguarding, for future generations as well as for ourselves, the mental and physical environment of the citizens, will presumably be exercised by the Local Authorities, under the general supervision of the Social Parliament (which might well have a Standing Committee on Common Amenity and Public Beauty), enforcing laws enacted by the Political Parliament. It need hardly be added that the enforcement of the Policy of the National Minimum in all its ramifications will not be required only in respect of the under-takings of capitalist profit - makers. The national industries and services, the enterprises of the Local Authorities and of voluntary associations of con-sumers—even the activities of the vocational organ-isations themselves—will all have to adopt, as the necessary basis of their activities, a corresponding " fencing off of the downward way," so that the emulation of all of them may be directed—really to the actual augmentation of their practical freedom in self-development—exclusively to the " upward way " that is not inimical to public well-being.[1]

---

[1] It is difficult to propose that there should be any enforcement of the Policy of National Minimum beyond national boundaries. Yet a grave problem is presented—not to Socialists only—by the evils accompanying unrestrained capitalist enterprise in countries in which there is no civilised government as European nations understand the term, or in which such a government refuses to adopt (or is prevented from adopting) measures that would prevent these evils. Apart from the aggressions of a Capitalist Imperialism (as to which see *Empire and Commerce in Africa*, by L. S. Woolf,

The Promotion of Efficiency and the Prevention of Extortion

It was one of the unexpected discoveries of governments during the Great War that the system of capitalist profit-making, as a method of producing commodities and services, habitually fell so enormously short of the maximum efficiency of which it was capable. It had been taken for granted that the competition of rival producers kept down prices. We had, most of us, not realised that this competitive rivalry, where it existed uninformed and unrestrained, involved, incidentally, an extraordinarily wasteful organisation, or rather lack of organisation, of the means of production, distribution and exchange on which the community depends. The public recognised during the war, what Socialists had long been pointing out, the wastefulness of the unnecessary multiplication of retailers, wholesalers and middlemen of every sort ; the colossal waste in the mendacious advertisement of

---

1919), which may, it is hoped, be voluntarily abandoned, or prevented by an effective League of Nations, the examples of the Congo and Putumayo, not to mention the African slave trade and " blackbirding " in the Pacific, demonstrate how unendurable it is, for a civilised community, to allow to capitalist enterprise a free hand for exploitation of the " Non-Adult " races. That a comprehensive Criminal Code may one day be rigidly enforced by the League of Nations on all aliens in all territories not under civilised government—such, for instance, as the British High Commissioner for the Pacific attempts to enforce on British subjects over a large part of the Pacific Ocean— is an aspiration for the future.   But not by mere prohibition and punishment of criminal acts can the problem be dealt with.   The obtaining of products from these territories, and the exportation to them of the commodities that the natives desire—it may be ardent spirits of deleterious nature, " trade guns " and explosives—cannot safely be left to the greed for gain of individual capitalists, unable, even if willing, to control those whom they send out to do the business.   The only alternative to an indefinite extension of the sovereignty of the civilised nations, ultimately covering the whole earth, seems to be the organisation of the commerce with the Non-Adult races that are not thus annexed, by some responsible corporate body, not acting for private profit.   The League of Nations should undertake it, or some civilised democratic community acting as the agent of the League, doing the work entirely by public officers, on lines that would exclude the possibility of profit-making, oppression or extortion ; any surplus of receipts over expenditure being devoted to purposes beneficial to the Non-Adult races themselves.

rival products ; the waste of unnecessary carriage of
goods to and fro ; the excessive cost involved, from
agriculture to engineering, from coal-mining to merchant
shipping, in the continued existence, not eliminated,
as had been assumed, by the " struggle for existence,"
of units of production uneconomic in size, insufficiently
equipped with machinery and managed with all degrees
of technical incompetence ; the further waste of
capital and wreckage of humanity involved whenever,
after a prolonged fight for life, any of these less efficient
establishments succumbed to bankruptcy ; finally,
the waste incidental to the lack of knowledge among
the capitalist proprietors themselves of what were
their costs of production, in comparison with those
elsewhere, and to the jealous secrecy, largely fostered
by this ignorance, by which the capitalists concealed
from one another (and therefore even from themselves)
what actually were the technical conditions of the
industry that they supposed themselves to be conducting.   The answer of the capitalists was simple,
if not convincing.   Their object was not output but
profit : they were not concerned even for the aggregate
profit of their industries as wholes, but exclusively
for the profits of their several establishments.   They
believed that isolated individualism, the absence of
any organisation of the industry as a whole, and the
secrecy in which each establishment wrapped its own
concerns—whatever it might mean in aggregate output
or even in aggregate profit—enabled the more successful
members of the crowd to amass larger fortunes than
they could do in any other way.   What the Government discovered during the Great War, and the point
on which it succeeded, largely, in convincing the
business world, was that—whatever might be the
effect on the profits of particular firms—the aggregate
output of commodities could be very greatly increased,
their average cost of production considerably lowered

and a valuable saving effected in the expense of transport and distribution, if only each industry were organised as a whole, in relation to its function in supplying the community with what was required— by collective purchases and importation of the raw materials ; by concerted allocation of production to the establishments best suited to each part ; by further standardisation and specialisation ; by elaborate comparative costing of each component and every item of expense, and the relentless application of the knowledge thus gained in the effecting of improvements wherever required ; by concerted distribution of the product so as to lessen the aggregate of handling and transport ; by collective selling and the elimination of unnecessary advertisement and expenses of distribution. It has been roughly estimated throughout British industry—even if, in each industry, only the present standard of efficiency in the best ten per cent of establishments could be universalised—the aggregate output could, without increasing either the numbers or the exertions of the persons employed, and without any new inventions, be at least doubled. Unfortunately, in the hurried return during 1918–20 of industry to private enterprise, a large part of the increased productivity and lessened cost which were among the social gains of the war, was sacrificed to the scramble for individual profit-making ; and in many industries there has been a rapid reversion to the unmeasured wastefulness of anarchic business competition. In other industries and parts of industries, the lesson has been more or less learned, although the knowledge has been applied, not to the advantage of the community of consumers, but, by the rapid aggregation into trusts and combinations, to an unparalleled increase in aggregate profits and to the unnecessary exploitation of the consumer. The situation, in short, is now dominated by the substitution, for unregulated competition, of capitalist monopolies. The dramatic world-shortage of commodities, and the frantic demand to make good the ravages of war, have made manifest what has long been suspected by the shrewder economists, namely, that there is no sort of assurance, even where business competition is supposed to prevail, that the prices charged to the domestic consumer will, taken as a whole, automatically oscillate closely about the real and necessary costs of production, or that the public can rely on business competition as an effective safeguard against the extortion of an entirely unnecessary price.

In the light of this advance of economic knowledge, alike on the side of efficiency of production measured in output, and on that of retail price in relation to necessary cost, no instructed statesman can nowadays honestly base his polity on *laisser faire*. Capitalist enterprise, as is now admitted, has, in and for itself alone, no logical claim to existence.   It can be regarded as justified only in so far as it fulfils a function in the social order ; and society has to be vigilant to see that the function is fulfilled. The constitution to be drafted, here and now, must accordingly provide for supervision and control of those activities that may, for the time being, be left to capitalist enterprise, notably during the transition to a predominantly Socialist community. The first thing to be ensured is the production, in adequate quantity and of proper quality, of what the community needs. Every one to-day realises that it will not do to leave entirely to the chance-medley of the capitalist greed for gain either the production of food or that of knowledge, the provision of dwelling-houses or that of the means of healthy and improving recreation. In the second place, it is imperative to ensure that a progressively increasing efficiency of production is obtained, in each industry as a whole, irrespective of the apathy or

ignorance or incompetence of the moiety of establishments which, at any one time, fall below the average
standard.   Finally, it is necessary to take care that the
prices charged to the consumers are not, as they are
apt to be in a world of capitalist combination, " all
that the trade will bear," or all that monopoly can
extort ; but, on the contrary, no more than can be
proved to be sufficient, with the most efficient organisation of the industry as a whole, to call forth the
productivity that we require.

THE STANDING COMMITTEE ON PRODUCTIVITY

Thus we may contemplate the appointment, by
the Social Parliament, of a Standing Committee on
Productivity, served by a department of which the
Board of Trade and the Board of Agriculture and
Fisheries will supply the beginning, although many
existing prejudices and conventions will need to
be shed in its development. It must realise that
its function will not be merely to get abuses
prohibited by the criminal law, or detected by its
inspectors ; but that it will exist primarily for the
assistance of the nation's industry, in all its branches,
by whomsoever conducted ; and that its main work
will be actually to help in the efficient conduct of industrial undertakings by doing for them, freely and
energetically, what the conductors can practically never
do for themselves.   Such a department would take, as
its guiding principles for the supervision and control
of capitalist, as of all other enterprise, that throughout
the whole range of industrial activity, Measurement
and Publicity will be everywhere secured ; that
industrial organisation requires to be as persistently
stimulated as industrial invention ; and that prices
everywhere need to be kept in close relation to the
ascertained necessary costs of production.   Such a

department would render to all industry the inestimable
service of constantly making available, for the directors
of industrial undertakings, the new knowledge which
no one among them can get for himself. In this work
it would employ not merely or even mainly its own
salaried staff, but would make constant use of independent professional experts ; applying, for instance,
the instrument of strict and accurate costing to every
establishment in every industry ; comparing, one with
another, the expense and output of every process
in all its applications ; supplying each establishment,
with the object of inducing it to increase its own
efficiency, with a stream of reports showing how it
compares with others at home and abroad ; providing
incessant comparative statistics of the cost of each
component or factor in all the establishments of the
same kind, and with full and varied information as to
what is happening elsewhere. All this information
should be communicated, not merely to the capitalist
or other conductors of enterprises, but also to the
Works Committees, so that the workers concerned
may know how their establishment compares in
efficiency with others ; and subsequently, in suitable
detail, to the scientific societies and other vocational
organisations, of manual workers and brain workers,
interested in the industry ; with eventual publication
to the world.

It is not suggested that, for the most part, there
should be any use of coercive powers to bring about
improvements.[1] The reports of the cost accountants

---

[1] Authoritative interference with the methods of industry—apart from
what may be involved in the enforcement of the Policy of the National
Minimum—would probably need to be exercised principally in the form of
covenants in a lease of the nation's land or other instruments of production ;
or when, as may well be the case, the Social Parliament supplies on loan from
public funds the whole or part of the capital required for a new or expanding
industry. It may, for instance, be thought necessary in the public interest
that a certain minimum acreage should be applied to wheat-growing ; or
that the production of food should not be hampered by individual desires
for the preservation of game.

and the auditors, the statisticians and the technical experts would, in no case, have any authoritative force. They would only furnish information and more or less explicit suggestions for improvement. They could be, and with great intellectual advantage to all concerned, doubtless would be in many cases disputed. Each establishment would be disposed to believe in their accuracy with regard to every other establishment, though not with regard to itself. But they would anyhow bring new light, and, what is of supreme importance, it would be known that they would be published. They would accordingly be eagerly scanned and discussed in the industry concerned, not less among the workmen than among the managers, and most of all by the technicians.

The Fixing of Prices

The searchlight of published knowledge will be the main instrument of increasing the productivity of industrial enterprise. But there will also be an indirect effect through prices. It will of course be at all times the duty of the Social Parliament to see to it that the current market price does not unduly exceed that which its departments will have ascertained, and its standing committees will have reported to be, for the time being, the socially necessary expense of production or of importation, assuming a standard of efficiency in practice attained at the moment by the better half of the establishments concerned. Any rise above this socially necessary return might have to be at once checked by the enforcement of a Legal Maximum Price, coupled with the demonstration, to each of the establishments complaining that such a price left them with insufficient profit, that they were falling below the average level of efficiency in the industry, and that the other establishments were quite capable of supplying the whole requirements at the statutory price.

Doubtless the average business man of to-day will not only be revolted at such an interference with his pursuit of private gain, but will also be honestly unable to understand how production could possibly be conducted at a profit if all the processes and working costs of his establishment were revealed to the world ; if he was expected always to keep up to a steadily rising standard of efficiency, and if he was never to be allowed (adequate provision being made for insurance against risk, for depreciation and even for reserves) to get a windfall of more than an average rate of profit. Nevertheless, once it is realised that the object of industry is not a maximum of profit, but, consistently with proper conditions and proper remuneration for all employed, a maximum of output, it will be seen that very much more is gained by universalising all the available knowledge than by each man trying, through secrecy, to get the better of his rivals. Moreover, to the ingenious inventor of some improvement in organisation, to the genius of a manager who has a new idea, to the discoverer of some new market or some new application, there will always remain the profit that is involved in priority. Measurement and Publicity, which are so much feared to-day by the capitalist profit-maker, operate, after all, only *ex post facto*. It is the past half-year's work that the auditor and the cost accountant will report upon. The energetic and ambitious manager, even if his past achievements are revealed to an admiring world, and even if he cannot be allowed to monopolise his ideas for the future, has always to-day in which to work for his own gain. And this gain, if gain be his inducement to efficiency, will be proportionate to the improvement that he makes. In a Socialist Commonwealth, so far as concerns any industry which is still being conducted

for private profit, the capitalist *entrepreneur* or manager
will have to become, in effect, a strictly regulated
intellectual piece-worker, remunerated according to
results ascertained by accurate scientific measurement.

The Method of Expropriation

But the community, as the experience of the past
half-century has taught us, will be always expanding
the sphere of its collective undertakings, in which it
is found that the profit-making motive can with
advantage be dispensed with.   We need not pretend
to forecast the future, but Socialists at least will believe
that the process of promoting a private business into
a public service will continue to prevail, and that it
will be rapidly extended.   It is therefore of importance
to make clear in what way, and with what consideration
to the persons concerned, a Socialist Commonwealth
will proceed to " nationalise " or " municipalise "
any industry or service heretofore conducted for
private gain.

In the first place, the Socialist Commonwealth
will put in force the principle of Freedom of Socialised
Enterprise.   The Social Parliament will certainly be
liberated from the prejudice that in all capitalist
legislatures to-day constantly seeks, if not to maintain an actual monopoly for capitalist enterprise, at
least to protect it (as if it were conscious of its inferiority
of service) against the competition of public undertakings.   Socialist legislators will not be much impressed by the " unfairness " of any National Board
created by the Social Parliament, or of the Co-operative
Movement, or of the Local Authority, supplying some
public need, or serving some generally useful purpose,
notwithstanding that the result may eventually be a
diminution of the profits of the private capitalists who
have done very well out of the business in the past.

Even under our present capitalist Parliament in Great Britain a Local Authority is statutorily permitted to supply electricity without compensating the local gas company; it is encouraged and subsidised to conduct its own schools far under cost price, or even gratuitously, to the ruin of the " private adventure " schools; it is allowed to provide a municipal burial-ground or crematorium without regard to its effect on the profits of the local joint-stock cemetery; it is authorised to run the local omnibuses off the road with its tramway service if it can do so; it is most strongly pressed to provide new dwelling-houses in direct reduction of the incomes of the landlords of the local slum property; and it is urged to supply milk below cost, or even free, to nursing-mothers and infants, without any test of indigence, and whatever the local milk-sellers may say to the contrary.

But although common sense, and the above precedents, will make for conceding as much Freedom of Enterprise to National Boards, Municipalities and Co-operative Societies as the individual *entrepreneur* has for a century enjoyed, when it comes actually to taking over a whole industry, or to dispossessing any owner of property, we expect and believe that the community, and therefore, as its representatives, the Social Parliament, will be influenced by a sense of both fairness and expediency in dealing very gently with " established expectations." It will let no " vested interests " stand in the way of improvement. It will " expropriate " without remorse individual owners from their lands, their house property, their factories and their enterprises, whenever this course seems to promote the general well-being. But the community will, it may be assumed, remember that those on whom the Tower of Siloam fell were not greater sinners than other men—that the particular men and women whom at any moment it finds necessary to deprive of their property ought not, in equity, to be made to suffer more than the other members of the class to which they belong. It will no doubt be necessary for the community to take over, for public purposes, a whole succession of industries, and, as Socialists have learnt from the economists, eventually to supersede, as completely as may prove to be practicable, the whole system of "living by owning." But landlords and capitalists, great or small, will not during their own lives be deprived of their means of livelihood. Much as the moralists may condemn "living by owning," it is not only humane but also expedient, and moreover, in the long run, less costly to the community, to treat fairly, and even liberally, not merely every employee whose livelihood is disturbed, but also each particular owner as he is dispossessed.

Accordingly, those British Socialists who have experience of administration, do not contemplate a method of expropriation essentially different from that which prevails to-day whenever a Local Authority takes over a local gas or water company, or acquires property for widening a street. Each owner should receive in compensation the fair market value of that of which he is compulsorily dispossessed, as between a willing seller and a willing buyer. Whether he is paid such a sum in cash, or in government securities at their own market value, or by an equivalent annuity for a term of years, or for life, is of no pecuniary importance. The community will, of course, be saddled with the interest and sinking fund, or the annuity ; and will thus, on the face of it, be no wealthier than before ; just as the expropriated person will be no poorer, and the aggregate tribute on production levied by ownership no less than before. The object of "socialisation" is "socialisation,"—that is to say, the transformation of profit-making enterprise into public service ; not the enrichment of the community by confiscation. But as the Socialist Commonwealth will certainly adopt the economists' emphatic canon of taxation, and levy its revenue on the citizens in proportion to their relative " Ability to Pay," the burden of compensation for expropriation will fall, in effect, almost entirely on the property owners as a class. They will, in short, in order to prevent the hardship which summary confiscation would cause to particular individuals among them, be allowed (like the holders of licences to sell alcoholic drink under the Licensing Act of 1902) gradually to extinguish each other's private ownership over a term of years, by the silent operation of the Death Duties and the graduated Income Tax and Super-tax. No expropriation without full compensation ; no payment of the annuities, or of the interest and sinking fund thereby incurred, otherwise than from the taxes on property ownership !

TAXATION

It will be seen that it is part of the conception of the Socialist Commonwealth that, at any rate during what we have referred to as the period of transition, the great instrument of taxation will be used—as Bentham vainly sought to teach the Liberal and Radical Parties a hundred years ago—as a means of reducing the inequality of wealth. The tribute of rent and interest which ownership, in this transitional period, will continue to levy on production—to use the phrase of the British Parliament itself, the " unearned incomes "—will naturally continue to be subjected to differential rates of taxation, in comparison with " earned incomes." But the other existing principle of progressive graduation according to the amount of the wealth, or of the income, will also be applied, with much more deliberate purpose than any British Finance Minister has yet had the courage to propose to a capitalist Parliament.

To take first the Death Duties. Socialists are, as will be explained in the following section, very far from desiring to abolish inheritance as such. But in a Socialist Commonwealth the Social Parliament would doubtless proceed, at an early date, to discriminate between the kind and the amount of heritage which is beneficial, alike to the family and to the community, and that which is demonstrably injurious, both to the children or other heirs (whom it now habitually demoralises, and often ruins, by tempting them to " live by owning ") and to the community as a whole, in its perpetuation of that evil. In the ensuing section will be discussed the principles on which something like a maximum of permissible testamentary disposition or inheritance would be fixed. Beyond this the Death Duties would rise very steeply to nearly 100 per cent.

Not accumulated fortunes only, but also incomes, even if " earned," would presumably be dealt with on similar lines ; but, as may be suggested, less drastically. If differential rates of tax are placed on " unearned income " (notably so as to obtain for the public as much as possible of the surplus that is of the nature of economic rent) ; and if Death Duties are used as the " abhorred shears " to reclaim in due course all but a reasonable family provision, the Socialist Commonwealth may afford to be more lenient to the incomes which are obtained during life, alike by the capitalist *entrepreneurs* who are left in possession of industries not yet expropriated ; by inventors who may enrich the community by their thoughts and their experiments; and by the brain-working professionals, from poets and artists of all sorts, and medical, financial and legal experts, down to the scientific and managerial technicians. But there is such a thing, even among professionals, as "exploitation" of the needs of individuals or of the public; and it is already condemned as "unprofessional" for even the most skilful surgeon, or the ablest inventor, actually to hold the community to ransom, and to extort the highest possible tribute for his exceptional talent. Even "captains of industry" may be, in the future, expected to be "gentlemen," with no lower standard of professional honour than the artists and the doctors; and when by valuable inventions or exceptional genius in management they obtain incomes which, commensurate though they may be with the service rendered to the community, are markedly above the standard of life of the highest public officials whom the Commonwealth delights to honour, it will be assumed that they would wish (by the device of a steep progression of the rate of Income Tax that they will pay) to surrender a large part of the surplus for public purposes.

THE RELATION OF PRICES TO THE NATIONAL REVENUE

With the gradual progress of socialisation, the steady advance in eliminating all "living by owning," and the approximation towards substantial equality of incomes, the place in the Socialist Budget filled by either Income Tax or Death Duties will eventually be a diminishing one. It need not be assumed, indeed, that there will ever come a time when there will be absolutely no surplus of heritable estates, or of bequests, to assess to Death Duties; and absolutely no incomes beyond the common standard of life from which the progressive graduation of the Income Tax can extract a contribution to the public revenue. Moreover, any important differential advantages of the main factors of production in the hands of Local Authorities or Co-operative Societies—of the nature of economic rent—should at all times be equitably distributed among the whole community by suitable taxation of Land Values. With these exceptions, however, the Socialist Commonwealth would ultimately find its national and local revenues accruing, almost entirely, in the receipts of the national and municipal industries and services, the net proceeds of which would depend essentially upon the fees or prices charged to the consumers or users of the several commodities and services. The budget of the Chairman of the Finance Committee of the Social Parliament, and those of the Chairmen of the Finance Committees of the various Local Authorities, like those of the existing Co-operative Societies and social clubs of mutual character, would therefore depend, almost entirely, on a fixing of fees and prices.

A simple adherence to the cost of rendering the service does not solve the problem. There are some public services which are of such a nature that they cannot be charged for at all, such as national defence, the conduct of relations with communities overseas, the general administration of the community's affairs, the promotion of public health, the provision for the non-effectives, and even the execution of justice. There are others, such as the maintenance of roads, the institutional treatment of the sick, and the education of children, in which it has already been found convenient to adopt the principle of Communism, in the sense of letting every one enjoy in accordance with his needs, whilst paying (by taxation) in proportion to his ability. There are other services, again, like those of the water supply or the Post Office, where the most convenient course is to make charges according to uniform scales, having little reference to the actual expense involved in each item of service. On the other hand there are other services, such as the supply of gas and electricity, where it is practicable to charge exactly according to the quantity supplied, and very closely proportionate to the cost of production. There are yet other cases, in which, whilst the community may be ready to provide the service or produce the commodity, it is one of which the use or consumption is not seen to be of any public advantage—it may, even, possibly be regarded as having disadvantageous consequences to the community, so that consumption or use, whilst not forbidden or prevented, may come to be discouraged by exceptionally high prices.

The prices at which the products of the national industries and services will pass into consumption or use will be determined by the Social Parliament, on the recommendation of its Standing Committee on Finance, according to the feelings and opinions of the community for the time being. The tendency towards Communism may, for instance, gather strength; and it may be generally desired to reduce to a minimum both postage rates and railway fares ; or even to make these services (with the necessary administrative safeguards) as " free " as we have already made our roads, our public libraries and museums, and our elementary schools. But the aggregate receipts must somehow be made to equal the aggregate outgoings ; and the price of coal, or of railway goods traffic, or of alcoholic drinks, or of imported tea and coffee, might need to be raised proportionately—just as, to-day, a Town Council will often make a large profit by charging high prices for gas and electricity, in order to be able to run its baths and washhouses at a loss, and to be munificent with its university college, or its parks and open spaces. On the other hand, the consumers of the surcharged commodities may resent this imposition ; they may press, in the alternative, for higher railway fares and postage rates, the reimposition of school fees and of charges for medical attendance. A simple plan, analogous to that adopted in capitalist industry with regard to " overhead charges," would be to require, in the first place, each national industry or service to include in its price a certain percentage on cost, so fixed, year by year, as to cover the whole expense of the non-remunerative services, which are, essentially, the " overhead charges " of the community.

The Continuous Increase in a Socialist Commonwealth of Private Property in Individual Ownership

It is apparently part of the " invincible ignorance " of the upholders of the Capitalist System to confuse the institution of private property with the right of private ownership, for the purpose of profit-making, of the instruments of wealth production. This leads to the constant reiteration of the accusation that Socialism involves the abrogation of private property. Yet the whole policy of the British Labour and Socialist Movement may be summed up as a determination to maintain, strengthen and extend private property by preventing its monopoly in the hands of a small fraction of the population. Far from being hostile to the institution of private property, it would necessarily be one of the fundamental objects of a Socialist Commonwealth so to broaden the base and extend the benefits of private ownership as continuously to increase its aggregate amount. At present, in Great Britain as in other countries of advanced industrialism, more than two-thirds of all the citizens find themselves, in fact, excluded all their lives long from anything that can reasonably be called private property—from anything beyond their current wages, their exiguous hoards against a rainy day, and " as much old furniture as would go into a cart." Of all the amenity and

charm and the development of family life that may
be given by the secure possession of a permanent home
the bulk of the wage-earners are, under modern
Capitalism, deprived. From that " development of
personality " which may be promoted by the ownership and gradual improvement, year by year, of house
and garden, as home and homestead, they are, for the
most part, debarred. Their chances of surrounding
themselves and their children with the refinements of
beautiful furniture, books, pictures and music are, so
far as concerns the mass of the people, the " common
lump of men," of the slightest. Their painfully maintained insurance, through Friendly Society and Trade
Union, against the stoppage of all income by sickness,
unemployment, chronic infirmity, or old age, is, when
adversity comes, in amount hopelessly inadequate to
the mere continuance of their accustomed standard of
life, low as this is ; and even when supplemented by
their little hoards, it seldom suffices either for competent care and nursing in ill-health, or for reasonable
comfort in old age. Hardly the smallest fraction of
working-class families find their earnings and their
savings sufficient to provide for their children, either
the constant personal care during the first few years,
or the educational surroundings during childhood, or
the skilled medical attention, or the technical training,
or even the outfit on leaving home, that fathers and
mothers in all classes yearn to give to their children,
and that the average parent of the professional class
considers absolutely necessary for the health and well-
being of his own progeny. When the manual-working
parent dies—on an average, prematurely, at a much
earlier age than among the class provided with property
—there is left, in nine cases out of ten, hardly sufficient
estate to pay the funeral expenses ; very seldom even
the most modest provision for a surviving spouse or
young children ; and practically never the sort of

pecuniary guarantee against suffering through misfortune which fond fathers and mothers in other classes aspire to leave for their own children. The awful insecurity and the continuous apprehension of privation involved in the lack of private property are the common lot to-day of at least three-fourths of all the families of the kingdom. " The Labouring Classes," remarks a British economist, " accepted from ignorance or powerlessness, or were compelled, persuaded or cajoled by custom, convention, authority and the well-established order of society, into accepting a situation in which they could call their own very little of the cake that they and Nature, and the capitalists were co-operating to produce."[1] It is exactly this absence of private property, with all the beneficent development of character and personality that it involves in the lives of the great mass of men and women, that the Socialist deplores and is determined to prevent.

What Socialists object to is the perversion of the institution of private property by the extension of the concept to things and rights which, in their judgment, are not fit objects of individual ownership. In no civilised community has the definition of private property been quite unlimited. Even in the Roman Empire a citizen could acquire no right of property in the city wall. To-day, in Great Britain, individual ownership is not permitted to extend to human beings, to public thoroughfares, to the organisation of postal, telegraph and telephone services, or to the particular public services monopolised by any Local Authority. The question of what things and what rights should be allowed to become private property is one to be decided from time to time ; but it does not involve any prohibition of private property itself. On the

---

[1] *The Economic Consequences of the Peace*, by J. M. Keynes (1920), p-. 16.

contrary, the very demarcation of the boundaries of private property implies, it will be seen, its maintenance and its endorsement. To the Socialist it seems that to extend private property to the ownership of the instruments of production is a perversion of the institution. " The original idea, essence and purpose of property," remarks an American Socialist, " was to secure to a person or group of persons the use and control of the things which that person or group needed for his or its own subsistence and welfare." This purpose, he explains, has been actually thwarted by the capitalist system. " The capitalist does not wish to own his railroads and factories, his rented houses and lands because he wishes to use them, but because some one else wishes to use them. He wants to own his clothes or his umbrella because he wishes to use them ; but he wishes to own his stocks, bonds and rentable real estate because he wants to be paid for owning them, and he cannot be paid for owning them unless some one else needs to use them. On a desert island they would be valueless to him. Thus the whole value of capitalistic property to the capitalist depends upon the disjunction between use and ownership—upon the complete reversal of the original purpose of property. It seems strange that an institution which started out to place the ownership of things in the hands of those who use them should have ended by placing the ownership of a large class of things, namely, the means of production of society, in the hands of those who do not use them, except as they constitute one fraction of the consuming public ; but this reversal of the purpose of property has taken place imperceptibly and without attracting attention, because the forms of transfer of property have not changed. Title to property is secured in the same way it always has been—by direct appropriation from nature, by gift, by inheritance, by purchase or other legal assignment. It is only the purpose of the institution which has been changed." [1]

A new demarcation of the sphere of individually owned private property, together with a preference for its universal diffusion throughout the whole community, instead of its aggregation in masses, or its limitation to a small class, does not involve any restriction on its aggregate amount. It may seem paradoxical, but it is literally true that, in the Socialist Commonwealth, the aggregate amount of the private property, or individual wealth, owned by the citizens may be expected greatly to exceed the total wealth at present owned by all the inhabitants of the United States or of Australia, which are to-day the richest of capitalist societies ; and it will be the constant endeavour of a Socialist community to promote its further increase.

The Socialist Commonwealth will be based fundamentally on the public provision of services, not on the prohibition of individual activity. There will be no desire to prevent each family from having, on a practically permanent tenure, at least so far as its own occupation is concerned, its own home and homestead, as commodious and as well appointed as its members desire. Clearly all the personal paraphernalia, from furniture and clothes to tools and apparatus, for individual use will be equally unrestricted. Every person will be free to devote his income to any one of these desirable things to any extent. All the ingenious difficulties suggested, as to what is to prevent these possessions being " lent " for hire, and so giving rise to " exploitation " and " tribute," in despite of all laws, are otiose, and based on sheer misunderstanding. There is no reason why anything that is individually owned in a Socialist Commonwealth should

[1] *Americanised Socialism · A Yankee View of Capitalism*, by James MacKaye (1920), pp. 34-5, 40-1.

not, subject to any conditions deemed necessary in the public interest, and to appropriate taxation, be freely saleable, rentable, transferable, inheritable and transmissible by testamentary disposition. Further, there will be not only complete freedom, but even the utmost possible encouragement to the accumulation, in each family, of its private hoard of savings, for future enjoyment, or by way of provision against adversity. This saving will take, it may be assumed, three main forms. There will be first the improvement of the home, to which sufficient reference has been made, but which must be noted as accounting in the aggregate for an amount of family thrift and individual saving of which the England of to-day has little conception. Secondly, it may be assumed that the habit of insurance will be greatly developed. Whatever common provision is made, locally or nationally (and possibly also vocationally), for sickness and infirmity, accident and old age—and of this there will be much —there will always be the desire to supplement this public provision, to provide against other contingencies, and to prepare something special and individual for the years to come. The insurance fund and reserve in the hands of the national, local or vocational departments of insurance will therefore become steadily more enormous as the opportunities which they offer are taken advantage of by the whole community. This capital will of course be used on such conditions as may be arranged (which may quite reasonably include a rate of interest if this is found necessary or desirable), for the industrial undertakings and public services of the several public authorities.

The third form of saving will be the simple accumulation of deposits in the national and municipal (and possibly also vocational) banks, on which, too, it may be quite permissible to pay interest, if such a stimulus to saving proves to be necessary or desirable.

All this range of activities may quite well be, so far as law or regulation is concerned, as free and unlimited as at present, and will in practice certainly be much more effectively open to all. The banks and insurance offices will all be publicly owned and administered, but with the increase in the number of their customers this will mean an increase, not a diminution in the extent and variety of their action. Where restriction will come in, as regards private accumulation, will be by progressive taxation of incomes, and of wealth passing by alienation or at death. The increasing steepness of the graduation of the Income Tax, and the differentiation against " unearned incomes " of more than small amount, can easily be made effective to prevent any incomes of a magnitude injurious to public morals. Similarly, the Death Duties—light as regards the home and homestead of reasonable value, as regards testamentary provision for family dependents, and even as regards a modest trust fund to safeguard children from pecuniary disaster—will rise steeply beyond a limit to be fixed from time to time. Whilst fortunes up to £5000 or even £10,000, taking the present level of prices, will be only lightly taxed, anything beyond such a sum, or at any rate any bequest of more than such a sum, would be virtually prevented by Death Duties rising to nearly 100 per cent of the excess. It will certainly be the intention of the Social Parliament so to levy taxation as to prevent—except in cases of ill-health or infirmity, under family settlements limited in amount—any " living by owning."

It is interesting to estimate that, in Great Britain to-day, if each family possessed in Home and Homestead, in Paraphernalia and in Hoard (whether in insurance or savings bank), private property to an aggregate value of only £5000, no one possessing more, this would represent a total capital wealth of fifty thousand million pounds, or at least three times as much as all the existing private riches of the inhabitants of the Kingdom.

How Capital will be provided

There is accordingly, in the Socialist Common-wealth, ample scope for individual saving, the best possible provision for its secure investment, free play to those motives for saving which have hitherto operated most powerfully on the minds of the masses of the people, and a greater margin out of which their savings will be practicable. This may well prove a sufficient substitute for the savings that the profit-making and wealthy classes have hitherto made out from the surplus of their incomes. But it is scarcely likely that the Socialist Commonwealth will make itself dependent, for carrying out the necessary annual improvements and extensions in every department, on borrowing any such voluntarily accumulated fund of savings.[1] It is more likely to arrange, so as to avoid

[1] It may be observed that there is an extraordinary delusion current in the capitalist society of to-day, to the effect that the normal and economical way — indeed the only practicable way — in which new enterprises or extensions of any magnitude can be undertaken is by borrowing. As a matter of fact, throughout the history of the world, by far the greater part of the extensions, increases and improvements by which the capital of the world's industries and services has steadily grown in magnitude have been effected without debt or borrowing at all, but merely, year by year, as part of the operations of the year. It was in this way, for instance, throughout the ages, that the land of England has been, by great landowner or small, gradually reclaimed from fen or waste. There is no record of public debt being contracted for the Cloth Hall at Ypres, or for the Cathedrals. The practice of borrowing at interest the capital required for any kind of in-dustrial enterprise is, indeed, as a general practice, only two or three centuries old. In our own day the national and municipal Authorities, whilst they are great borrowers, are also constant savers on a large scale. The Post Office is only one of the departments which have silently accumu-lated a large aggregate property, without (apart from the telegraph and telephone systems, and some recent purchases of additional sites) having any debt or capital account at all. The British Local Authorities to-day own property worth at least three times the total of their indebtedness. The Co-operative Movement in the same way has accumulated relatively large reserves which constitute no small part of its working capital. The Govern-ment of the Federated Malay States itself constructed the extensive and well-equipped railway system of that community, without borrowing any capital,

incurring any burden of interest, that each National Board should provide in its budget for the year for the execution of the extensions and improvements that it is considered desirable to execute within the year. In this way there would be, in favour of the future, a " loading " on the cost of production of the commodities or services produced in the year, but (as experience has taught the British municipal financiers) a smaller loading than would be necessitated, year in and year out, by the payment of interest and sinking fund of borrowed capital.

The Transition and its Dangers

There are those who will be impatient of discussion of transitional arrangements, and who would prefer to think only of the organisation by which an entirely " socialised " community would conduct its completely " socialised " life. How short or long may last any transitional stage, during which exceptional provision must be made for controlling industries and services still in profit-making hands, and for taxing incomes and inheritances of abnormal amount, no one can predict. We venture on one prophecy. The period of transition, inevitable though it is as one social order passes into another, is necessarily a disheartening and a dangerous one for all concerned. So long as there is a whole class of persons who " live by owning "—so long as there are in a community any considerable number of able-bodied men and women who ostentatiously refuse to render a social service which, in the opinion of their fellow citizens, is

---

incurring any debt or paying any interest, simply by making just whatever extension, year after year, could conveniently be undertaken as part of the year's budget. The Commonwealth Bank, now the largest banking institution of Australia, was started, within the last decade, by the Commonwealth Government without any other capital than an office and a suite of office furniture, both of them lent gratuitously for the purpose.

equivalent to the commodities and services that they consume [1]—an embittered " class war " will continue to diminish the total product. So long as those who direct the productive energies of the nation, instigated by the motive of " making a fortune," are heaping up for themselves and their families wealth and power, we may expect other sections of workers by hand and by brain to attempt to follow their example ; and to seek to better their own material conditions, and even to increase their own arbitrary power, without regard to the well-being of the whole. And, seeing that the advent of political and industrial Democracy has endowed the multitude who use the instruments of production with potential authority in the State, whilst the Capitalist System reserves the effective authority to the relatively small class of persons who

---

[1] A question which troubles not a few public-spirited and conscientious citizens possessing property, and finding themselves " living by owning," is what they ought to do with their wealth. We may note, first, that the duty of work for the community—of rendering continuous and useful service in return for one's livelihood—is incumbent on all adults so long as health and strength lasts, whether or not they possess what are called " independent means." Their possession of " an independence " merely adds to their social responsibilities that of freely choosing the vocation in which they can be of the greatest use. Those with tender consciences have been known to refuse to accept or to retain income-yielding property, preferring to earn their subsistence in the competitive market, a course which may possibly not lead to their adopting the vocation in which they can be of most use. But by refusing to accept or to retain what is lawfully their property they do not escape responsibility for the use that is made of the wealth of which they have, to soothe their own consciences, abandoned the control ; whether the transfer be to the next heir or some other member of their family, or to some charitable foundation. If they cast their wealth upon the Exchequer, intending to present it to the community, they are really making a donation to their fellow landlords and capitalists, by relieving them of a proportion of the Super-tax that would otherwise be levied on them. It cannot be deemed wise or economical to " give the money away " for purposes (such as the ordinary treatment of the sick, or the ordinary school education, or the relief of the destitute), which merely relieve the rates ; still less should it be distributed in alms (otherwise than by way of substantial assistance for individual cases known to the donor). The wisest course appears to us to be to use whatever means are available for the utmost possible increase of one's own specific function ; and then for the creation or promotion of additional efficiency in suitable persons, preferably young persons of promise whose means are insufficient to enable them to render as much service as they are capable of. In corporate work, what is most needed to-day is the endowment of research in economic and political science.

live by owning and organising these instruments of production, we may possibly be confronted with an interval of costly social friction and degrading strife, during which the rapid disintegration of the modern industrial system might drag, into an abyss of privation, disease and civil war, all that we now recognise as Western civilisation.

What is needed to avert the possible disasters of the transitional period is a development of the spirit of social service, on the one hand, and of science on the other. It is our faith as well as our hope that the Democracies of the world are capable of responding to these two fundamental requirements for the establishment of a Co-operative Commonwealth.

The Spirit of Service

The disastrous assumption on which the Capitalist System was based—an assumption as immoral as it was fortunately untrue—that man in society is and should be inspired, in the exercise of his function, by the passion for riches, was a morbid obsession into which Western Europe passed less than three centuries ago, and out of which it is now emerging. The assumption was never accepted by the learned professions, nor, in Great Britain, by the typical civil servants. It never even penetrated to the bulk of the manual workers, who were saved from the assumption by the fact that, as a class, they had only the smallest possible opportunity of acquiring riches. The equivalent in their case was the equally demoralising motive of the fear of starvation. We think that the tide has now turned. The rapid growth of the consumers' Co-operative Movement on the one hand, and of State and Municipal enterprise on the other, has given the community a large and constantly growing class of administrators and technicians who are debarred by economic circumstances and by professional honour from making profit out of each day's transactions. From these men and women society is accustomed to ask and to receive assiduous and honest public service in return for their accustomed livelihood. It is this assumption of honest public service that, with a better organisation of industry, we hope and expect to generalise. And we mean by honest public service no Utopian altruism. Martyrs and saints, like poets and inventors, are needed for the progress of the human race to ever higher planes of feeling and intellect. But no Socialist expects, or even desires, a race of self-sacrificing saints who deny to themselves that enjoyment of life which they seek to maximise in the lives of other people, any more than he expects or desires that all men shall be artistic geniuses or scientific discoverers. What the establishment of a genuine Co-operative Commonwealth requires in the way of an advance in morality is no more than that those who have the gift for industrial organisation should be as public-spirited in their work, and as modest in their claims to a livelihood, as is already normally the case among scientific workers, teachers in schools and colleges, the whole army of civil servants of every degree and kind, municipal officers of every grade, the administrators of the Co-operative Movement and the officials of the Trade Union world. And this substitution of the motive of public service for the motive of self-enrichment will be fostered by the change already beginning in public opinion, which will make " living by owning " as shameful as the pauperism of the wastrel ; and will, moreover, regard the exceptionally gifted man who insists on extorting from the community the full rent of his ability as a mean fellow —as mean as the surgeon who refuses to operate except for the highest fee that he can extract. Equally influential will be the social approval and public honour given, not to success in amassing riches, but to disinterested and zealous public service. Is it cynical to suggest that, for one pioneer in a higher morality there are hundreds of worthy citizens whose lack of moral imagination will lead them to accept a higher morality as a new convention, to which they automatically conform ? New and better conventions in morality, which are at all times within the capacity of the community, are, in fact, the normal way of standardising and generalising the moral discoveries of the race, just as the new scientific school-books serve to standardise and generalise our widening knowledge. Men are, in their manners and morals, to a far larger extent than is yet realised, what their fellows expect them to be. It is in this sense that Socialist institutions within a community, exacting from the average man a higher level of morality than that of the Capitalist System—like a genuine League of Nations among communities themselves—bring about an actual change of heart, and are thus the effective instruments of religion.

The Need for Knowledge

It is, indeed, not any failure in public spirit that presents, at least in an Anglo-Saxon race, the greatest obstacle to social amelioration. More difficult, in our view, will it be to induce the whole body of citizens—the wealthy and the college-trained no less than the manual workers—to realise the imperative need for a rapid development of science in its widest sense, alike in the discovery of new knowledge and in the universal dissemination of scientific methods of thinking. This is necessary if we are to get a greater output. Not the least of the shortcomings of the Capitalist System has been its calamitous failure to produce, in the aggregate, anything like enough commodities and services even to keep the community in health and efficiency, let alone enough to constitute a decent mental and physical environment for the whole people. In the Great War, indeed, this failure in production was so glaringly revealed that a capitalist government had, perforce, hastily to improvise a different organisation, in order merely to survive.[1] More science in the organisation of production (not of material commodities only) is therefore indispensable. If we wish to divide among the whole community a larger quantity and a higher quality of commodities and services than the painfully exiguous yield of the Capitalist System of to-day, the necessary increase in output has to be secured. And goodwill alone will not secure it. Even the replacement of the desire for riches by the motive of public service, as the dominant stimulus of personal effort, will not give us the needful larger and better production, without the application of much more science to the work than the Capitalist System has yet known how to harness. The need is, of course, not for physical science only. It was one of the disastrous mistakes of the Victorian era that physical science seemed to be the only science worth cultivating. There is no reason to fear that mechanics, physics and chemistry will be neglected, even if discoverers have no chance of

---

[1] Now that the war is over, we find again put forward the (surely ironical ?) defence of private property in the instruments of production, that, however inadequate may be its provision for the mass of the workers, it, at least, affords to a small minority of landlords and capitalists the ease and plenty on which alone such of them as are active administrators can put forth their full powers ! Apart from the disquieting fact that the community, in thus feeding luxuriously a whole class, has no guarantee that any one of the class will devote himself to the public service—apart also from the still more disquieting doubt whether the possession of riches can be relied on as a stimulus to productive effort—the validity of this defence of the Capitalist System depends, perhaps, on whether it is any longer possible to compel the great majority of the people, whom the system does not seem to fatten, and who are no longer either so ignorant or so powerless as they were, to continue to work upon such terms. A refusal might lead, at least temporarily, to a dead level of economic disaster. Unfortunately the disaster to the rich that an economic upheaval might produce would not bring wealth to the poor; and might, conceivably, not be even a stage on the road to a decent social order.

accumulating personal riches. There is, indeed, good ground for expecting discovery in physical science to go forward by leaps and bounds, in a way that may presently transform all our dealings with forms of force and kinds of substance. But what is no less needed than this greater knowledge of things, is the greater knowledge of men : of the conditions of the successful working of social institutions. That on which the world to-day most needs light is how to render more effective every form of social organisation : how to make more socially fertile the relations among men. And this nascent science and art of democratic institutions, in which, for all that has so far been done, a hundredfold yet remains to do, must be, in the generation that is to come, as effectively opened up to the masses of manual workers as to the administrators and technicians. Without this community in knowledge there will, very shortly, be no popular consent. There is no need so imperative to-day as increased economic and political science. There is no peril so dangerous as the failure to get community of education among all classes.

It is, perhaps, in this respect that Parliamentary institutions have most lamentably fallen short. They have had no regard for knowledge. If they are now so rapidly losing public respect, and the support of popular consent, it is because Members of Parliament and Cabinet Ministers show themselves not only so ignorant of their job, but also so complacently unaware that they have anything to learn ; and therefore quite unconscious of the need for making the electorate any better educated than they are themselves.

But our present failures are to be ascribed, not merely to deficiencies in knowledge, but also to the impossibility, with our existing institutions, of bringing into play such knowledge as is available. The House of Commons and the Cabinet, as they exist to-day, are

as incapable of organising the industrial and social
life of Great Britain, so as to make a decent social
order, as the Capitalist System has proved itself to be.
It is for this reason that thoughtful Socialists lay so
much stress on quite a different conception of Government. They are insistent, for the new social order,
not only on a varied and highly developed organisation
of knowledge, and of an "Adult Education" far
transcending the present imagination of the Board of
Education, but also on such a transformation of administrative institutions, from the House of Commons
to the Trade Union, as will provide an environment of
free initiative and personal activity, which are now so
much restricted, and without which there can, in the
long run, be no full social efficiency. It is with this
object that, far from heaping up all government on a
centralised authority, they propose the widest possible
variety in the forms of socialisation—calling in aid a
far-reaching reorganisation of the vocational world,
a vast extension of the consumers' Co-operative Movement, a great development of Local Government and
even the splitting into two of the powers of Parliament
itself. The same sense of the need for much more
detailed knowledge and much more widely disseminated personal interest in production and distribution
than the Capitalist System has been able to afford, lies
at the back of the proposals for a constantly increasing
participation of employees of all kinds and grades in
the management of the enterprise. We ourselves lay
equal stress on the freedom of the independent professional, and even on the continuance, unabsorbed,
of individual producers themselves owning the instruments with which they labour. What we visualise
is a community so variously organised, and so highly
differentiated in function as to be not only invigorated
by a sense of personal freedom, but also constantly
swept by the fresh air of experiment, observation and

verification. We want to get rid of the " stuffiness " of private interests which now infects our institutions ; and to usher in a reign of " Measurement and Publicity." It is to a free Democracy, inspired by the spirit of social service, and illumined by ever-increasing knowledge, that we dedicate this book.

INDEX

357

THE END